P9-DWU-576

Women's Social Rights and Entitlements

Women's Rights in Europe Series

Series Editors: **Christien L. van den Anker, Audrey Guichon, Sirkku K. Hellsten and Heather Widdows**

Titles include:

Audrey Guichon, Christien L. van den Anker and Irina Novikova (*editors*)
WOMEN'S SOCIAL RIGHTS AND ENTITLEMENTS

Sirkku K. Hellsten, Anne Maria Holli and Krassimira Daskalova (*editors*)
WOMEN'S CITIZENSHIP AND POLITICAL RIGHTS

Heather Widdows, Itziar Alkorta Idiakez and Aitziber Emaldi Cirión (*editors*)
WOMEN'S REPRODUCTIVE RIGHTS

Forthcoming title:

Christien L. van den Anker and Jeroen Doormernik (*editors*)
TRAFFICKING AND WOMEN'S RIGHTS

Women's Rights in Europe Series
Series Standing Order ISBN 1–4039–4988–3

You can receive future titles in this series as they are published by placing a standing order. Please contact your bookseller or, in case of difficulty, write to us at the address below with your name and address, the title of the series and the ISBN quoted above.

Customer Services Department, Macmillan Distribution Ltd, Houndmills, Basingstoke, Hampshire RG21 6XS, England

305.4094
G941

Women's Social Rights and Entitlements

Edited by

Audrey Guichon, Christien L. van den Anker and
Irina Novikova

WITHDRAWI

LIBRARY ST. MARY'S COLLEGE

Editorial matter, introduction and selection
© Audrey Guichon, Christien L. van den Anker and Irina Novikova 2006
Chapters 1–11 © Palgrave Macmillan Ltd 2006

All rights reserved. No reproduction, copy or transmission of this
publication may be made without written permission.

No paragraph of this publication may be reproduced, copied or transmitted
save with written permission or in accordance with the provisions of the
Copyright, Designs and Patents Act 1988, or under the terms of any licence
permitting limited copying issued by the Copyright Licensing Agency,
90 Tottenham Court Road, London W1T 4LP.

Any person who does any unauthorised act in relation to this publication
may be liable to criminal prosecution and civil claims for damages.

The authors have asserted their rights to be identified
as the authors of this work in accordance with the Copyright,
Designs and Patents Act 1988.

First published 2006 by
PALGRAVE MACMILLAN
Houndmills, Basingstoke, Hampshire RG21 6XS and
175 Fifth Avenue, New York, N.Y. 10010
Companies and representatives throughout the world

PALGRAVE MACMILLAN is the global academic imprint of the Palgrave
Macmillan division of St. Martin's Press, LLC and of Palgrave Macmillan Ltd.
Macmillan® is a registered trademark in the United States, United Kingdom
and other countries. Palgrave is a registered trademark in the European
Union and other countries.

ISBN-13: 978–1–4039–4992–9 hardback
ISBN-10: 1–4039–4992–1 hardback

This book is printed on paper suitable for recycling and made from fully
managed and sustained forest sources.

A catalogue record for this book is available from the British Library.

Library of Congress Cataloging-in-Publication Data
Women's social rights and entitlements / edited by
    Audrey Guichon, Christien van den Anker and Irina Novikova.
       p.   cm. — (Women's rights in Europe)
    Includes bibliographical references and index.
    ISBN 1–4039–4992–1 (cloth)
    1. Women's rights—Europe.   2. Women—Europe—Social conditions.
    3. Europe—Social policy.   I. Guichon, Audrey.   II. Anker, Christien
    van den, 1965–   III. Novikova, Irina,   IV. Series.
    HQ1236.5.E85W647 2006
    305.42094—dc22   2005058648

10   9   8   7   6   5   4   3   2   1
15   14   13   12   11   10   09   08   07   06

Printed and bound in Great Britain by
Antony Rowe Ltd, Chippenham and Eastbourne

Contents

List of Tables and Figures

Tables

Figures

List of Abbreviations

BWS	Battered Woman Syndrome
CEDAW	Convention on the Elimination of all Forms of Discrimination Against Women
CEE	Central and Eastern Europe(an)
CEEP	European Centre of Enterprises with Public Participation
CIS	Commonwealth of Independent States
DALY	Disability Adjusted life Years
DEVAW	Declaration on the Elimination of Violence Against Women
EC	European Commission; European Communities
ECJ	European Court of Justice
ECHR	European Court of Human Rights
EMU	European Monetary Union
EO	Equal Opportunity
ETUC	European Trade Unions Confederation
EU	European Union
EWSI	Employment and Women's Studies: The Impact of Women's Studies Training on Women's Employment in Europe
HBR	Latvian Household Budget Report
HE	Higher Education
HEWPSP	High Level Working Party on Social Protection
ICCPR	International Covenant on Civil and Political Rights
ICFTU	International Confederation of Free Trade Unions
ILO	International Labour Organisation
NEWR	Network for European Women's Rights
NGOs	Non-Governmental Organisations
OECD	Organisation for Economic Co-operation and Development
OMCT	Organisation Mondiale Contre la Torture [World Organisation Against Torture]
PTSD	Post-Traumatic Stress Disorder
TEC	Treaty of the European Community
UDHR	Universal Declaration of Human Rights
UK	United Kingdom

UNECE	United Nations Economic Commission for Europe
UNICE	Union of Industrial and Employers' Confederation of Europe
UNIFEM	United Nations Development Fund for Women
USSR	Union of Soviet Socialist Republics
WHO	World Health Organisation
WIDE	Women in Development in Europe

Acknowledgements

This series is the result of the involvement of a large number of people in the work of the Network for European Women's Rights (NEWR). We would like to thank them all for their input, although we cannot name them all here.

We want to thank especially those who spent time and energy discussing the four themes of NEWR during a series of intensive and engaging workshops across Europe and in the final conference in Birmingham.

We would also like to thank Donna Dickenson for initiating the project and leading it for two years and Christien L. van den Anker for taking over this leadership for the final year of the project, as well as the project partners, Itziar Alkorta Idiakez, Francesca Bettio, Krassimira Daskalova, Jeroen Doomernik, Aitziber Emaldi Cirión, Anne Maria Holli, Maria Katsiyianni-Papakonstantinou, Lukas H. Meyer and Irina Novikova for their contributions.

We could not have done the project without the commitment and persistence of Audrey Guichon and the consistent support of José R. Vicente. We thank Rebecca Shah for taking over from Audrey in the final months of the NEWR project and for her thorough editing work of all four volumes in this series.

We thank the European Commission for funding the NEWR project under its 5th Framework Programme.

We hope that this series of books will contribute positively to the debate on women's rights and to improving the lives of all women in Europe.

Audrey Guichon, Christien L. van den Anker and Irina Novikova

Foreword

This series is a timely initiative to counter the mounting opposition and challenge to the progress made thus far in transforming mainstream human rights discourse from a feminist perspective. Expansion of the concept of human rights to address violations experienced by women due specifically to their sex has considerably altered international and domestic law and demystified the public/private distinction that justified women's subordination.

The Convention on the Elimination of All Forms of Discrimination Against Women, adopted in 1979 by the United Nations General Assembly was an important step in the recognition of the universality of human rights, a view that became officially endorsed at the Vienna World Conference on Human Rights in 1993. Also referred to as the International Bill of Rights of Women, the Convention enjoys the ratification of 180 member states today. Yet, after over quarter of a century since the adoption of the Convention and the numerous human rights instruments that have followed, what remains universal is the gross violation of women's rights worldwide.

Notwithstanding the notable progress achieved in the advancement of women in the past decades, women in all parts of the world still face obstacles in accessing rights, such as those to education, health, political participation, property and to decide over matters related to their sexuality, reproduction, marriage, divorce and child custody, among others. Women's bodies are the zones of wars and the sites of politics and policies, as revealed in the armed conflicts around the world, transgressions over their reproductive and sexual rights, trafficking, dress codes, as well as immigration and refugee policies, etc. Even in countries where traditional patriarchy is transformed, as in the European experience, gender-based discrimination and violence against women persist in modified, subtle and discrete forms.

In many of the countries in the European region, where human rights standards and institutions are in place, women's formal political participation is still extremely low, reproductive rights are an area of continuous contestation and struggle, social entitlements are at risk and single mothers and minority and immigrant women are at the greatest risk of poverty. We need to learn more and understand how gender hierarchies are reproduced under diverse conditions and in different

places. The books in this series promise to do that. They illustrate the
need for increased attention from researchers, NGOs and policy-makers
throughout Europe for these instances of violations of women's rights.

This series comes at a time when the EU process of enlargement has
shown that respect for women's rights within different regions in Europe
is diverse. It is fascinating to see that specific rights for women are
protected better in some countries than in others, while it may also be
the case that in the same region other rights for women are less well
observed. By illustrating these trends and inconsistencies, this series
allows for comparison across the region as well as for reflection on the
policy gaps across Europe.

The four books in this series cover the areas of trafficking, political
participation, social entitlements and reproductive rights in detail, from
a multidisciplinary perspective and with contributions from activists,
professionals, academics and policy-makers. State-of-the-art debates are
reflected on and burning issues in women's rights are brought together
in one series for the first time. The depth of the arguments, coverage
of recent developments and clear focus on their implications for gender
equality are most commendable aspects of the series. The books push
forward the agenda for all of us and remind us that women's rights
are not protected equally and intrinsically. In fact, the contributions
confirm that we still have a way to go to achieve women's equality in
contemporary Europe.

This unique and compelling collection is a must for everyone striving
for rights, equality and justice!

Yakın Ertürk
United Nations Special Rapporteur on Violence Against Women

Notes on the Contributors

Christien L. van den Anker is Principal Lecturer in Politics at the University of the West of England. Her research interests are global justice, human rights (especially women's rights, contemporary slavery and ethnic/racial discrimination) and the ethical implications of globalisation. Her most recent publications include *Essentials of Human Rights* (editor with R. K. Smith, 2005) and *The Political Economy of New Slavery* (editor, 2004).

Anneli Anttonen is a Professor of Social Policy in Tampere University, Finland. She has participated in many cross-national research projects, and written widely on women, social policies and citizenship. She also leads a research group, Care and Social Policy, at Tampere University (see www.uta.fi/laitokset/sospol/tutkimus/caso/). Among her latest publications is *The Young, the Old and the State: Social Care Systems in Five Industrial Nations* (editor with John Baldock and Jorma Sipilä, 2003).

Inge Bleijenbergh is Assistant Professor at Radboud University, Nijmegen. In 2004 she presented her PhD thesis on the issue of European social citizenship rights, in particular on combining work and family life. In 2000 she was a research visitor at the European University Institute, Florence. Her most recent publications include articles in the *European Journal of Industrial Relations* and *Transfer* and a policy paper on *Equal Opportunities in Collective Bargaining in Europe* (with Linda Dickens and Jeanne de Bruijn) for the European Commission.

Virginia Bras Gomes was born in Goa and has lived and worked in Lisbon for many years. She is currently Head of the Department for Social Research and International Relations of the Directorate General of Social Security. In June 2000 she was one of the main negotiators on behalf of the EU at the 24th Special Session of the UN General Assembly which adopted the further initiatives for the implementation of the commitments of the World Summit for Social Development. She was elected to the UN Committee of Economic, Social and Cultural Rights from 1 January 2003. Among her most recent publications are 'The Future of Economic, Social and Cultural Rights', in K. M. Smith and C. van den Anker (eds), *Essentials of Human Rights* (2005) and 'The Role of the Commission for Social Development: a Forum for Institutional Collaboration and Professional Exchange', in Federal Ministry for Family Affairs, Senior Citizens, Women and Youth, *The Global Dialogue on Social Issue. The role of the Commission for Social Development of the UN* (2005).

Morag Gillespie is Research Fellow at the Scottish Poverty Information Unit, Glasgow Caledonian University. She has a long history of working with voluntary and community groups. Her research interests include welfare rights; women, poverty and employment issues; welfare to work; and equality mainstreaming. She was previously the Parliamentary Liaison and Development Worker for the Scottish Women's Budget Group, an organisation that promotes gender awareness in public spending in Scotland.

Audrey Guichon holds an LL.M in international human rights law. She is currently employed as a researcher at INCORE, University of Ulster and was the project officer for NEWR. Before that, she worked as an intern at the International Secretariat of Amnesty International, London and at the South Asia Human Rights Documentation Centre, New Delhi. She has published in the area of women's rights and human rights in general.

Theodora Hiou Maniatopulou is Associate Professor at Panteion University, Athens. She holds a Jean Monet Chair, specialising in EU enlargement and the social policy of the European Community. She was formerly a collaborator of the Legal Service of the European Commission and was national representative at the European Union – China Human Rights Dialogue, Beijing 2003. Her publications include: 'La Charte Sociale Européenne', in R. Wtervulzhe (ed.), *Droit General Communautaire*, Université de Louvain La Neuve. She was a partner of the NEWR project.

Maria Katsiyianni Papakonstantinou was born in Athens and has lived and worked there ever since. She holds a BA in Political Sciences from the Faculty of Political Science at the Panteion School of Political Sciences and a BA in Law from the Faculty of Law of the Kapodistrian University of Athens. She is Doctor of Public International Law and has acted as a solicitor in Athens for the past 28 years. She is presently Lecturer at the Department of International and European Studies at Panteion University of Social and Political Sciences, and specialises in Public

International Law, International Institutions and the European Law. She was a partner of the NEWR project.

Eleonore Kofman is Professor of Gender, Migration and Citizenship, at the School of Health and Social Science, Middlesex University. Her research focuses on gendered migrations in Europe, especially in relation to entitlements and changing welfare regimes and skilled female migrants, and feminist political geographies. She has co-authored *Gender and International Migrations in Europe* (2000), and co-edited *Globalization: Theory and Practice* (2nd edn, 2003), *Continuum and Mapping Women, Making Politics: Feminist Perspectives on Political Geography* (2004), and special issues of *Feminist Review, Geoforum* and *Women's Studies International Forum* on global gendered migrations. She also co-authored 'Gendered Migrations: Towards a Gender-sensitive Policy in the UK', for the *Institute of Public Policy Research Working Papers on Migration and Asylum* no. 6 (2005).

Tana Lace is Vice Dean of the Faculty of European Studies, Riga Stradins University, Latvia and teaches courses in the Department of Sociology. Her scientific interests are in gender equality, social policy, poverty and social inclusion. She has participated in many research projects including with UNDP and UNICEF. She is now the Latvian expert in the network of independent experts in the fight against poverty and social exclusion at the European Commission.

Nicky Le Feuvre has worked as an Assistant Professor of Sociology and Gender Studies at Toulouse-Le Mirail University, France since 1992. She is currently director of the Simone-SAGESSE interdisciplinary research and doctoral training centre in Toulouse, where she has carried out several cross-national comparative research projects on women's labour market experiences, particularly in the professions (medicine, law, pharmacy, speech therapy, etc). She has recently been involved in three projects funded by the European Commission. Her recent publications include: (with Muriel Andriocci) 'Employment Opportunities for Women in Europe', in G. Griffin (ed.), *Doing Women's Studies: Equal Opportunities, Personal Impacts and Social Consequences* (2005) and 'The Impact of Women's Studies on Women's Employment Opportunities and Experiences in France', in G. Griffin (ed.), *Employment, Equal Opportunities and Women's Studies. Women's Experiences in Seven European Countries* (2004).

Ruth Lister is Professor of Social Policy at Loughborough University. She is former Director of the Child Poverty Action Group and served on the Commission on Social Justice, the Opsahl Commission into the Future of Northern Ireland and the Commission on Poverty, Participation and Power. She is a founding Academician of the Academy for Learned Societies for the Social Sciences and a Trustee of the Community Development Foundation. She is currently a member of the Fabian Commission on Life Chances and Child Poverty and Donald Dewar Visiting Professor of Social Justice at Glasgow University. She has published widely on poverty and social exclusion, welfare state reform, gender and citizenship. Her most recent books are *Citizenship: Feminist Perspectives* (2nd edn, 2003) and *Poverty* (2004).

Osnat Lubrani was appointed as UNIFEM Regional Programme Director for Central and Eastern Europe (CEE) in April 2001 and has been with UNIFEM since 1997. Prior to that, she was seconded to support the UNDP in Macedonia. As Acting Deputy Resident Representative, she supported the work of the Country Office during the ethnic crisis that erupted in the North west region of the country in early 2001. Formerly, Ms. Lubrani served as Executive Officer to the Executive Director of UNIFEM. She also helped to set up and served as the first manager of a UNIFEM Trust Fund to End Violence against Women. She has worked in Rwanda and the Democratic Republic of Congo on human rights, peace building and development initiatives, with a focus on local capacity building.

Irina Novikova is Professor in the Department of Culture and Literature, and Director of The Centre for Gender Studies, University of Latvia. Her research interests are gender and genre in film and literature; and gender, citizenship and ethnicity in post-socialism. She has published *Gender and Genre: Women's Autobiography and Bildungsroman* (2004) and (co-editor with Dimitar Kambourov) *Men in the Global World: Integrating Postsocialist Perspectives* (2004).

Giedre Purvaneckiene is an Associate Professor in the Department of Educology, Vilnius University. She graduated from Vilnius University in 1968, and worked for the five following years at the Institute of Semiconductors in the Academy of Sciences. Since 1973 she has been based at Vilnius University where she has participated in numerous scientific conferences, and underwent training in Norway, Sweden and the US. She is the author of more than 50 scientific and other publications in

Lithuania and abroad, took part in the drafting of the *Conception of Lithuanian Family Policy* (1995), led the drafting of the *Action Plan of the Advancement of Women of Lithuania* (1996) and *Conception of Lithuanian State Policy on Child Welfare* (2003). From 1994 to 1997 she worked in the Prime Minister's Office as a State Counsellor on Women's Issues and was Adviser to the Government on Family and Women's Issues. Between 1997 and 2000, she worked at the United Nations Development Programme country office as Gender in Development Adviser. From 2000 and 2004, she was an elected representative in the Parliament of the Republic of Lithuania.

Rebecca Shah is a researcher on the NEWR project at the Centre for the Study of Global Ethics, University of Birmingham. Her research interests include human rights, HIV/AIDS, gender and women's rights and international development. Rebecca has been an acting research fellow at the UK Department for International Development's Governance Resource Centre, and has conducted research in Tanzania and for the Institute of Child Health, Great Ormond Street Hospital, London. Her recent publications include 'The Right to Development', in R. Smith and C. van den Anker (eds) *The Essential Guide to Human Rights* (2005) and 'HIV/AIDS, Women and Human Rights', in the *Network of European Women's Rights Newsletter*, Issue 3 (2005).

Elizabeth Villagómez holds a BA in Economics from the Universidad Autónoma Metropolitana (Mexico) and holds a postgraduate diploma in Quantitative Development Economics from Warwick University, England. She gained a doctorate in Economic Science at the Universidad de Alcalá de Henares, Spain in 2000. She received two awards for her thesis on informal labour markets in Mexico. She is a specialist in applied economics in the areas of social policy and labour market issues with 17 years' experience in Mexico, CEE and EU countries and has been active in both the academic and activist fields. During 2001–2 she was Economic Governance Adviser for UNIFEM in New York managing the global programme on gender responsive budgets. She currently carries out consulting work as a founding and senior partner of Almenara, Estudios Económicos y Sociales, S.L. and in particular for the UNIFEM CEE office.

Introduction: Women's Social Rights and Entitlements in Europe

Audrey Guichon, Christien L. van den Anker and Irina Novikova

This volume brings together some of the findings and conclusions that emerged from the Network for European Women's Rights (NEWR), a three-year collaborative project funded by the European Commission between 2002 and 2005. Developed by a partnership of nine universities across Europe, NEWR aimed at identifying and researching the most burning issues in the field of women's rights in Europe, with particular emphasis on four issues: trafficking in women, women's reproductive rights, women's political participation and women's social entitlements. This book is therefore one volume in a series which consists of one book on each of these themes. The NEWR approach was multidisciplinary in nature and concentrated on the concerns and needs of women and organisations working on women's rights across Europe and beyond. This book focuses on the issues related to 'Women's Social Rights: Entitlements in Europe'.

The NEWR project found that gender equality in the area of social entitlements is still lacking in Europe. In response to the pressures of globalisation, post-socialist transition, enlargement of the European Union, ageing populations and mass migration, new models of social policy have been created and the role of the traditional welfare regimes has changed. Recognising the differences between types of welfare regime, we conclude that none of the existing models has found satisfactory ways to guarantee gender equality in social entitlements. Despite social policy initiatives on a European-wide level, women in Europe still earn less, have smaller pensions and are more at risk of poverty than men.

In this volume, we analyse the circumstances for women and show that gender discrimination in the labour market as well as the unequal distribution of care tasks in the household plays a large role in keeping women at a disadvantage. The pressure on women to enter the formal labour market (in part due to a move from a breadwinner model to individualisation in welfare regimes) and absence of child care provision leave women with a double burden, dependent mostly on mothers and grandmothers (and grandfathers) as well as on migrant domestic and care workers. The balance between work, care and a personal life has been discussed in the Nordic states, but even with generous parental leave and sabbaticals, women still take up such leave far more than men and also carry the burden of loss of earnings and pension entitlements if they work part-time. We identified particular groups of women who are especially vulnerable to poverty. These include lone mothers, widows, elderly women, migrant women and women who experience domestic violence.

The chapters in this volume address these issues in different ways.

In Chapter 1, 'Gendered Social Entitlements: Building Blocks of Women's Citizenship', Ruth Lister discusses the meaning of women's social rights and entitlements and places them at the centre of gendered politics and other rights which are often given higher priority in understandings of citizenship. Lister discusses some of the key notions related to gendered social entitlements. She focuses on three issues, emphasising their implications for gendered social entitlements: the relationship between care and paid work as citizenship responsibilities; the gendered division of labour and time; and income maintenance, economic dependence and poverty. In addition to specific policies, the author formulates more general goals to underpin demands for improved gendered social entitlements: a more equitable gendered division of different forms of labour and of time, as an essential platform for women's effective political citizenship; adequate support for the care of children and older people and a high quality social infrastructure; greater economic equality between women and men and the economic independence and well-being of *all* women.

In Chapter 2, 'Individualisation and the Crumbling of the Welfare State', Virginia Bras Gomes offers an analysis of social protection models in European welfare states. She discusses the influence of political and institutional systems, of levels of economic and social development and of cultural backgrounds. She discusses conceptions of the welfare state in relation to combating poverty and social exclusion and promoting individual and collective well-being. Bras Gomes argues that the crumbling of the welfare state is linked to its difficulties in responding to a number of challenges: the demographic; the economic, posed by the employment crisis; changes in the political and economic systems in many

European countries; and globalisation. The changing gender balance is an important economic, social and cultural challenge faced by the state, 'relating, for instance, to activities that were traditionally provided free of charge as informal care but are now paid for and will continue to be so in the future'. In this context, Bras Gomes discusses four dimensions of individualisation as well as arguments for and against individualisation.

The author argues that the individualisation of rights raises two major problems – how to guarantee that participation in the labour market ensures a sufficient level of social benefits for women, subject to professional and vertical segregation in the labour market; and how to ensure social protection that respects human dignity even for those who do not work, through universal social protection. Furthermore, a more focused gender equal approach requires the adoption of reconciliation measures between work and the family, which would also represent a central step for the individualisation of women's rights.

In Chapter 3, 'Gendered Configurations of the Nordic Model: Civil Society, the State and Social Citizenship', Anneli Anttonen identifies welfare states as the most important pillar of modernisation and democratisation in Nordic democracies. Her focus is mainly on that part of the welfare state she calls the 'social services state': social care services have a special importance for women whose labour market participation is dependent on collective care arrangements. Anttonen pays particular attention to care services and their historical development to evaluate the emancipatory dimension of the Nordic welfare state model in order to explain and highlight its distinctiveness. Her main argument is that the Nordic model is based on conceptions of emancipation and democratisation where the ethical role of the state is important. The analysis contributes to the theoretical debate on the woman-friendliness of the Nordic model by demonstrating that the Nordic welfare state model is based on a well-developed civil society and a special form of social citizenship. However, the author concedes that the ideology of the social services state is changing and new challenges and social issues – e.g. violence against women and the struggle over 'sexual citizenship' – are appearing which may well impact on women's lives and choices.

In Chapter 4, 'European Social Policies on Combining Work and Family Life: The Gap between Legislation and Practice', Inge Bleijenbergh discusses the gap between legislation and practice in European social policies on the issue of combining work and family life. She addresses the theoretical debate on the nature of the welfare state, social policy-making, types of care policies and gender equality, as well as the ways in which the issue of combining work and family life entered the EU policy agenda. Since the 1990s concrete European policy measures have been introduced on maternity leave, parental leave, part-time work and, to a lesser extent, child care services. Nevertheless, the author discusses at length the realities of the rights to time for care recognised at the European level, in particular with regard to the need for a re-division of care-giving between men and women. The author argues that 'the development of a common European market shows an intrinsic drive for developing public care giving support to allow the participation of women to the labour market', but adds that 'full social equality for women and men will only be possible when inclusive citizenship rights are fully realised at European level'.

In Chapter 5, 'The Adoption and Enforcement of Equal Opportunity Measures in Employment: The Case of France in Comparative Perspective', Nicky Le Feuvre develops an argument on the adoption and implementation of equal opportunity measures with regard to gender equality in employment in EU member states. She focuses on the case of France, with a view to illustrating the influence of the societal context on the manner in which equal opportunity measures are defined, adopted and implemented in other national settings. Cross-national differences are illustrated with regard to three sub-themes: the variations in the visibility and legitimacy of equal opportunity discourses and practices in national contexts; the degree to which the enforcement of equal opportunity legislation rests on the good will of the protagonists or on legally binding means of enforcement, control and policy evaluation; and the degree to which equal opportunities have been 'professionalised' in different national contexts as well as the role of women's studies in providing training for employment in the equal opportunities field. The author shows that a lack of understanding of the impact of the societal level gender relations on men's and women's employment experiences is one of the major barriers to more effective implementation of equal opportunity measures in many EU member states.

In Chapter 6, 'The Risk of Poverty among Women in Europe', Morag Gillespie discusses the factors that increase the risk of poverty for women in Europe, including the impact of the recent EU enlargement. The chapter discusses the 'feminisation' of poverty and outlines key issues affecting the risk of poverty among women. The discussion of welfare state regimes, the labour market, skills and education, and caring roles also highlights the interaction of gender with a wide range of other factors that need to be considered more fully in moving towards gender-sensitive analysis and policy development. Gillespie offers illustrations and an analysis of the influence of single motherhood, disability, nationality and migration, work, education, care and age on women's vulnerability to poverty and, in doing so, makes a significant contribution to the realities of inter-sectionality between gender and other factors in relation to poverty.

In Chapter 7, 'Migration, Ethnicity and Entitlements in European Welfare Regimes', Eleonore Kofman engages with the discussion of gendered patterns of migration by addressing the livelihoods and differential rights and entitlements of third country women, i.e. non-EU nationals who enter on their own for work and education, as family migrants or as asylum seekers and refugees. The analysis focuses on first-generation migrants, those who were born in a country other than the country of residence, and on the situation in the EU before its enlargement in May 2004. The first section of the chapter outlines the various migrations patterns (labour, family and asylum) and their gendered nature. The second explores key forms of employment in changing welfare regimes and in particular those sectors linked with the globalisation of care and social reproduction. The final section focuses on rights and entitlements arising from migration policies which have generated complex systems of stratification, racism and cultural differences based on the interplay of routes of entry and labour market position.

In Chapter 8, 'Violence as Violation: Understanding Domestic Violence against Women as a Matter for Human Rights', Audrey Guichon and Rebecca Shah develop a position on domestic violence against women and its nature as a topic of particular concern in the field of women's social entitlements and rights. Their analysis focuses on domestic violence as violence perpetrated by men against their female partners and as one of the most widespread violations of human rights worldwide, while at the same time being one of the most silent and pernicious forms of violence against women. In pursuing the objective to determine whether the issues raised by domestic violence can be answered by international human rights law, the authors take a multidisciplinary approach to domestic violence in Europe, drawing on sociological, psychological and legal perspectives to address these issues, presenting the international legal framework and contextualising the legal discussion. The chapter is primarily concerned with the impact on the psycho-social well-being of victims as individual women to reveal and discuss the multifarious causes of domestic violence. The authors stress the need to ensure better national implementation of the international standards applying to domestic violence and further evolution of the international human rights framework by, for example, offering an adapted and fair response to the specificities of women's rights. Finally, they suggest that the human rights framework needs to be equipped to challenge the causes of rights violations.

In Chapter 9, 'Women's Social Rights and Entitlements in Latvia and Lithuania – Transformations and Challenges', Tana Lace, Irina Novikova and Giedre Purvaneckiene bring together issues in women's social rights and entitlements in Latvia and Lithuania in the transitional period from the socialist welfare system, the Soviet model, to the welfare state, structured by the demands of the capitalist market economy. Gender policy in the Soviet period, derived from the socialist model of citizenship, is discussed to contextualise the argument about the gendered impact of economic transformation and liberalisation on women's social entitlements in Latvia and Lithuania. The authors argue that occupational segregation and a growing wage differential have become distinctive features of gendering the national labour markets in Latvia and Lithuania, and discriminatory practices have been affecting all age groups, particularly young women entering the labour market and women of pre-retirement age, who are especially vulnerable to recruitment into part-time jobs and to impoverishment. The argument is located in a comparative perspective, as the formations of social welfare regimes in Latvia and Lithuania have been developing according to different scenarios and choices. Nevertheless, as the authors argue, both countries have shared the 'divorce' between gender equality policy and family policy whose gendered effect is buttressed by the steady imbalance between family and employment, feminisation of poverty, professional deskilling, social dumping and a gendered information technology gap.

In Chapter 10, 'The Impact of Globalisation on Women's Labour Market Situation in Eastern Europe', Osnat Lubrani and Elizabeth Villagómez address the main trends in the situation of women in Central and Eastern Europe (CEE) and the former USSR (part of which is now known as the Commonwealth of Independent States, or CIS) and discuss the ways in which globalisation and regional transition processes have influenced women's economic opportunities, outcomes in terms of women's situation in society and the status of gender equality and women's human rights. The chapter reviews the results and conclusions of one initiative, which specifically centred on the impact of globalisation on women in three countries in the CEE/CIS region: Bulgaria, Hungary and Kazakhstan. The project concentrated on the development of national-level studies of women's participation in the labour market, women's education and training, the gendered nature of social security and social services for women, the main trends of discrimination for men and women, the increasing difference among women, and changes in societal attitudes on the role of women. The authors conclude that the trends identified through this initiative are directly linked to the type of work that UNIFEM is carrying out in the region. From improving the knowledge about women's economic situation to advocating specific changes in polices, the project work has contributed to building up the knowledge of women's NGOs themselves.

Finally, in Chapter 11, 'Current Approaches to Gender Equality in European Social Policies', Theodora Hiou Maniatopulou and Maria Katsiyianni Papakonstantinou offer a legal approach to the content and implementation of the principle of gender equality in EU legislation, through various legal instruments and jurisprudence. More specifically, they offer an insight into the field of European social policy and question whether we are witnessing the establishment of a European system of social security and its potential role for women.

We hope this volume will contribute to increased multidisciplinary research into these issues, attention from policy-makers for these gender imbalances and sustainable collaboration between non-governmental organisations, professionals, academics and policy-makers.

The specifics of long-term gender-sensitive social policy can be worked out only if the voices of women experiencing inequality and reflecting on alternatives are heard.

1
Gendered Social Entitlements: Building Blocks of Women's Citizenship

Ruth Lister

Women's social rights and entitlements are critical to gender politics. Which rights and entitlements figure prominently in political debate varies among countries. The exact configuration depends on factors such as the type of welfare regime, the quality of the social infrastructure and the level and nature of women's labour market participation. They vary also between different groups of women so that, for example, the priorities of disabled women may differ from those of non-disabled, and women from different ethnic groups may have different priorities. Whatever the specific perspectives, however, it is important to emphasise the importance of social rights and entitlements to the other dimensions of rights that are often given higher priority in understandings of citizenship.

It is necessary to consider what is meant by 'women's social entitlements'. The notion of 'entitlements' is broader than that of rights. It is commonly attributed to Amartya Sen, who defines it as 'the commodities over which a person can establish her ownership and command' (1999: 162). This is not just a question of legal rights but also of social rules and norms. Arguably, it could be broadened to include collective commodities – that is, the social wage or social infrastructure. In practice, the distinction between rights and entitlements is not always that clear.

It is probably true to say that the only social entitlements or rights that accrue to women *qua* women are those around reproduction, embracing contraception, abortion and reproductive health. Their importance to women's autonomy and citizenship has been a key tenet of modern feminism and has now been given official recognition by bodies such as the United Nations. However, these rights are not always absolute and unconditional. Thus, for example, in some countries effective entitlement to an abortion rests not only on a legal right but depends also

8

on the adequacy of social rights to the services necessary to exercise the right (Shaver, 1993/94). This illustrates a wider point: because of the distinction that has to be made between *de jure* and *de facto* women's rights, the ease with which women can exercise their rights as well as the rights themselves are crucial to any assessment of whether they constitute an effective entitlement (Norris, 1987).

Other than reproductive rights, it is possible to talk about *gendered* social entitlements/rights in two senses: first, as deriving from women's position in the gendered division of labour, which in turn raises the question of *men*'s social entitlements and as well as their responsibilities; and second, as affecting both women and men but in different ways because of the division of labour in both the private and public spheres and because of their differential economic position. Examples might include access to transport and rights to user-involvement in and the democratic accountability of welfare services.

This chapter focuses on three issues, drawing out their implications for gendered social entitlements: the relationship between care and paid work as citizenship responsibilities; the gendered division of labour and time; and income maintenance, economic dependence and poverty. It concludes by setting out some possible goals.

Care and paid work as citizenship responsibilities

The first set of issues derives from women's continued main responsibility for the unpaid work of care – of both children and adults – within families. It raises general questions about the relationship between unpaid care and paid work as citizenship responsibilities and the more specific and politically charged implication of this relationship for lone mothers' social rights and entitlements (Lister, 2003).

Policy in many European countries is moving in the direction of what Nancy Fraser (1997) has dubbed the 'universal breadwinner' and Jane Lewis (2000) the 'adult worker' model. All adults capable of paid work are expected to be full-time members of the labour market, although in practice where there are high levels of part-time female employment it is more of a $1\frac{1}{2}$ adult worker model. Yet, as Lewis (2000: 61) observes, care work still has to be done; the question is by whom and 'on what terms'.

One expression of this question is the current preoccupation, at both EU level and within individual member states, with the so-called work–life balance (more accurately termed the work–rest-of-life balance). For those with care responsibilities it is primarily about how to balance paid and unpaid work (see Chapter 4). More fundamentally, the terms on which care work is done raises a question with which feminists have grappled in various guises for years: how to provide due recognition and valorisation of care work without locking women further into a private caring role, which serves to exclude them from the power and influence that can derive from participation in the public sphere of the economy and polis (Lister, 2003). Part of the answer lies in addressing the question of who does care work, which is central to the chapter's second theme.

Nevertheless, whoever does the care work, there is an issue of what social entitlements should be available to support that work. This in turn raises questions about the level of social investment and about whether social entitlements are geared towards enabling parents and other carers to take paid work or towards providing financial support for them to provide care themselves at home. Three types of resources are involved: financial support, services and time (Daly, 2002).

The issue of adult care is all too often ignored in debates around the work–rest-of-life balance. Yet it is of growing significance in the ageing populations of Europe. There are various models of payment for adult care which differ in two main ways. The first is whether they represent a social security wage replacement or wages for care undertaken (McLaughlin and Glendinning, 1994). Second is whether such wages are paid direct or are 'routed' via payments to care users (Ungerson, 1997). The nature of the entitlement is different in each case. Whatever the scheme of financial support, it needs to balance the needs of those providing and those receiving care, many of whom are also women. It also needs to be sufficiently flexible to enable carers of working age to combine their caring work with paid work, if they so wish. This requires flexible working hours, care leave provisions and appropriate community support services.

The care of children is the more common focus of work–rest-of-life policies. The main social entitlements to support the care of children are: publicly funded child care; payments to care for children at home; and various forms of leave, the last of which will be discussed in the next section.

The availability of affordable, accessible, good quality child care is an essential social entitlement, which in some countries, notably the Nordic states, is expressed as the right of the child. For instance in Sweden:

> Enrolling children from age 1 in full-day pre-schools has become generally acceptable. What was once viewed as either a privilege of

the wealthy for a few hours a day or an institution for needy children has become, after 70 years of political vision and policy making, *an unquestionable right* of children and families. Parents now expect a holistic pedagogy that includes health care, nurturing and education for their pre-schoolers. (Lenz Taguchi and Munkhammer, 2003: 27, cited in Moss, 2005; emphasis in original)

It is an entitlement that is not simply about enabling parents to combine paid work and family responsibilities, but also about the right of the child to a holistic child-centred service. It is important not only for pre-school children but also for younger schoolchildren during school holidays and out of school hours.

In the United Kingdom (UK), it is only recently that child care has been acknowledged as a public as well as a private responsibility for the generality of children. Although it does not go nearly as far as the Swedish model, the UK government's ten-year strategy for child care, published at the end of 2004, does talk of parents' 'entitlement' to early education for three and four year olds, which will gradually be extended in terms of hours and 'integrated with high quality, affordable, child care from 8 am to 6 pm all year round' (HM Treasury, 2004: 33). It also promises that local authorities will be given a 'new duty to secure sufficient provision to meet local child care needs' (ibid.).

The other approach to supporting care of children is to pay parents to stay at home. There has been something of a trend towards this in recent years in some continental European welfare states. The impact on gender equity appears to be mixed, depending to a large extent on the motivation behind the policies and on their precise nature. Nevertheless, even if ostensibly gender-neutral, such allowances tend to be seen as for mothers.

The extent to which mothers actually make use of them can depend on the adequacy of child care provisions, unemployment levels and cultural factors. Overall, though, such policies 'have produced a substantial decline in the numbers of mothers with children under three who are in paid employment' (Morgan and Zippel, 2003: 76). The fear thus remains that they will cement rather than loosen the traditional gendered division of labour. They may also widen class divisions, as analysis shows that working-class, less educated and lower paid women are more likely to take advantage of them (Morgan and Zippel, 2003). The conclusion reached by a study of such policies is that:

It is difficult to superimpose a right to extensive child care leave on highly gendered labor markets and traditional cultural norms without reinforcing the current division of labor in both the workplace and the home. Until there are wider social, economic, and attitudinal changes, women will continue to make up the vast majority of recipients and child care leaves and benefits will simply reproduce the norms and structures that feminists have been fighting. (Morgan and Zippel, 2003: 77)

A universal payment to all those raising children after the end of any parental leave period, regardless of whether a parent takes paid work or not, would reduce the risks but is unlikely in the context of welfare state containment and increased targeting. Many, therefore, take the view that a payment to look after children at home is a social entitlement that feminists should be very wary of demanding.

With regard to the specific position of lone mothers, policy has tended to swing between treating them as primarily mothers or primarily paid workers (Lewis, 1997). Increasingly, European welfare states are treating them as primarily the latter, although policies vary according to the level of compulsion and the age of the youngest child at which paid work is expected to take over from full-time motherhood.

The UK is unusual in that lone parents still have the right to claim social assistance until their youngest child is aged 16. Nevertheless, increasingly, policy is framed in terms of the expectation that lone parents should be in paid work and the right to social assistance is now conditional on attendance at work-focused interviews. Two defensible positions have been articulated in debates on the issue.

One is that adopted by the Commission on Social Justice (1994).[1] The Commission argued that it is not in the interests of lone mothers or their children for them to be out of the labour market for a long period. Thus, after a decent breathing space, lone mothers should be expected to look for at least part-time work when their youngest child reaches a certain age, subject to various provisos and safeguards. Cross-national evidence shows that paid work is the best route out of poverty for lone mothers, even if it is not an automatic route. It also suggests that, where a clear line is drawn requiring lone parents to be economically active when their children reach a certain age, an implicit contract sometimes (though not always) emerges under which more generous benefits are provided for lone parents with younger children and better services and financial support for those in paid work (Millar and Rowlingson, 2001).

The alternative position is grounded in the belief that the current heavy emphasis in European social policy on the obligations of paid work is devaluing care work and denying its status as an expression of citizenship responsibility (Sevenhuijsen, 1998; Williams, 2004). It is also influenced by research, which shows that some lone mothers do not feel that it is right to take paid work (Duncan and Edwards, 1999; van Drenth et al., 1999). Moreover, in the UK lone mothers face what are sometimes conflicting expectations. Not only is the expectation increasingly that they will take paid work, but also policy is stressing the parental role in regulating children's behaviour and in supporting their education (Standing, 1999). For lone mothers with the sole day-to-day responsibility for their children, the resultant time pressures can impose severe strains. The UK does not yet have the infrastructure of child care and family-friendly employment rights needed to minimise the stress of juggling paid work and the sole care of children.

I have moved uneasily between these two positions. While I still believe that it is not in lone mothers' longer-term interests to spend a long period outside the labour market, I would now pay more attention to the second set of arguments than I did previously. Certainly, at present there is not a sufficiently strong social infrastructure in place to take conditionality any further than work-focused interviews, which evaluation suggests are proving helpful (Thomas and Griffiths, 2004).

The gendered division of labour and time

An alternative to the increasingly dominant universal bread-winner/adult carer model, which assumes all adults will be in the work-force (at least part-time in the case of women in many countries) is Nancy Fraser's (1997) 'universal caregiver' model. In this model men become more like women, combining the obligations and responsibilities of paid work and care. In this way, both women and men are constructed as 'citizen-earner/carers' and 'carer-earners'.

Critical to this model are policies that will encourage a more equitable gendered distribution of different kinds of labour and of time. This means considering men's as well as women's right to time to care for young children. Cross-national experience suggests that, from the perspective of gender equity, this right – and responsibility – is best achieved through decent parental leave schemes and working time policies. Critical components are:

- *Adequate parental leave.* The optimum length of parental leave is open to discussion. What is crucial is that it is adequately paid. Important too is that leave is structured so as to emphasise the parent's links with the labour market (Bruning and Plantenga, 1999).

- *Some form of quota for fathers*, with strong governmental encouragement to them to take it and a culture change in the workplace that supports paternal use of the leave. Unless parental leave schemes encourage male use, they can represent a 'poisoned chalice', which reinforces the gendered division of labour (Fagnani, 1999).
- *Generous leave for family reasons* – again there should be emphasis on encouraging fathers as well as mothers to use it.
- *An entitlement to work shorter hours*; more effective regulation of paid working hours and possibly the goal of a shorter working day as the norm. A culture of long working hours constrains male participation in caring and domestic work, while creating barriers to mothers' and carers' full integration and advancement in the workplace. The converse of an entitlement to shorter paid working hours is the entitlement to 'time for care' (Knijn and Kremer, 1997).

Income rights

One consequence of the still dominant gendered division of labour in both the private and public sphere is that women tend to be economically disadvantaged over their lifetime relative to men. They are vulnerable to economic dependence and poverty so that the very experience of poverty is gendered (Lister, 2004; and see Chapter 6). In addition to the kind of rights and entitlements discussed so far, it is therefore also necessary to consider including women's rights and entitlements in the workplace and to social security.

Workplace

In relation to the workplace, in many countries it is a question of the effectiveness of existing rights and entitlements as enshrined in equal opportunity, sex discrimination, equal pay and minimum wage policies. Women are more likely than men to be low paid, largely because of the poor rewards attached to part-time work and of the under-valuing of the jobs women typically do (Howarth and Kenway, 2004). Throughout the EU women suffer a pay gap, to a greater or lesser degree. Fagan and Rubery warn that 'there are no grounds for optimism that the gender pay gap will close progressively over time' (1999: 26). The gender pay gap is to a large extent a reflection of the vertical and horizontal segregation that characterises women's employment despite equal opportunities and anti-discrimination legislation. It is important to remember, however, that women's position in the labour market also reflects other social divisions such as class, 'race' and disability.

Social security

Women are more likely to claim social security – particularly social assistance – than men, therefore the level of benefits provided is of critical importance. The present UK government has made significant improvements to benefit levels for children, especially younger children, but not for their parents. Inadequate adult rates of benefit make it harder for mothers to protect their children from hardship (Women's Budget Group, 2005). Particular concern has been raised in the UK about the position of first-time mothers-to-be and young mothers living on benefit.

A long-standing feminist demand has been for an individual right to benefits for women in heterosexual couples on the grounds that rights mediated by dependence on male partners cease to be genuine rights. Black feminists, however, have been critical of white feminists' preoccupation with the general issue of economic independence. There has also been a more general lack of agreement as to how to achieve that independent right – through a reformed social insurance scheme, through disaggregation of means-tested benefits, or through the more radical idea of citizens/basic income or the half-way house of a participation income?

My preference has been to argue for a reformed social insurance scheme, which better reflects the needs of women. However, policy in the UK is moving in the opposite direction. With a few exceptions, social insurance benefits are becoming more marginal in the face of increased reliance on means-testing. Moreover, the introduction and extension of means-tested tax credits, in which the couple, and not the individual, is the basic unit, can be 'seen as a threat' to independent taxation, defined broadly to mean that 'the amount of income tax that one partner pays should not be affected by the decisions of their partner about earnings and income' (Bennett, 2002: 573).

The total individualisation of means-tested benefits is neither feasible nor, many would argue, desirable. Research suggests it might not be what women themselves want (Goode et al., 1998). However, Australia has shown that it is possible to achieve partial individualisation. This suggests, Jane Millar observes, that:

> means testing need not mean that the aspirations for a more individualised system are completely lost. Some combination of individual- and family-based system may be the best way to recognise both

independence and interdependence in people's lives. (2003: 73; see also McLaughlin et al., 2002)

For some, a more inspiring longer-term vision of individualisation is provided by the idea of a citizen's or basic income (McKay and VanEvery, 2000). This would provide all adults with an independent, unconditional and non-means-tested income in their own right. There are arguments for and against from a feminist perspective (see Lister, 2003). A rather less controversial variant is the idea of a 'participation income', advocated by the economist A. B. Atkinson (1993) and endorsed by the Commission on Social Justice. Like citizen's income, this would provide a non-means-tested benefit on an individual basis, but it would have attached to it a condition of 'active citizenship' (caring or voluntary work as well as paid work or education/training) for those of working age capable of work of some kind (Oppenheim, 2001; White, 2003).

Finally, when considering social security rights from a European perspective, it is imperative that these rights should attach to all women in Europe and not just European women. Of particular concern are the social rights and entitlements of women asylum-seekers (Mcleish et al., 2002; Women's Budget Group, 2005).

Conclusion

This chapter has discussed some of the key debates raised by the notion of gendered social entitlements. It has focused, in particular, on the tensions between care and paid work; the gendered division of labour and time; and income rights. In addition to specific policies, it is helpful to formulate more general goals to underpin demands for improved gendered social entitlements. These goals might include: first, a more equitable gendered division of different forms of labour and of time, which is also an essential platform for women's effective political citizenship; second, adequate support for the care of children and older people and a high quality social infrastructure; and third, greater economic equality between women and men and the economic independence and well-being of *all* women.

Note

1. The Commission on Social Justice was established by the former leader of the Labour Party, the late John Smith, to advise the party on a strategy for social and economic reform.

References

Atkinson, A. B. (1993) *Beveridge, the National Minimum, and its Future in a European Context*, London: STICERD/LSE.

Bennett, F. (2002) 'Gender implications of current social security reforms', *Fiscal Studies*, 23(4): 559–84.

Bruning, G. and Plantenga, J. (1999) 'Parental leave and equal opportunities: experiences in eight European countries', *Journal of European Social Policy*, 9(3): 195–209.

Commission on Social Justice (1994) *Social Justice: Strategies for National Renewal*, London: Vintage.

Daly, M. (2002) 'Care as a good for social policy', *Journal of Social Policy*, 31(2): 251–70.

Duncan, S. and Edwards, R. (1999) *Lone Mothers, Paid Work and Gendered Moral Rationalities*, Basingstoke: Macmillan.

Fagan, C. and Rubery, J. (1999) 'Gender and labour markets in the European Union', paper presented at *COST 13 Workshop, Gender, Labour Markets and Citizenship*, Vienna, 19–20 March.

Fagnani, J. (1999) 'Parental leave in France', in P. Moss and F. Deven (eds) *Parental Leave: Progress or Pitfalls?* Brussels: NIDI/CBGS Publications.

Fraser, N. (1997) *Justice Interruptus*, London and New York: Routledge.

Goode, J., Callender, C. and Lister, R. (1998) *Purse or Wallet? Gender Inequalities within Families on Benefits*, London: Policy Studies Institute.

HM Treasury (2004) *Choice for Parents, the Best Start for Children. A Ten-Year Strategy for Childcare*. Available at http://www.everychildmatters.gov.uk/_files/C7A546CB4579620B7381308E1C161A9D.pdf [Accessed 8 December 2005].

Howarth, C. and Kenway, P. (2004) *Why Worry Any More about the Low Paid?* London: New Policy Institute.

Knijn, T. and Kremer, M. (1997) 'Gender and the caring dimension of welfare states: towards inclusive citizenship', *Social Politics*, 4(3): 328–61.

Lenz Taguchi, H. and Munkhammer, I. (2003) *Consolidating Early Childhood Education and Care under the Ministry of Education and Care: A Swedish Case Study*, Early Childhood and Family Policy Series No. 6, Paris: UNESCO.

Lewis, J. (ed.) (1997) *Lone Mothers in European Welfare Regimes*, London and Philadelphia: Jessica Kingsley.

Lewis, J. (2000) 'Work and care', in H. Dean, R. Sykes and R. Woods (eds) *Social Policy Review 12*, Newcastle: Social Policy Association.

Lister, R. (2003) *Citizenship: Feminist Perspectives* (2nd edn), Basingstoke: Palgrave.

Lister, R. (2004) *Poverty*, Cambridge: Polity Press.

McKay A. and VanEvery, J. (2000) 'Gender, family, and income maintenance: a feminist case for citizens basic income', *Social Politics*, 7(2): 266–84.

McLaughlin, E. and Glendinning, C. (1994) 'Paying for care in Europe: is there a feminist approach?' in L. Hantrais and S. Mangen (eds) *Family Policy and the Welfare of Women*, Loughborough: Cross National Research Group.

McLaughlin, E., Yeates, N. and Kelly, G. (2002) *Social Protection and Units of Assessment*, London: Trades Union Congress.

Mcleish, J., Cutler, S. and Stancer, C. (2002) *A Crying Shame: Pregnant Asylum-Seekers and their Babies in Detention*, London: Maternity Alliance.

Millar, J. (2003) 'Squaring the circle? Means testing and individualisation in the UK and Australia', *Social Policy & Society*, 3(1): 67–74.

Millar, J. and Rowlingson, K. (eds) (2001) *Lone Parents, Employment and Social Policy*, Bristol: Policy Press.

Morgan, K. J. and Zippel, K. (2003) 'Paid to care: the origins and effects of care leave policies in Western Europe', *Social Politics*, 10(1): 49–85.

Moss, P. (2005) 'Getting beyond child care . . . and the Barcelona targets', paper presented at Challenges and Opportunities faced by European Welfare States: The Changing Context for Child Welfare, University of Oxford, Oxford, 7–8 January.

Norris, P. (1987) *Politics and Sexual Equality: The Comparative Position of Women in Western Democracies*, London: Wheatsheaf.

Oppenheim, C. (2001) 'Enabling participation? New Labour's welfare-to-work policies', in S. White (ed.) *New Labour: The Progressive Future?* Basingstoke: Palgrave.

Sen, A. (1999) *Development as Freedom*, Oxford: Oxford University Press.

Sevenhuijsen, S. (1998) *Citizenship and the Ethics of Care*, London and New York: Routledge.

Shaver, S. (1993/94) 'Body rights, social rights and the liberal welfare state', *Critical Social Policy*, 39: 66–93.

Standing, K. (1999) 'Lone mothers and "parental" employment: a contradiction in policy?' *Journal of Social Policy*, 28 (3): 479–95.

Thomas, A. and Griffiths, R. (2004) *Integrated Findings from the Evaluation of the First 18 Months of Lone Parent Work-Focused Interviews*, Sheffield: Department for Work and Pensions.

Ungerson, C. (1997) 'Social politics and the commodification of care', *Social Politics*, 4(3): 362–81.

van Drenth, A., Knijn, T. and Lewis, J. (1999) 'Sources of income for lone mother families: policy changes in Britain and the Netherlands and the experiences of divorced women', *Journal of Social Policy*, 28(4): 619–41.

White, S. (2003) *The Civic Minimum*, Oxford: Oxford University Press.

Williams, F. (2004) *Rethinking Families*, London: Calouste Gulbenkian Foundation.

Women's Budget Group (2005) *Women's and Children's Poverty: Making the Links*, London: Women's Budget Group.

2

Individualisation and the Crumbling of the Welfare State

Virginia Bras Gomes

Social protection models in welfare states may be influenced by political and institutional systems, economic and social development levels and cultural backgrounds, but the notion of welfare is inextricably linked to combating poverty and social exclusion and to promoting individual and collective well-being.

Although the terms 'welfare' and 'social protection' are sometimes used interchangeably, the concept of the welfare state goes beyond social protection systems to include social policies and various other fields, whether economic or cultural, in which the state maintains forms of systematic intervention.

Social security is a universal component of social protection systems of welfare states. In this chapter, the focus on individualised social rights for women allows for the materialisation of the broader concept of social protection through social security systems that include interconnected measures within a common framework system. The purpose of such measures is to ensure benefits in cash or in kind in situations of economic or social need due to the occurrence of legally defined risks or insufficient lack of personal or family resources.

The notion of social protection as an instrument of poverty eradication and, therefore, one almost exclusively restricted to means-tested benefits and basic social services, is shared by countries in certain developing regions of the world. At the other end of the spectrum are social protection systems inspired by the European social model that cover individuals and groups through a range of benefits and services to ensure protection against social risks like unemployment, sickness, maternity, family charges, old age and disability.

In between social protection solely for poverty eradication and social protection as a productive factor that contributes to economic and political stability and towards making the EU the most competitive knowledge-based economy in the world there are many options open for individual states.[1]

The differences in the nature and scope of social protection systems do not depend on financial resources only. It is true that in many developing countries social protection is very limited, leaving a large proportion of the population without adequate coverage, but it is equally true that in some of the most developed industrial countries, individuals and families in need are also left without coverage due to the large gaps in public social assistance systems.

The European social model

Notwithstanding the differences in their national economic, social and cultural contexts, EU member states consider the European social model as a shared goal and a joint commitment. Countries to a greater or lesser extent inspired by this goal are generally grouped under four historic social protection models (Kerschen, 2000). Though the countries included in a certain group may not share all the characteristics of the model and some of them may in fact have a certain mix of elements from more than one model, the general grouping is useful to highlight the elements in all the models that are relevant to the discussion about the individualisation of social protection and social security rights, specially for women.

The items used in the left-hand column of Table 2.1 to illustrate the characteristics of the social protection models are intended to draw attention to the differences in their nature and scope. There are also common, across-the-board constraints that impact negatively on all protection models and require innovative solutions to balance the sustainability of financial resources with the need to maintain the extent and levels of social protection in covering not only traditional social risks but also new factors of social exclusion.

The Scandinavian model is the one most conducive to the individualisation of rights and is, therefore, referred to in various arguments in the course of this chapter. The discussion about the role of the welfare state and the ideal welfare mix to guarantee social security/social inclusion by extending people's entitlements has been high on the political agenda for the last two decades and its importance is increasing.

On the one hand, individual and collective social risks are becoming more complex and interrelated as the links between drug addiction/ AIDS/disability; between longevity/dependency/pensions/health and

Table 2.1: Social protection models in Europe

	Scandinavian (Denmark, Finland, Iceland, Norway, Sweden)	Continental (Germany, Austria, Netherlands)	Anglo Saxon (UK, Ireland)	Mediterranean (Italy, Spain, Greece, Portugal)
Nature	Universal / Caring State	Insurance-based	Redistributive	Redistributive
Guiding principles	Gender equality and well-being of citizens, specially children	Work-related and family-oriented; recognition of the worker and his family	Notion of need or of vital minimum; social protection in insecurity; welfare-to-work policies	Work-related and family-oriented; traditional solidarities (family, neighbourhood)
Access	Individual access to work-related social rights. Rights-based access to services (children)	Connected to the head of the family as the right-holder but fast-changing (e.g. splitting of pension rights after divorce)	Insufficient access to work-related social rights due to high percentage of part-time work	Individual access to work-related social rights
Funding	Taxation	Contributions	Taxation and contributions	Taxation and contributions
Formal and informal social care services	Collective child care; social care services; parental and family leaves; different ways of organising work time	Subsidiarity; individual arrangements (part-time work, leave)	Provision of services at the best level possible; lack of affordable public or private collective child care	Insufficient collective child care; informal care of children and adult dependants
Constraints	Economic setbacks, unemployment, labour precariousness, demographic pressures, internal and international migration, changing living and family patterns			

social care; or between globalisation/poverty and vulnerability/social safety nets show. On the other hand, the welfare state is coming under severe pressure and financial constraints which have led to its philosophy being challenged and to the erosion of its scope, personal and material coverage and protection measures.

The crumbling of the welfare state is related to its difficulties in responding to a number of challenges. One of the most important of these, one that is bound to become even more important in the future, is the demographic challenge. The world is ageing in a process of radical demographic change at both ends of the age pyramid – a decrease in birth rates and an increase in life expectancy. Between 2000 and 2050, the percentage of people aged 65 and over will double from 10 to 21 per cent. The older population itself is ageing. The oldest elderly (80 years or older) is the fastest growing segment of older population. As a result, the dependency ratio[2] poses major problems for the financial sustainability of public pensions and long-term health and social care systems in terms of both old age pensions and expenses with health care and social services for very old and dependent persons.

The second challenge is the economic one posed by long-term unemployment, youth unemployment, underemployment and low labour market participation rates due to the weakening of the correlation between economic growth and employment rate as well as the high cost of jobs and fragmented work careers. The employment crisis has a significant impact on public finances, leading to an increase in public expenditure on unemployment benefits and training and retraining policies, as well as to a huge decrease in revenues from taxation and social security contributions. This is a serious shortcoming, because in order to sustain itself, a welfare state needs enough workers to contribute to the social security system and to pay the taxes that support welfare programmes and benefits for the non-working.

Partly linked to this challenge, but also to changes in the political and economic systems in many European countries, are the efforts to rethink and reorganise the role of the state, no longer as the sole provider of social security and social services, but as the enabler of the overall framework to ensure universal and equitable access to basic benefits and services that allow all its citizens, and especially the most vulnerable, to live in dignity. These efforts are far from successful in many countries where the state is still grappling with the need to balance long-term financial sustainability concerns with meeting its overall function of ensuring an acceptable level of social protection to all its citizens, especially the most vulnerable.

The changing gender balance is an important economic, social and cultural challenge faced by the state, relating, for instance, to activities that were traditionally provided free of charge as informal care but are now paid for and will continue to be so in the future. This is particularly true for what we might consider the production of family well-being, which was almost exclusively entrusted to women, but for which we need to find good alternatives so that 'l'état providence caché' (Schulte, 2000) – the hidden welfare state – once almost exclusively supported by women, gains new support. The increased participation of women in the labour market has reduced the availability of unpaid informal family carers and consequently increased the demand for child care, as well as for family support services and institutional long-term care facilities. But many women still perform the role of informal carers and, therefore, are not in gainful employment, either because they have never entered the workforce or because they have interrupted professional careers that would have allowed them to contribute towards immediate or long-term benefits. They are often left without adequate individual social protection.

Globalisation is a complex, politically influenced process that carries a number of international challenges and still poses threats to national political and social institutions and decision-making power. In its report 'A Fair Globalisation – Creating Opportunities for All', the World Commission on the Social Dimension of Globalisation states that 'seen through the eyes of the vast majority of men and women around the world, globalisation has not met their simple aspiration for decent jobs, livelihoods and a better future for their children' (2004: 10). While highlighting ways in which all relevant players can work towards the common goal of fair globalisation, the report refers to 'persistent imbalances in the current workings of the global economy which are both ethically unacceptable and politically unsustainable' (p. 3).

As recognised by developing and developed countries alike, the benefits of globalisation have not been equitably shared among regions, nations and peoples. On the contrary, the gap between and within countries has widened, because the opportunities provided by globalisation require material, technological and organisational capacities that are unevenly distributed. Furthermore, social development policies have been mistakenly considered as being contrary to economic growth and international competitiveness and the establishment of social safety nets absolutely necessary to cushion the unwanted or unexpected effects of globalisation on poor persons, families and communities has not been considered a national political priority.

All these challenges threatening the welfare state need to be tackled without diluting its socio-political content and ethical approach. They call for ongoing adjustments and adaptation in the architecture of public systems and continuous monitoring of public policies. In fact, in the era of globalisation and weakening institutional protection mechanisms, the need for consolidated national social security systems is even greater.

Modern welfare states have to cover traditional risks as well as face new ones in an active and preventive manner, within a context of dwindling resources. Success in this endeavour calls for priorities in line with concerns of social justice without trade-offs between equality and efficiency, and for clear goals[3] and strategies for integrated economic and social policies. These should include improved educational and employment opportunities, qualified human resources and a wide range of benefits and quality social and health care services to respond to new social needs, namely the reconciliation of professional, family and personal life. Central to these goals and strategies is the principle of 'equality of rights, conditions and opportunities, which refer broadly to ways in which people are able to participate in society as citizens, to exercise their entitlement to resources, and their ability to contribute to the well being of themselves, their families and their communities' (UN Secretary General, 2005: 5).

Although there is no globally recognised definition of social rights, they are normally understood as rights that call for state intervention in their materialisation for all, through legislation, policies and operational programmes. At the international level, the UN International Covenant on Economic, Social and Cultural Rights sets out a vast range of economic, social and cultural rights. State parties to the Covenant need to comply with their obligations to promote, protect and fulfil the rights set out therein, either through immediate measures to fulfil core obligations or through the promotion of adequate policies for the progressive realisation of the Covenant rights.

At the regional level, instruments such as the European Social Charter and the Revised European Social Charter, as well as the Additional Protocol to the American Convention on Human Rights in the Area of Economic, Social and Cultural Rights (Protocol of San Salvador), provide an international framework for governments to adopt the necessary measures for the purpose of achieving progressively the observance of the rights contained in them.

Access to social rights and their effective materialisation, in the context of this chapter, depends on the nature, scope and provisions of social protection/social security systems.

The dimensions of individualisation

Let us now consider four dimensions of individualisation: individualisation as a personal identity trait; individualisation of social protection; individualisation of rights; and direct rights versus derived rights.

Individualisation is part of identity-building in modern societies, especially in the more industrialised countries where people need to respond positively to growing demands throughout their life-course, without being able to rely on solutions inherited from the past (to face and overcome new problems).

The crumbling of institutional social protection systems, the weakening of informal support networks due to changing family and living patterns, together with new factors of social exclusion in highly competitive environments push people into believing that they have to assume full control of their lives and that they depend entirely on their own resources and skills. This feeling does give individuals a greater autonomy in relation to traditional state structures, but also enhances the conviction that social problems are personal shortcomings that call for individual solutions.

Social protection is one of the great institutions of individualisation in the twenty-first century, whether through social insurance or social security. In Europe, the issue of individualisation of social security rights has its root in article 119 of the Rome Treaty, and is further consolidated in more recent documents. For more than twenty years, social law and various socio-economic instruments of the EU have clearly moved towards the individualisation of social protection.[4] Individualisation implies the acquisition by an individual of his/her own security, that is, the acquisition of rights related to his/her needs. This can be done through universal access to social rights on a non-contributory residence basis or through individual contributions and entitlements. In terms of options for women, the first is relevant for non-working women, in so far as it allows them not to depend on their working husbands, and for poor women heading one-parent families who need to support their children. The second option is certainly an encouragement for women to engage in paid labour so as to earn individual entitlements to social benefits and services.

According to Henri Sterdyniak (2004), a system is individualised if social rights and taxation have the individual as their subject, without taking into consideration whether he/she lives with others, sharing common resources. In such cases, needs evaluation for taxation and concession of social benefits, whether through universal access (for example, to child allowances or residence-based old-age pensions) or in return for contributions under mandatory or voluntary public social insurance schemes, relate to the individual. By opposition, in a family-oriented system (in whatever form the family may exist), needs evaluation, social benefits and taxes are family-based since workers' contributions to the social protection system allow for direct rights and derived rights (or subordinate rights).

Individualisation further implies the distinction between these rights. Direct rights are normally residence-based or work-related contributory rights materialised through social security benefits funded by employer and employee contributions. Derived rights are based on a family or partner relationship of children or non-working adults with a holder of direct rights. Derived rights ensure social protection for those considered to be *à charge de* (a dependant) of a direct right holder. The two elements that constitute a derived right are the absence of a direct right for an adult and the link to a direct right holder. Derived rights are often means tested.

In the context of this chapter, individualisation of social protection rights is favoured by the 'from the cradle to the grave' approach to the materialisation of citizenship-based social rights (Kuhnle and Hort, 2004) in the Scandinavian model[5] referred to in Table 2.1. Based on the principle of universality, this model has implied strong state and local government interventions and comprehensive public policies.

In the other models, individualisation could be ensured by abolishing the notion of the rights holder (since it could lead to indirect discrimination in access to benefits like a sickness benefit), in favour of universal access on condition of residence and, therefore, no longer work-related. It could also be achieved by suppressing joint household resource calculations in case of the social minima so as to prevent inactivity traps for women with low remunerations.

However, in no country is there a purely universal system or a purely work-related system. It is relatively easy to recognise an unemployment benefit as a work-related individual right, to replace lost earnings, but when it comes to social solidarity benefits[6] the problem is more complex: when the notion of risk insurance is replaced by the guarantee of a minimum living standard, there is good reason to take into account the household resources to calculate necessary differentials arising from the savings of living in a couple or in a family.[7] As an example, in some Central and Eastern European countries with economies in transition, the minimum level income, provided by the municipalities, is calculated as a differential means-tested benefit.

Arguments against individualisation are based on the perception that individual rights are contrary to family solidarity, by considering the development of individual social protection rights as a replacement for family and group solidarity. In fact, some authors fear that policies in favour of the individualisation of rights will contribute to the disappearance of traditional horizontal solidarity networks and the weakening of welfare protection for families, groups and individuals. This is a particular concern in countries where the taxation system is based on the family unit and less on the effort to make work pay for everybody, which is more in line with a policy focus on gender equality. In fact, individualisation of rights is positive for non-workers who live alone and do not hold any derived rights. But the situation changes if the option becomes an obstacle for non-workers living with workers who have chosen to pool their resources (of whatever nature these might be).

Turning to individual social security rights for women, let us now look at how individualisation of rights affects women along their lifecycle or in especially difficult situations. Gender is a generally recognised source of inequality; women experience greater obstacles in exercising their social rights than men. Gender discrimination is the cornerstone for women's lack of access to individual social rights. This is not to say that the other grounds of discrimination referred to in article 13 of the Amsterdam Treaty and in the 2002 Racial Equality and Employment Equality EU Directives[8] are not as important, all the more so because many women experience distinct forms of discrimination due to the intersection of sex with the other discrimination factors 'resulting in compounded disadvantage'.[9]

As early as 1997, the European Commission, in its Communication on the modernisation of social protection in the European Union, indicated the progressive realisation of individual rights as one of the solutions needed to adapt social protection to the new gender balance. The document considers that derived rights entail three negative consequences: they create dependency on the direct rights holder; they discourage women from joining the labour market and encourage them to work in the informal economy (since they are entitled to social protection through their husbands); and they are unfair in the case of survivor pensions granted without a contributory career.

For those who consider the integration of women in the labour market as an essential goal for overall economic growth, women's financial independence by avoiding the inactivity trap, and increased equality between men and women, one of the measures to undertake is the reduction of the income of one-worker families, either by decreasing the level of benefits or by increasing taxation. But this option can have a negative effect if it further jeopardises the situation of many one-worker families who are generally poorer than two-worker families or workers without families. The positive outcome of the entry of women into the labour market is that they are acquiring more and more individual work-related social rights and are thus no longer dependent on their husbands or partners as breadwinners. But the reverse side of this coin is the need for a vast range of measures to reconcile professional, family and personal life, so that men and women share both worlds – the outer world of work and professional satisfaction and the inner world of the family and emotional satisfaction. For this to happen, parents need to have clearly defined rights of securing a place for their children in child care services, individual and non-transferable entitlements to paid paternity and parental leave, and crediting of contributions during these leave periods as work periods and not as periods of incapacity to work. This is a very important issue for the individualisation of rights for women and for men. Even in countries inspired by the European social model, until a few years ago, paternity rights and benefits were conditioned by the fact that the father was expected to step in and assume parental responsibility only when the mother was physically or mentally unable to care for the newborn child. Welcome changes in some national legislations now establish a non-transferable right to paternity leave.

Parental and family leave are part and parcel of employment protection and social security in a growing number of countries. However, these periods of leave sometimes remain unpaid or are paid through a means-tested social security benefit. Such policies are in no way conducive to women's individual rights because, due to various obstacles, it is still mostly women who use parental leave or family leave to care for sick children or children with handicaps, or frail, dependent elderly people. Among the most relevant of these obstacles is discrimination against women in the workforce (non-compliance with the principle of equal pay for work of equal value as well as professional and vertical segregation practices) and the negative cultural stereotypes of the roles of men and women at home and in the outside world. Fortunately, in some countries, changes are being introduced in entitlement to benefits for parental leave. For example, the Czech Republic abolished the earnings limit for parental allowances in 1 January 2004. They are now paid regardless of the mother's or father's income. What are still not common are national laws that guarantee men a non-transferable right to part of parental leave. But the issues around leave and career breaks along the life-course of men and women provide clear examples of how the individualisation of rights for men impacts on the individualisation of rights for women.

What we need is a change of mentality, culture, policies and organisational structures in order to improve women's employment and career prospects. This will eventually lead to a more equitable sharing of the costs incurred by employers for paid parental and family leave and allow men and women to achieve a better balance between work, family and personal lives.

However, in spite of shortcomings in protection systems, it remains clear that the steep increase in the numbers in the female labour force in the last thirty years and the resulting entitlement to contributory retirement pensions as well as the trend towards universal non-contributory pension schemes with the corresponding individualisation of rights have significantly reduced the number of women, especially older women, who are entirely financially dependent on their direct right-holding husbands.

But lack of rights to adequate social security still remains a problem for non-working women and part-time women workers. Women's work typically includes looking after the welfare of others. Women are, therefore, welfare agents. In order to compensate for services traditionally ensured by women and usually related to motherhood, children's education and care of older family members, some systems take into account the economic and social importance of non-remunerated family activities by linking individual rights to their family context. Often, these derived rights acknowledge women's non-remunerated work as welfare agents, protecting them from falling into poverty, for example, through sharing pension rights after divorce in recognition of the contribution of the non-working spouse. But, in certain situations, derived rights can become unfair and discriminatory, for example when a non-worker married or living with a direct right-holder is considered to be *à charge de* (a dependant) even though she may have important property revenues, whereas an adult non-working woman living alone will not benefit from derived rights. Another example is the survivor pension. A non-working woman could be entitled to a survivor pension calculated as a percentage of the contributions of her deceased working husband or partner, which results in a higher pension than that paid to a single worker, who might have worked all his/her life for a lower salary. In both cases, the redistribution of resources is in favour of dependants or survivors of workers with higher earnings at the expense of workers with average or lower earnings.

Given the high unemployment rates and the situation of women in the labour market, they will probably stand to lose a lot if they lose the right to a survivor pension in favour of a non-contributory universal pension that would necessarily have to remain at a modest level, thus depriving non-working spouses of deceased workers of the resources needed to maintain their standard of living. This is a difficult choice, since the individualisation of rights will impact on persons as well as on public budgets, depending on the social protection branches that are covered by public systems. Individualising non-contributory pension rights implies the end of derived benefits for non-workers, for example the replacement of survivor pensions. In this case, workers would no longer contribute to survivor pensions, further leading to the need to reformulate social security systems in which employer and employee contributions are disaggregated to cover specific social risks.

A different standpoint on women as welfare agents is taken by those systems that consider the period of childrearing and informal care activities as entitlement periods for old age pensions, non-contributory pensions or other allowances, resulting in individualising rights for informal carers. Recent illustrations of such options are referred to in documents published by the International Social Security Association (2004/5).

In Norway, where the issue of non-work has been the focus of considerable political attention during the last decade, a White Paper on pension reform recently presented in Parliament refers to the need to improve rules for pension entitlements for unpaid care work, to introduce a life expectancy adjustment ratio and an amendment to take into account pension entitlements in the event of divorce. In Cyprus, the Mother's Allowance Law, which entered into force on 1 January 2003, provides an allowance to mothers with at least four children who have ceased to be eligible for child benefit after their children reach 15 years of age (or older under special conditions). In Belize, a new non-contributory pension covers women aged 65 and over who have not had the opportunity to contribute to a retirement benefit because they have stayed in the home caring for their family. Even more important is the fact that the new scheme recognises their contribution to the country's national development. Nevertheless, in general terms, it is hardly to be expected that public contributory systems subject to major financial constraints will be able to allocate resources for non-contributory pensions. In fact, in an effort to maintain long-term sustainable pension schemes, European public social security schemes are looking for ways to limit future spending on pensions, by increasing the retirement age, by introducing a contributory ceiling in order to avoid the payment of high pensions and by encouraging individuals and families to adhere to supplementary systems under state supervision.

The only way out for non-contributory pensions to become individual rights for women in return for their 'work' as informal carers would be for them to be funded by the state's budget from revenues derived from general taxation.

Voluntary affiliation

In some countries, individual rights are achieved through voluntary affiliation to social insurance security schemes, whether public or private. Voluntary affiliation under public management enables non-workers and people engaged in socially useful activities, for example volunteering, to acquire individual rights. These schemes allow beneficiaries to choose from among different options for contributions and corresponding benefit, but as with private insurance, affiliation requires that potential recipients are able to make contributions.

The crisis of the welfare state and financial cutbacks in social security have led public systems to lose their monopoly as providers of protection against social risks and, consequently, to the erosion of trust in the public system. Workers, especially those whose earnings are above nominal fixed ceilings and who wish to maintain their standard of living, especially after retirement, are being encouraged to acquire individual rights through private social insurance systems, for example, health insurance and supplementary pension funds for old age and invalidity, in order to augment protection afforded by the public system. This is true for developed countries as well as for countries with economies in transition. Hungary, Poland, Bulgaria, Latvia and Estonia are scaling down public, pay-as-you-go schemes and putting commercially managed individual savings schemes in place alongside them (Fultz, 2004: 12).

However, besides the fact that it does not guarantee benefits to cover risks traditionally covered by public systems (e.g. family benefits such as child allowances), individualisation through private schemes is not accessible to everyone, especially not to non-workers and low-income workers: it requires the ability to make financial contributions, information, planning and organisational capacity.

Social services

Maternity and paternity rights and benefits, paid parental and family leave, career breaks and child care services are extremely relevant for the reconciliation of professional and family life for men and women and for the materialisation of women's work-related individual rights. Personal social services involving professionally provided assistance for older persons in need of long-term care are also becoming increasingly important due to population ageing and increased life expectancy. For many middle-aged employed women, care of dependent parents and relatives is a major constraint to career advancement and often to better work-related social protection.

From a socio-economic perspective, social services are an important component of the infrastructure required for the smooth functioning of the economy through the full integration of women in the labour market, and for social integration through the harmonious development of children and the care of older or dependent persons. The demand for child care and other personal social services is based on the idea of collective responsibility of for society's children and its more vulnerable and disadvantaged citizens. However, even in Europe, where, irrespective of different female employment patterns, reconciliation of work and family is high on national agendas, child care costs are to a large extent still supported by the oldest solidarity network, i.e. the family.

Access to social services is crucial to the acquisition of individual work-related rights for women. Lone parents and low-income persons and families are especially dependent on affordable (if need be, subsidised) social services to be able to work and escape from benefit dependency. The absence or insufficiency of adequate, accessible and affordable social services is likely to reinforce old divisions of social welfare and give rise to new ones.

In spite of welcome changes in the stereotyped roles of men and women, especially among the younger generations in urban settings, reconciliation between work and family life is still largely considered a woman's problem, in the same way as it is taken for granted that it is still a woman's job to raise children and look after older relatives. It is probably because of the double burden to which mothers and grandmothers have been subject that some young women in developed countries do not consider combining full-time work and family life as an option, preferring to work part-time or not at all, while their children are small. This choice should of course be respected, but one may wonder if, faced with readily available, quality child care services and other measures to reconcile professional and family life, young women would still make the same choice.

The crumbling of the welfare state has particularly impacted on the provision of social services. The state is no longer the sole provider of social services but rather the enabler of an overall favourable environment for social development with increased responsibility for ensuring equitable delivery of, and access to, quality social services through an effective legal and fiscal framework and an accountable public sector.[10]

Issues of subsidiarity and complementarity of social services were very much brought to the fore by the changes in the role of the public sector. It is assumed that these services can, in most cases, be delivered most effectively and efficiently by entities closest to local communities and, therefore, more aware of their needs. It is also part of present public policy formulation and practice to consider decentralisation, privatisation, public/private partnerships and the introduction of competitive, market-based structures as complementary and alternative approaches to the delivery of social services.[11]

Specially vulnerable groups of women

Women in particularly difficult situations are in special need of guaranteed access to their social rights. The issue here is less of direct versus derived rights, but of women's rights as human rights enabling women to live in dignity. I would like to point out a few examples – women victims of domestic violence and migrant women.

Many women are subject, at some point in their lives, to violence within their family and/or community. Tradition, cultural assumptions and the stereotyped roles of men and women are at the heart of various causes of domestic violence, which may range from child and forced marriages in traditional communities, to the still hidden phenomenon of physical and psychological violence.

Notwithstanding the fact that cultural changes do not happen overnight and require an immense effort of awareness-raising as well as better educational and employment opportunities for girls and women, it is the responsibility of the state to enact legislation to ensure full respect for the human rights of victims of domestic violence, providing them with immediate protection and long-term rehabilitation

Documented and undocumented migrants face a number of different problems, including discrimination and xenophobia, now enhanced by the widespread fear of terrorism. Respect for the principle of non-discrimination in relation to migrants implies equal treatment in access to rights for their economic and social integration in receiving countries.

Women living in developing countries or in countries with economies in transition are particularly vulnerable to migration problems. Faced with increasing barriers to family reunification in the more developed countries, they suffer the worst of both worlds. When alone in their home countries, they hold no rights and often live in poverty with their children. In receiving countries, they suffer the greatest discrimination in the labour market for a number of reasons, including negative racial or social stereotypes. Often the only employment opportunities open to low-skilled migrant women are as hired home-helpers, dish-washers or supermarket workers, subjecting them to long working hours and other forms of labour exploitation and inadequate social protection. The way out for many migrant women is to work in the informal sector, with low wages, no employment security or social protection coverage in maternity or sickness. The fact that the informal sector is still unregulated also jeopardises their entitlement to an individual work-related pension.

Conclusion

The underlying goal in strengthening social security should be to maintain, and when necessary restore, the universal approach to social protection (Palme, 2003) so that not only population groups are covered, but also that benefits and services are adequate enough to ensure protection and care for people of different income levels.

In most EU countries, a substantial part of social security rights is based on individual participation in the labour market. The individualisation of rights on the basis of this participation raises two major problems. The first is how to guarantee that this participation ensures a sufficient level of social benefits for women, given the fact that they are subject to professional segregation[12] and vertical segregation[13] in the labour market, normally due to overlapping factors like recruitment, promotion and training. The second problem is more complex – how to ensure social protection that respects human dignity, even for those that do not work, through universal social protection.

Within the development of the EU along the lines of a 'social' Union, individualisation of social security rights calls for a combination of models. If putting in place a universal sickness benefit constitutes an advance for women's rights, such an option may not be appropriate for retirement pensions, which, being universal and non-contributory, would necessarily remain modest.

The model proposed by the European Commission in its 1997 Communication involves the idea of a universal, flat-rate old age pension complemented by a professional contributory pension. This option could provide women pensioners with some income security as long as the first pension element ensured an adequate living standard to all those who became beneficiaries after a certain age. However, once again, the financial constraints faced by public pension schemes due to demographic pressure and the low level of contributions entering into the system do not lead us to think that this might be a feasible solution.

Another option, that of individualisation of benefits based on calculations that do not take into account household resources for the attribution of minimum income benefits, cannot solve the problem of gender inequalities that arise from differences in the status of men and women in the labour market and within the family.

In a broad sense, for individual rights to be materialised in the context of wider equality, socio-economic systems have to respond positively to a number of issues concerning the improvement and adequacy of work-related schemes, changing labour market rules and regulations and unemployment protection. This will allow for the reduction of job precariousness and part-time working constraints, and reinforce the protective role of the unemployment benefit.

In a more focused gender equality perspective,[14] the widespread adoption of reconciliation measures related to the organisation of work and the needs of persons and families (work hours, child care, organisation of time) is a highly relevant step for the individualisation of women's rights.

The Scandinavian universal welfare model of social protection, based on tax-financed social programmes with a strong emphasis on economic efficiency, has been successful not only in combating social inequalities but also in promoting the individualisation of women's rights. This was achieved by increasing their employment and participation opportunities through improved employment incentives and investment in human resources, not least in the social service sector, as well as the adoption of a wide range of measures to reconcile professional, family and personal responsibilities. It is also a system that pays universal old-age pensions, including pension rights for housewives and others who have not been in gainful employment (Kuhnle and Hort, 2004).

The responsibilities of the actors that together ensure social protection through many different provisions of the 'welfare mix' – the state through policy formulation and social security systems, the family, the local community and the individual him- or herself – are continuously shifting under the influence of changing social needs. Nevertheless, no doubt remains with regard to the importance of safeguarding the welfare state to individualise social rights. 'The welfare state is unquestionably one of the noblest accomplishments of the 20th century,' writes Pranab Chatterjee (1999), because 'all of us are welfare recipients in one way or another...the stereotypical welfare person is just one small part of it'.

Notes

1. These options and the contradictions between them were made clear at the 41st Session of the UN Commission for Social Development, in 2001, on the theme *Enhancing Social Protection and Reducing Vulnerability in a Globalizing World*, in which government representatives could not arrive at the customary set of agreed conclusions issued at the end of every session because it was not possible to overcome the major differences in the definition of the concept of social protection.
2. The ratio between working-age population and those who are dependent (under 15 and over 64).
3. The Millennium Development Goals, adopted by the heads of state and government, at the Millennium Summit, September 2000, establish quantitative targets to be achieved within a certain timeframe, thus contributing towards a more demanding implementation of national and international benchmarks.
4. Important directives: 75/117/CEE (equal pay); 76/207/CEE (equal opportunities in access to employment, training, promotions and working conditions); 79/7/CEE (equal treatment in social security); 86/378/CEE and 96/97/CEE (equal treatment in the professional social security schemes); 86/613/CEE (equal treatment for the self employed, including in agriculture and in maternity protection); 97/80/CE (burden of proof in the case of gender discrimination); 96/34/CE (parental leave).
5. In this model, the concept of the welfare state normally covers social security schemes; family benefits; maternity benefits; social assistance; public health system; labour market policies; basic education; social services; and public subsidies for housing.
6. According to Alain Euzéby, solidarity is a 'humanist ideal which provides the basis for the concept of collective responsibility in relation to others within a community' (Euzéby, 2004: 109).
7. In order to have the same standard of living, a household made up of two adults only needs $1\frac{1}{2}$ times the revenue of an isolated person. The increase of fixed charges, such as housing, for example, is not proportional to that of the size of the household.
8. Referred grounds of discrimination are race, national or ethnic origin, religion/belief, age, sexual orientation, marital status and family status.
9. Draft General Comment no. 16 on article 3 of the International Covenant of Economic, Social and Cultural Rights, on the equal right of men and women to the enjoyment of all economic, social and cultural rights, under discussion by the UN Committee on ESCR, adopted in April 2005.
10. Agreed Conclusions on the priority theme *Social Services for All* adopted during the 37th Session of the UN Commission for Social Development (1999).

11. Agreed Conclusions on the priority theme *Improving Public Sector Effectiveness* adopted during the 42nd session of the UN Commission for Social Development (2004).
12. A significant proportion of women work in the service and care sectors, offices, nursing and teaching.
13. Fewer women than men are in management positions.
14. The equal right of men and women to the enjoyment of all human rights calls for the mainstreaming of the gender perspective in all policies and programmes.

References

Chatterjee, P. (1999) *Repackaging the Welfare State*, Washington, DC: NASW Press.

Council of Europe, European Proposal for a Directive of the European Parliament and of the Council on the implementation of the principle of equal opportunities and equal treatment of men and women in matters of employment and occupation COM/2004/0279 final – COD 2004/0084.

European Union, Employment and Social Affairs (2002) *MISSCEEC 2002, Social Protection in the Central and Eastern European Countries: situation on 1 January 2002 and evolution*, Brussels: European Commission.

Euzéby, A. (2004) 'Social protection: values to be defended!' *International Social Security Review*, 57(2): 107–15.

Fultz, E. (2004) 'Pension reform in the EU accession countries: challenges, achievements and pitfalls', *International Social Security Review*, 57(2): 3–21.

Gomes, M. V. B. (2005) 'The role of the Commission for Social Development: a forum for institutional collaboration and professional exchange', paper presented by the German delegation at the *43rd Session of the Commission for Social Development*, United Nations, New York, 9–18 February.

Hespanha, P. (2002) 'Individualização, fragmentação e risco social, nas sociedades globalizadas', *Revista Crítica de Ciências Sociais*, 63: 21–30.

ISSA (2004/5) *Trends in Social Security: An International Update*, Geneva: International Social Security Association.

Kerschen, N., (2000) 'L'individualisation et les modèles historiques de protection sociale', *Redistribuer les Responsabilités pour Moderniser et Améliorer la Protection Sociale*, AISS. Série Européenne, 27: 21–8.

Kuhnle, S. and Hort, S. E. O. (2004) 'The developmental welfare state in Scandinavia. Lessons for the developing world', *United Nations Research Institute for Social Development. Social Policy and Development*, paper no. 17.

Neves, I. das (2001) *Dicionário Técnico e Jurídico de Protecção Social*, Coimbra: Coimbra Editora.

Palme, J. (2003) 'Foundations and guarantees of social security rights at the beginning of the 21st century', paper presented at the *Conference on the ISSA Initiative*, venue of the conference, city, 10–12 September. Available at: http://www.issa.int/pdf/initiative/2find-op8.pdf [accessed: 4 May 2005].

Peemans-Poullet, H. (2000) 'L'individualisation des droits', *Redistribuer les Responsabilités pour Moderniser et Améliorer la Protection Sociale. AISS. Série Européenne*, 27: 47–64.

Saunier, J. M. (2000) 'Minima sociaux: droit individuel ou droit familial?' *Droit Social*, 7–8: 722–9.

ISSA (2004) *Social Security Programs Throughout the World: Europe*, Washington: Social Security Administration.

Ministry of Social Affairs and Health (2004) *Socius*, Helsinki: Ministry of Social Affairs and Health.

Schulte, B. (2004) *Defending and Enforcing Rights to Social Protection. ISSA Initiative Findings and Opinions*, Munich: ISSA no. 16.

Schulte, B. (2000) 'Une nouvelle solidarité familiale', *Redistribuer les Responsabilités pour Moderniser et Améliorer la Protection Sociale. AISS. Série Européenne*, 27: 101–15.

Sterdyniak, H. (2004) 'Contre l'individualisation des droits sociaux', *Revue de l'OFCE*, 90: 419–45.

UN Secretary General (2005) 'Review of further implementation of the World Summit for Social Development and the Outcome of the 24th special session of the General Assembly', report presented at the *43rd Session of the UN Commission for Social Development*, United Nations, New York, 9–18 February.

UN (2000) Resolutions adopted by the General Assembly A/RES/S-23/2 and A/RES/S-23/3, on the report of the Ad Hoc Committee of the Whole of the 23rd Special Session of the General Assembly, 16 November.

Vandenbroucke, F. (2001) 'The active welfare state: a European ambition', paper presented at the *41st Session of the UN Commission for Social Development*, United Nations, New York, 10–21 February.

World Commission on the Social Dimension of Globalization (2004) *A Fair Globalization: Creating Opportunities for All*, Geneva: International Labour Office.

Zaidman, C. (1998) 'L'individualisation des droits réduirait-elle les inégalités hommes/femmes?', *Droit Social*, 6: 590–5.

3
Gendered Configurations of the Nordic Model: Civil Society, State and Social Citizenship

Anneli Anttonen

The Nordic welfare state: a twentieth-century emancipatory project

In northern Europe, the welfare state was defined very early on as an emancipatory project that would guarantee social justice and a good life for its citizens. We know that 'real welfare states' have been the most important pillars of modernisation and democratisation in the Nordic democracies. For a long time there has been a consensus over the fact that the Nordic model has been exceptional in promoting solidarity and equality among different social groups and between men and women; and it has been effective in solving social problems such as poverty and the marginalisation of vulnerable groups and individuals. It was in the 1980s when feminist scholars started to pay attention to the distinctive nature of the Nordic model as a 'woman-friendly state' where women's needs and interests as mothers/carers and as workers are acknowledged much more widely than in any other modern welfare society (Siim, 1988; Leira, 1992; Anttonen, 1997). It was argued that Nordic social policies are exceptional in promoting gender equality and in particular women's labour market participation. The Nordic model has meant a radical redefinition of social citizenship.

During the last fifteen years or so, comparative welfare state research has given much support to the proposition that Nordic welfare states make a difference in Western democracies. From the 1990s, the welfare regime approach has been the most influential school in comparative social policy analysis: it aims at modelling whole welfare state systems. Gøsta Esping-Andersen's *The Three Worlds of Welfare Capitalism* (1990) inspired much interest in developing typologies of welfare states. His approach also produced a broad critical debate about the bases of formation of regimes. Feminist scholars in particular have criticised regime theorists for concentrating on the situation of male wage-earners in formal employment and on those social policy areas which are linked to the status of citizen as worker and breadwinner (e.g. Lewis, 1992; Brush, 2002).

The regime approach has since been extended to cover other social policy issues such as social care and social services (Anttonen and Sipilä, 1996; Daly, 2001). The debate on the decline of the male breadwinner model (Lewis, 2001; Pfau-Effinger, 1998) and the feminist insight that families as well as markets and states are sources for welfare have meant a vital corrective to welfare regime studies (Brush, 2002: 169). The other side of the coin is that these extensions and corrections have not fundamentally changed the positioning of the Nordic countries: the 'Nordic regime' tends to be the most consistent and coherent one when compared to other regime types. One can even go further and argue that the 'Nordic regime' is the only regime that can be formed without any substantial difficulties: all other regimes include a lot of incoherence and heterogeneity when it comes to their construction. There really are good grounds to argue that a 'Nordic model' or a 'Nordic regime' exists – irrespective of its founding elements – and that it really is different from all other welfare state models.

According to Mikko Kautto et al. (1999: 13) the most distinctive features of the Nordic model are the following:

- The scope of public social policy is large, it encompasses social security, services, education, housing, employment, etc.
- The state's involvement has been strong in all policy areas.
- The Nordic welfare system is based on a high degree of universalism, meaning that all citizens/residents are entitled to basic social security benefits and services, regardless of their position in the labour markets.
- Income security is based on two elements. In most schemes, there is a flat-rate basic security and an earnings-related part of those with a work history.
- The share of social expenditure of GNP has been high.
- The Nordic countries have also been characterised as (social) services states.
- The role of local democracy is strong.
- Income distribution is relatively even and there are no big cleavages between different income groups.
- Gender equality is one of the guiding principles of the Nordic welfare states.

Although gender equality is an explicit aim of the Nordic model, it is important to point out that other characteristics mentioned above also have much to do with the woman-friendliness of the model. When the scope of social policy is large and the leading principle of redistribution of resources is universalism, it means that different kinds of social risks are covered – not only those related to the status of waged worker. The concept of 'social services state' ensures that the well-being of citizens is guaranteed not only through various kinds of income transfers (such as pensions and family allowances) but also through education, health care and social care. In this chapter my focus is mainly on that part of the welfare state I have named 'social services state' because social care services have a special importance for women whose labour market participation is dependent on collective arrangements of care. Women's access to paid labour is highly dependent on care services; and these services make it possible for women to stay at work when children or adult family members need help and care in the case of sickness or disability. Care services also create new job opportunities for women. The notion of social services or social care here means that education and health care are left out of the analysis: I shall pay particular attention to care services and their historical development.

Although there seems to be a wide consensus about the fact that the Nordic model is successful in solving social problems and promoting gender equality, criticism of the model has increased during the last decade. There have always been commentators saying that the Nordic model threatens the fluent operation of a market economy and weakens a citizen's moral and civic responsibilities. Today, it is often argued that the Nordic model is unable to meet all the new challenges caused by the globalisation of the economy and the labour market.

In this chapter, my intention is to evaluate the emancipatory dimension of the Nordic welfare state model in an historical context to understand better the distinctive nature of the model. My main argument is that the Nordic model is based on conceptions of emancipation and democratisation where the *ethical role of the state* is important. I shall describe some of the historical processes through which Finland became a woman-friendly welfare state. My analysis shows that civil society and its organisations played a crucial role in bringing in the 'women's nation'. It again was a precondition for the Nordic social services state to develop. Civil society and the state already operated in a close relationship at the beginning of the twentieth century; and the same is true throughout the twentieth century.

Before moving on to the historical part of my chapter, I shall briefly speak about 'Nordic welfare statism' in the context of liberalism and communitarianism. The reason for this is that civil society, market and family now are seen as the main representations of 'individual and collective emancipation' instead of the state. Commentators from these camps tend to think that what we need is 'less state' and more citizen participation. The idea of the ethical role of the state is undervalued in much of today's political and social thought. Against this background the whole ideology of Nordic 'welfare statism' seems to be false. In the Nordic countries, social protection is formed by state-driven rather than family-based or market-reliant activities. The state and municipal authorities have assumed a large responsibility for the well-being of citizens. It is, however, important to stress that all welfare states and models are historical and social constructions. Therefore, we should be careful when making universal claims about the nature of the state or civil society or their relation to each other in particular countries. We really need a deeper understanding of the historical and cultural under-currents of welfare state development. In this chapter I shall concentrate on the situation in Finland that is a good representative of the Nordic model. The main features of the model listed above are all typical to Finnish social policies. Also the comparative welfare state research sees Finland as a Nordic welfare state.

Nordic welfare statism: a threat to civil society?

Today, it is often asked if the Nordic countries are able to carry on their state-driven social policies. In European societies, the political and social situation has changed due to several ongoing economic and social processes such as the globalisation of the economic system, the internationalisation of the European Union, the collapse of the Soviet Regime, and changes in gender relations, family patterns and lifestyles (Boje, 1999). There are also cultural changes taking place that seem to lead us to a more diversified value system and everyday life. Nearly ten years ago, Nancy Fraser (1997: 2) suggested that the twentieth-century 'emancipatory projects', such as 'socialism' and 'welfare statism', have lost much of their critical and transformative potential. It is therefore valid to ask if the 'Nordic welfare statism' has grown old and turned into a fossilised project.

I started my chapter by saying that the Nordic welfare state was understood from an early stage to be an 'emancipatory project' that would guarantee a good life for citizens. It was the state that became a central actor in the process of democratisation and modernisation of these societies. Social policies became a central vehicle to promote equality and solidarity among social groups and between men and women. Now, commentators from different theoretical and political camps try to persuade that the Nordic model has grown old. In the beginning of the 1990s, Alan Wolfe (1991: 108) wrote that the Nordic model has declined the importance of civil society and citizen's political participation; today, the same kind of arguments are often presented by social capital theorists (e.g. Putnam, 2000; Seligman, 2000).

Civil society has been used as a critical concept including an idea of citizen participation and empowerment in relation to state power. There is, however, no political or theoretical agreement over the meaning of civil society and active citizenship as its essential partner. Tuija Pulkkinen (1998: 17–45) sees a difference in the way that the concept of civil society is used in the two main tradition of political thought: the Hegelian-Marxist tradition and liberalism. In liberalism civil society is usually defined as a realm of individual freedom, while in the Hegelian-Marxist tradition civil society (*bürgerliche Gesellschaft*) is a sphere of egoism and self-interest (or of necessity). This distinction is of great importance when trying to understand the relations between the state and civil society both historically and in contemporary societies.

Ann Showstack Sassoon (1997) has noted that civil society represents a concept that has not traditionally dealt with gender relations. She also says that the revitalised debate on civil society and citizenship is something not to reject. A major problem, according to Showstack Sassoon, is that no concept of civil society, which is adequate today, can ignore relationships within and between family, voluntary organisations and the state or the gendered configurations of real civil societies.

The distinction made by Pulkkinen suggests that there is a difference between the more continental European tradition of defining civil society and the Anglo-American tradition which rests primarily on liberalism. In the continental tradition the ethical role of the state as well as positive connections between state and civil society has often been articulated by political theorists (Showstack Sassoon, 1997). The distinction is, of course, simple and does not do justice to different forms of liberalism, such as to social liberalism, for instance. However, I have found the distinction useful when tracing the historical roots of the Finnish welfare statism. My understanding of civil society rests on the continental European way of defining civil society.

Liberalism has been the main doctrine to challenge the legacy of 'welfare statism'. In the 1990s, Finland saw a rise of neoliberalism with claims of minimal state and maximal freedom of the market economy. According to neoliberalists the Nordic model has reached its limits both financially and socially: the welfare state threatens not only the autonomy of its citizens but also the effective use of labour power. Antti Hautamäki (1996), the leading neoliberal in Finland, suggests that the welfare state should be replaced by a 'spontaneous society' that is based on the very classic values of liberalism: the autonomy and freedom of citizens, self-employment and privacy. Neoliberalism does not speak in favour of a stronger civil society. Families and individuals should take more responsibility for individual lives. In neoliberalism individuals are seen as separate and atomistic monads rather than active members of communities (Young, 1990: 45).

Another critical line follows the neo-Aristotelian thinking where the state is not seen as a main enemy but as something like an 'enabling state' (Sihvola, 1996). In this doctrine civic responsibilities are strongly emphasised: individuals are not seen as atomistic monads but rather as moral beings constituted by a community. Neo-Aristotelianism comes close to communitarianism (see e.g. Avineri and De-Shalit, 1992) which again has the strongest foothold in the US. American political theorists often define civil society as separate from the state. For instance, Jean Cohen and Andrew Arato (1992) reject the idea that the state and its authorities could be in charge of creating the good life for its citizens. According to Sihvola (1996) a new balance between state and civil society is needed and the new condition can be achieved only through strengthening communal values and civic activities. The task of the state is, however, to guarantee that citizens are able to develop self-determination and active citizenship, which in turn lead to a more minimal role of the state.

Neoliberalism and communitarianism represent two main alternatives to welfare statism. Liberalism has its focus on individual emancipation. In its vocabulary 'active' citizenship means that everyone should earn a living through work or self-employment; moreover, family obligations are strongly emphasised. In the communitarian doctrines active citizenship is equated with political participation and collective organisation of citizens. Most communitarians, though, do not pay any attention to gender relations and gender differences when talking about civic responsibilities and activities. Such crucial things as who is responsible for caring and childbearing or what an ideal community for women is are easily excluded from the debate.

It really is important to ask: what is the critical potential of civil society? To reach a more comprehensive understanding of the changing relationships of the state and civil society I shall first look into the historical formation of civil society in the context of the development of the Finnish welfare state and then turn back to the present-day situation. My main argument is that the development of the Nordic welfare state has rested on a well-developed civil society that, however, has been and remains today divided along gender lines. Civil society and citizenship are gendered notions and highly contextual phenomena. We have to remember that every conception of civil society and citizenship is embedded in specific historical and cultural contexts; yet, we can learn from other countries' experiences. My aim is to contribute to the theoretical debate on the woman-friendliness of the Nordic model by paying attention to the historical formation of civil society and social citizenship in Finland. My main argument is that the Nordic welfare state model is based on a well-developed civil society and a special form of social citizenship.

Democratic civil society: a precondition for welfare state development

The idea of welfare statism where 'a centralized state has a capacity to design and execute its plans independent of the pressures of particular groups in society' (Cox, 1998: 4) has been implemented variously in different countries. The Finnish welfare state is an historical and discursive construction that has its roots in the democratisation of society as well as in the processes through which political and social citizenship were developed. In the nineteenth and early twentieth centuries, Finland was a predominantly agrarian and Protestant society: cultural homogeneity has played a crucial role in building up both a nation-state and a modern welfare state.

Since the early nineteenth century, the construction of being a Finn or a Finnish citizen was closely linked to nation-state building. The transformation from loyal subjects to individuals in Finland was fuelled by the nationalist Fennomanian movement of the first half of the nineteenth century when the idea of a nation-state began to gather momentum, especially among the Finnish-speaking upper classes. In their struggle against Russification and the Swedish-speaking ruling elite, the upper classes had a more powerful position in politics and in the emerging public sphere to gain. In this struggle the upper classes needed the support of the common people (Alapuro and Stenius, 1987; Pulkkinen, 1987; Satka, 1995). During the second half of the nineteenth century people's movements, such as the temperance movement, workers' associations and women's societies, were established: 'women took an active part in these nation-wide popular movements, often as the founders and leaders of local branches', as Irma Sulkunen (1990: 48) has shown.

Through these movements the idea of democratic citizenship equal to all members of society was developed. The idea of democratic citizenship was not only expressed in terms of civil and political rights, but also included a strong moral commitment to the welfare of the whole nation. It was thematised in terms of education and enlightened civilisation. In Finland, the works of J. V. Snellman (1806–81) and S. Alkio (1862–1930) share the heritage of the Danish N. F. S. Grundtvig (1783–1872) in their reliance on the power of education against ignorance and immorality. Snellman's conceptions of family, state and civil society were based on the Hegelian philosophy where the state represents the most developed level of moral reason. In Snellman's political thought, adopted by the Fennomanian movement, an individual was seen as a moral being constituted by a community that is the nation. The family is the place to raise moral and decent citizens. Individuals were seen not so much as autonomous and abstract monads brought together incidentally on the market, as teleological and moral agents. Later, this kind of 'communitarian' thinking became fertile soil for welfare statism.

During the first half of the nineteenth century it was mainly the liberal bourgeoisie that led political mobilisation and the building-up of the nation-state. In the 1880s, the situation started to change due to the organisation of the workers' movement. Until the early twentieth century these movements, however, unified Finns in their struggle against their oppressors (Hentilä, 1996). As the state was understood as the main source of protection against Russification, close ties of loyalty were constructed between people's movements and the emerging nation-state.

Even before independence which came late, in 1917, Finland had obtained a unicameral parliament in 1906 as a result of the weakness of Russia and the strength of the people's movements. The parliamentary reform of 1906, at that time the most radical in Europe, rested on Finland's political tradition which had a well-developed civil society (Hentilä, 1996: 3). Finland's parliamentary reform gave adult men and women not only universal and equal suffrage, but also the right to stand for elective office; this was unprecedented (Sulkunen, 1996: 10). But parliamentary reform offering universal and equal suffrage did not guarantee peaceful democratisation: the harmonious ties between the national government and the people's movement proved to be illusory.

The governing upper classes faced an uprising by the working class and landless population: the Finnish Civil War of 1918 triggered a political and mental crisis that froze the democratisation of civil society. The 'red' (or socialist) side was beaten and radical workers' organisations lost power for decades: the relationship between state and civil society was thoroughly transformed. The main task of the ruling bourgeoisie was to reintegrate the Finnish nation by strengthening the state by means of a loyal and unified civil society based on the revitalisation of conservative peasant values, strict Protestantism and absolute conformity. It is worth mentioning that fascism played only a minor role in Finland, but certainly there was little space for Western individualism and liberalism.

The relationship between the state and civil society seems to be full of contradictions and paradoxes. On the one hand, at the beginning of the twentieth century, Finland had a well-developed civil society and the democratisation process was determined by civic movements and organisations. On the other hand, a strong centralised state was a common goal for most political actors, although for different reasons. The late nineteenth- and the early twentieth-century developments show that civil society can lose the emancipatory power it has gained. In Nordic countries, there are also common features when trying to understand the mental and political culture of these societies.

When tracing the common roots of civil society and political citizenship in the Nordic countries, we should, according to Henrik Stenius (1997), pay special attention to the cultural homogeneity of these societies and the impact of Lutheranism on the Nordic political and mental culture. Lutheran cultural homogeneity has dominated Nordic countries: the relationship between state and church is unique. Even the Reformation was a state-driven project, not a protest from below. Furthermore, the laws and norms created by the state were compatible with the laws and norms of the Lutheran Church (Satka, 1995: 191). Secular local administration among other things was separated from ecclesiastical administration as late as 1865, when the functions of relief for the poor were delegated to local governments.

The unification of state and church has fostered a culture of belonging to one religion, to one (imaginary) community and to one nation. What is also important is that the Lutheran orthodoxy embraced the concept that work holds society together: through work one becomes part of the society as a *Gemeinschaft* (community). All Nordic countries have a strong work ethic: the status of good citizen has to be earned through (hard) work. The Nordic-Lutheran labour code covers poor and rich, women and men. The agrarian legacy of Nordic societies has favoured work-related citizenship ideals.

Protestantism and agrarianism have played an important role in the process of making of the Finnish nation and its citizens. Compared to many other European countries, industrialisation and urbanisation were delayed in Finland. We also have to remember that after Finland seceded from Sweden in a war of 1809 it was, until 1917, an autonomous part of the Russian Empire (the Grand Duchy of Finland). Especially during the first half of the nineteenth century it was extremely difficult to carry out legislative or any other reforms. After the Finnish Civil War legislative reforms, such as the social security programmes introduced in the other Nordic countries, were delayed. As the early welfare state development was slow, the 1920s and 1930s became the heyday of voluntary organisations. However, these acted in close co-operation with state authorities (Satka, 1994: 279).

Civil society and 'women's nation'

The mainstream narratives of civil society, citizenship and nation-state building tell us one part of the story of the making of Finnish citizens and civil society. Civil society and citizenship are, however, gendered concepts and practices as many of today's feminist scholars have shown (Hernes, 1987; Pateman, 1988; Lister, 1997; Showstack Sassoon, 1997; Williams, 2001). Feminist researchers have paid attention to the exclusionary processes of citizenship formation, where women and femininity have fallen outside the category of 'universally defined' citizenship, and only later were included.

In Finland, the idea of the modern citizen was defined in terms of moral self-government and willingness to serve the welfare of the whole nation. Sulkunen (1987; 1990: 121) has pointed out that:

> the very concept of democratic citizen is and has always been gender-biased. It did not offer any promises of unshared equality: all the rights and the duties it implied tied down the citizenship of women primarily to the family and to the private, while the citizenship of men was accordingly linked up with the public and with working life.

Men were expected to be respectable workers and breadwinners, while women were expected to show high moral standards as mothers and educators of new generations.

Women's status as (emerging) citizens and their special role in making the 'women's nation' – an expression used by Tuija Pulkkinen (1998) – was compatible with the social and political order advocated by J. V. Snellman. According to Hegel, women do not have any task to perform in the sphere of the state where the communal unity of the people turns into a self-conscious political nation – the new moral agency was male and represented by men.

As I have mentioned above, according to the elite Finland needed enlightened citizens who had to be informed about new, emancipating ideas, such as the importance of education, health and a well-ordered family life. While the family was understood as a realm for bringing up a new generation of healthy, decent and responsible citizens, women's role as mothers and caretakers was emphasised. In Finland, women's citizenship and women's civic responsibilities have been influenced by what Sulkunen (1987; 1990) calls 'social mothering'. Hence, even if excluded from the new moral agency, women took an active role in civil society and in building up the nation-state. They became integrated into the project of individualisation and modernisation as different moral agents, 'citizens' on their own terms.

Women started to build up a 'women's nation' partly as political actors in people's movements and partly through their own organisations. New emancipating doctrines, such as domestic economics, social work and public health care, were introduced to promote self-governance among common women and men. By the turn of the twentieth century women had already taken a leading role in social and health care organisa-tions (Satka, 1995). 'Social mothering' became a legitimate pathway for women from the private to the public sphere. It is a concept that is very close to maternalism, maternal citizenship and maternal social policies (see Koven and Michel, 1990; Bock and Thane, 1991). Interestingly, feminist scholars in different countries have reached very similar conclu-sions in relation to women's citizenship formation. When looking at the period between the 1880s and 1950s, maternalist discourses and politics are identifiable in most Western societies.

National projects and politics may well have been motivated by the same endeavour to bolster the nuclear family and women's role as mother-carers, but over time they have evolved differently and assumed different forms. Maternalism also means different things in different countries and eras: the situation in Finland during the early decades of the twentieth century resembled the situation in France more closely than that in the UK and US. As Jane Jenson (1989: 240–1) has noted: 'In France prevalent gender identities included the assumption that economic activity of both single and married women was valid... even if women workers were not exactly the same as men, women were nonetheless workers.'

This was very much the case in Finland too. Even if there were different norms and expectations for men and women, the idea of modern citizenship was not divided into feminine and masculine parts. The decent citizen was a productive and responsible man or woman whose duty was to serve the nation by denying his or her egoistic interests and drives. In Finland, work became the most important dimension of citizenship. Furthermore, women's paid work in factories and unpaid work on the farms was, in a poor and agrarian country, more of a necessity than a way to emancipation and economic independence – at least for working-class women and women living on smallholdings.

It would be wrong to argue that women were totally excluded from the sphere of civil society and the struggles for democratic citizenship. Before Finland's independence the issue of the right to vote unified men and women in their struggle for democratic citizenship, especially within workers' movements. As different moral agents women were mainly positioned outside the political power structure, but were creating civil society through their own activities and agendas (Saarinen, 1992: 216). Many social activities were run by philanthropic and voluntary organisations which promoted the well-being of children, mothers and families: maternity and children's clinics, for instance, started as voluntary organisations at the beginning of the 1900s, and only became part of public health care system in 1944, when national laws on clinics, health visitors and midwives came into force (Kuronen, 1993: 15–17).

Since the 1830s, voluntary organisations had been influential in running children's day care, hostels for working girls and boys, schools, hospitals and so on. In the late 1920s there were 1,532 voluntary organisations listed by the Ministry of Social Affairs that were running 'welfare' activities (Satka, 1994: 283–9). Most of today's social and health care services run by public authorities have their roots in voluntary work mainly carried out and organised by women. In the field of social and health care services the state was acting more as an extension of civil society than as an independent agent until the 1950s.

Women's active role in civil society led to social policy reforms that had special importance for women, children and the well-being of families. There are good reasons to argue that the early developments of social policies had a maternalist origin. During the first decades of the twentieth century maternal policies were at the centre of social reforms, although strongly influenced by the poor law tradition and population policy. In the 1930s a law on maternity grants, addressed to poor women, came into force. Furthermore, a special allowance for low-income families with more than four children was introduced. In the late 1940s Finland introduced universal child benefit and maternity allowance which represented the first nation-wide and universal social security systems in the history of Finnish social policy.

Women politicians campaigned for these benefits. Maternalism (or 'social motherhood') was a hegemonic discourse shared by bourgeois and working-class women, but they did not have the same ends in view. Bourgeois women were deeply concerned about the increasing employment of women in factories, which was thought to be a serious threat to the morality not only of the women themselves but also of homes, future generations and society at large (Vattula, 1989; Julkunen, 1994). For working-class women maternal values were important, because motherhood was a social and economic risk at a time when no support systems or benefits for mothers and children existed. This explains why working-class women demanded state intervention: it was the state that represented a sphere where women's issues could be solved. Also women living in the countryside gave their support to state social policy rather than civil society solutions. Most voluntary organisations were working in (big) cities and offered no help to those living in the countryside.

While the ideal of social motherhood unified women in some issues, it did not solve the class question. Maternalism was constructed on a hierarchical sisterhood, where upper-class women defined the content of womanhood. On the one hand there was a strong emphasis on mothering, on the other, both poor agrarian families and more affluent industrial families needed the labour input of women. It took decades before this kind of conflict was resolved. It came to the fore immediately after the Civil War. According to the winning side the rebellious working class had betrayed the national project. Widows and their children, as well as thousands of orphans on the 'red' side, were treated as second-class citizens during the postwar decades (Nätkin, 1997). In this situation the bourgeois women's movement naturally took the leadership in defining womanly citizenship duties. Woman's role as mother was celebrated more than ever and maternal values became extremely important. Consequently, working-class organisations lost their legitimacy on the level of both civil society and the state. Maternalism took a conservative turn and lost its emancipatory power.

When looking at the early developments of social policies in Finland, we cannot avoid paying attention to the 'women's nation' and 'social motherhood' as its feminine representation. It is evident that civil society and the state were not seen as two opposite spheres but rather as complementary and co-existing. Many social activities were started by voluntary organisations, which again were working in a close and friendly relationship with state and municipal authorities. Moreover, these associations were among the most important interest groups demanding social reform and state intervention. It is important to remember that voluntary organisations were established along class lines, so that bourgeois and working-class associations co-existed, for instance, in the field of child welfare. Gradually, working-class associations gained more legitimacy in Finnish society. There have always been bourgeois parties that have given strong support to the autonomy of voluntary and other welfare organisations, while leftist parties and interests groups have relied more on the power of the state in social policies.

My conclusion is that civil society formed the foundation for a modern welfare state in Finland. Nevertheless the role of the state was central by the late nineteenth century. Voluntary organisations worked in close co-operation with municipal and state authorities demanding state interventions, or at least state financing, for the activities they were running. The cultural and religious homogeneity helped in reaching a consensus on social policy issues, although the Finnish Civil War delayed consensual politics in a significant way, especially when Finland is compared with other Nordic countries. The role of women in making Finnish citizenship and civil society is of utmost importance when looking at the early developments of social policies. During the first decades of the twentieth century maternalism influenced the work of voluntary organisations in the field of social and health care. Yet, women's labour market participation internationally was on a high level. It was only after the Second World War that maternalism started to lose its hegemony.

The post-Second World War welfare state development: from 'women's nation' to social services state

In most countries modern social policies have been premised on the idea of compensating the wage-earner for lost income. The institutionalisation of workers' social rights was an important turning point for the redefinition of citizenship. The modern welfare state with social rights became possible only when paternal rule broke down and paved the way for a stronger political civil society and people's movements. Through the idea and practice of social citizenship, positive liberties, such as education, health and welfare, became integrated into citizenship rights.

The language of social citizenship and social rights challenged the legacy of economic, and partly also political, liberalism; it also defined an individual as a member of a larger community, especially the nation.

When speaking about the postwar period and its dominant vocabulary of citizenship and civil society in Nordic countries, we cannot avoid looking at the grand idea of 'social citizenship'. As a concept and idea it was introduced by T. H. Marshall (1950), who posited a relationship between class and citizenship in his famous sequence of civil, political and social rights. The Marshallian doctrine of social rights can be seen as an expression of a change in liberalism's vocabulary of citizenship in England. Marshall's intention was to support a 'social-democratic' turn in a situation where capitalism limited citizen's full participation in the democratic society organised through the principles of market liberalism. Marshall's definition constructs the citizen as a member of a community evoking 'a strong "sense of belonging" and of national identity that citizenship can provide' (Yuval-Davis, 1997: 7).

Gøsta Esping-Andersen (1985; 1990) and Walter Korpi (1985) developed Marshall's classic formulation in the Northern European context. One of the main ideas in Marshall's theory is that in obtaining political rights workers are able to establish social rights through the exercise of political power. According to Esping-Andersen (1990: 27) social democracy, together with political civil society, were clearly the dominant forces behind social reforms and social rights in Scandinavian countries. Rather than tolerate a dualism between state and market, between working class and middle class, the social democrats pursued a welfare state that would promote equality of the highest standard. His famous conclusion is that Sweden and the other Scandinavian countries have carried the practices of social rights and social citizenship further than any other country.

Welfare state development is deeply embedded in the 'communit-arian' tradition of Nordic societies. The internationalisation of social political practices (such as workers' social insurance) as well as strong economic growth during the postwar decades made it possible to transform collectivity based on conformity into large-scale social solidarity. This happened much earlier in Sweden and Denmark than in Finland: it was only in the 1980s that Finland reached the level of other Scandinavian countries when comparing social rights and entitlements (Alestalo and Uusitalo, 1986; Kröger, 1996). Thus, Finland is a latecomer among the Nordic nations.

The Nordic experience is evidence that solidarity and individual autonomy can be legislated through the idea of social citizenship.

It has meant that marginalised and other oppressed groups such as women have become part of the social policy contract. Women have succeeded in combining the dual role of mothers and workers: it has been extremely important for women to extend social rights to cover caring for young children, the elderly and sick and disabled members of society. In the 1970s and 1980s, the Nordic welfare states became distinctively social services states (Anttonen, 1997). This makes a difference when comparing Nordic countries to other kinds of welfare states.

The feminisation of social citizenship and social rights did not, however, happen without a struggle. Starting in the early 1960s a new women's movement actively campaigned for women's rights. The task they set for the state was to facilitate the fitting together of wage labour and the home: there were increasing calls for better day-care services for children, longer maternity leave and the right of parents to stay at home to look after a sick child. This line of politics has been successful: in Nordic countries the state has played an active role in creating equality between men and women and in promoting women's dual role as mother-carers and workers.

Jane Lewis (1992) speaks about a weak or a dual breadwinner model where woman's status has been transformed from a dependent mother-wife to worker through the promotion of women's economic independence. This has been done by means of separate taxation, abortion rights, generous service provision for small children, the disabled and elderly members of society, and by individually determined benefits. The 1970s and 1980s saw a huge expansion of social care services. We might argue that caring has become an acknowledged component of social citizenship. From a feminist point of view a radical extension of social citizenship and social rights was established, in particular, when citizens won rights to certain social care services. A comprehensive municipal day-care system is a good example of this process. In Finland, children's day-care has been a qualified right for parents who have children under three years of age since 1990, and since 1996 has covered all children under school-age. There are only a few countries in the world where parents of children under three years of age are entitled to full-time day care.

The Nordic democracies differ from most post-industrial welfare societies to the extent that informal caring has been transformed from a private matter for families to a public matter for the state. The comparative literature on welfare states shows that extensive public provision of social care services for adult citizens who need regular help in their daily life exists in Nordic welfare societies (e.g. Anttonen and Sipilä, 1996; Rostgaard and Fridberg, 1998; Daly, 2001; Anttonen, Baldock and Sipilä, 2003). The Nordic societies are also generous in their support for families with small children. Jorma Sipilä et al. (1997: 39–40) have argued that in all Nordic countries (with the exception of Iceland) social care services are widely available to children and adults who need help, and the service system at large responds to the interests of women. Thirdly, the middle and upper classes are among the users of public social services. Finally, the municipalities are responsible for service provision. For all these reasons it is justified to talk about a 'Nordic social care regime' or 'Nordic social services state'.

The Nordic social care regime is based on the dual breadwinner or adult worker model (Lewis, 1992; 2001). One of the most important aims is to support women's right to paid labour and help women (and men) reconcile home and work, caring and paid work. Overall, social care policies have served as an important goal for social policies in the Nordic countries and shaped the grand idea of social citizenship. Originally, social citizenship was strongly tied to the status of the male worker citizen; only gradually, were women's needs acknowledged. In this section I have used social care services as an example of the feminisation of social citizenship. At least as important are such rights as the right to abortion and other reproductive rights, even if I have paid no attention to these rights here.

Conclusion

Although Nordic countries have been exceptional in solving social problems and in promoting gender equality, there are plenty of old and new problems in the field of social policy. When talking about social citizenship in the Nordic countries, it is important to note that social rights are not complete. For instance, the services available to the frail elderly, whether institutional or home help services, does not always meet demand. Likewise, the idea of equal services for the poor and rich does not always work in practice. There has always been private service provision alongside municipal provision. In fact, the Finnish system of social services and social security at large is not nearly as 'public' as is declared. Local governments are by no means the only providers of social services; various civil society and market-based organisations are involved. A good example is home-help services: in the late 1990s, non-profit and for-profit providers accounted for about 20 per cent of all services in the home help sector (Kröger, Anttonen and Sipilä, 2003: 35).

In Finland, the social services state encountered new problems during the economic recession of the early 1990s. One of the main victims of cost containment was the state subsidy to local government, which hit the municipal social services hard. The economic recession, together with the growth of a neoliberal ideology, has led to a profound restructuring of social care policies. There has been a strong tendency to reduce the costs of institutional care and now there seems to be a tendency to increase selectivism and self-financing especially in the field of old age services (Anttonen, 2001). When looking at social and health care services, we can easily identify new principles in providing these services. Marta Szebehely (2004) speaks about the informalisation of care relations: families have assumed a larger responsibility for caring for their old and sick members than during the golden age of welfare statism (in the 1970s and 1980s). There are also signs of increasing privatisation of service provision: private or market provision is increasing, municipalities are contracting out services instead of providing services themselves; and privatisation means 'new public management' in public sector service provision.

The whole ideology of the social services state is changing; and these changes may have many impacts on women's lives and choices. First, women have to rely more than men on formal service provision because they live longer: men are often cared for by their spouses when they need help. Secondly, women form the majority of care workers, thus, all changes in the field impact on women's lives. Finland is a good example of a country where one important aim of social care policy has been the professionalisation of service provision: the majority of municipal home-helps get three years' vocational training which is internationally exceptional. The same applies to child care and many other female care professions. If there is a trend to limit the scope of municipal service provision and increase competition among different sectors, the training of care workers might be reduced. Finally, women are also a clear majority of those who bear the main responsibility of family-based informal caring. If in the future there are fewer subsidised services, women's access to paid labour might be threatened and we can expect the market and civil society sectors to become stronger in social care policies.

When looking at social policy developments in Finland, it is easy to conclude that social activities started and run by civic or welfare organisations have gradually been absorbed into the public sector. In the postwar years in particular, the state and municipalities assumed a much greater responsibility for welfare functions. The same applies to activities run by industrial companies: beginning in the nineteenth century many industrialists were providing services for workers and their families. In Finland, these were at their height in the interwar period (Kröger, 1999). Today such activity has all but disappeared. Therefore it is often argued that civil society has lost its emancipatory power; and that welfare statism in the Nordic countries threatens the idea of social solidarity and altruism.

It would be wrong, however, to argue that the state has taken the place of civil society because many activities were handed over to the state and municipalities without any real resistance. Increasing state participation in social policy had already become an important aim for most political parties and welfare organisations by the beginning of the twentieth century. The women's movement is no exception here: it demanded state intervention and legal action to promote women's well-being as workers and as mothers or care-givers.

Despite some activities being turned over to the public sector new activities have been established. It is also important to remember that Finland is a leader among the Nordic countries in terms of citizen memberships of different associations. Against this background we cannot say that civil society and civic responsibilities have been withering away alongside welfare state development. Since the 1970s, changes have occurred that could lead to a partial depoliticisation of civil society. Certainly political party membership has declined in recent decades and the same is true of other traditional associations. At the same time new forms of associations and activism have become popular: voluntary work in welfare associations, for instance (Ilmonen and Siisiäinen, 1998). Thus, it is extremely difficult to say if the overall importance of civil society is declining.

The other side of the coin is the question Bo Rothstein (2000) has raised: What is the impact of the universal welfare state on relationships of trust and the accumulation of social capital? According to his studies the Nordic welfare states represent societies with high levels of social capital and trust. This certainly has something to do with the special relation of civil society and the state in the Nordic democracies. Citizens have relied on the state and its authorities and given strong support to welfare services such as health care, education and social care, which again seem to increase social capital among citizens.

Civil society is still a sphere in which new social questions and initiatives are articulated and developed. Among the new social issues is, for instance, violence against women. It has been raised in public political debate by agencies that are part of civil society and its publicity today.

The same applies to citizenship struggles: it might be that social citizenship is no longer central to citizenship struggles in the Nordic countries. There are new struggles, such as the struggle over 'sexual citizenship' or the struggle over 'ecological citizenship'. A fundamental issue today is: who is a citizen? What about children's rights and migrants' rights? And what about the nation? What is a nation in today's world?

References

Alapuro, R. and Stenius, H. (1987) 'Kansanliikkeet loivat kansakunnan', in R. Alapuro (ed.) *Kansa liikkeessä*, Helsinki: Kirjayhtymä.
Alestalo M. and Uusitalo, H. (1986) 'Finland', in P. Flora (ed.) *Growth to Limits. The Western European Welfare States since World War II: Volume 1*, Berlin: Walter de Gruyter, pp. 198–292.
Anttonen, A. (1997) 'The welfare state and social citizenship', in K. Kauppinen and T. Gordon (eds) *Unresolved Dilemmas: Women, Work and the Family in the United States, Europe and the Former Soviet Union*, Aldershot: Ashgate, pp. 9–32.
Anttonen, A. (2001) 'The politics of social care in Finland: child and elder care in transition', in M. Daly (ed.) *Care Work. The Quest for Security*, Geneva: International Labour Office, pp. 143–58.
Anttonen, A., Baldock, J. and Sipilä, J. (eds) *The Young, the Old and the State: Social Care Systems in Five Industrial Societies*, Cheltenham: Edward Elgar.
Anttonen, A. and Sipilä, J. (1996) 'European social care services: is it possible to identify models?' *Journal of European Social Policy* 6(2): 87–100.
Avineri, S. and De-Shalit, A. (1992) *Communitarism and Individualism*, Oxford: Oxford University Press.
Bock, G. and Thane, P. (eds) (1991) *Maternity & Gender Policies. Women and the Rise of the European Welfare States 1880s–1950s*, London: Routledge.
Boje, T. (1999) 'Introduction', *European Societies*, 1(1):1–7.
Brush, L. D. (2002) 'Changing the subject: gender and welfare state regimes', *Social Politics*, Summer: 161–86.
Cohen, J. and Arato, A. (1992) *Civil Society and Political Theory*, Cambridge, MA: MIT Press.
Cox, R. H. (1998) 'The consequences of welfare reform: how conceptions of social rights are changing', *Journal of Social Policy*, 27(1): 1–16.
Daly, M. (2001) 'Care policies in Western Europe', in M. Daly (ed.) *Care Work. The Quest for Security*, Geneva: International Labour Organisation, pp. 33–55.
Esping-Andersen, G. (1985) *Politics against Markets: The Social Democratic Road to Power*, Princeton, NJ: University of Princeton Press.
Esping-Andersen, G. (1990) *The Three Worlds of Welfare Capitalism*, Princeton, NJ: University of Princeton Press.
Fraser, N. (1997) *Justice Interruptus. Critical Reflections on the 'Postsocialist' Condition*, New York and London: Routledge.
Hautamäki, A. (1996) 'Individualismi on humanismia', in A. Hautamäki et al. (eds) *Yksilö modernin murroksessa*, Helsinki: Gaudeamus, pp. 13–44.
Hentilä, S. (1996) 'Finland's leap into democracy – 1906', *Finfo*, 7: 3–8.
Hernes, H. M. (1987) *Welfare States and Woman Power: Essays in State Feminism*, Oslo: Norwegian University Press.

Ilmonen, K. and Siisiäinen, M. (eds) (1998) *Uudet ja vanhat liikkeet*, Tampere: Vastapaino.

Jenson, J. (1989) 'Paradigms and political discourse: protective legislation in France and the United States before 1914', *Canadian Journal of Political Science/Revue canadienne de science politique*, XXII(2): 235–58.

Julkunen, R. (1994) 'Suomalainen sukupuolimalli – 1960-luku käänteenä', in A. Anttonen, L. Henriksson and R. Nätkin (eds) *Naisten hyvinvointivaltio*, Tampere: Vastapaino.

Kautto, M. et al. (eds) (1999) *Nordic Social Policy. Changing Welfare States*, London: Routledge.

Korpi, W. (1985) 'Power resources vs. action and conflict: on causal and intentional explanation in the study of power', *Sociological Theory: A Semi-annual Journal of the American Sociological Association*, 3(2): 31–45.

Koven, S. and Michel, S. (1990) 'Womanly duties: maternalist politics and the origin of the welfare states in France, Germany, Great Britain and the United States, 1880–1920', *American Historical Review*, 95: 1076–108.

Kröger, T. (1996) 'Policy-makers in social services in Finland: the municipality and the state', *Scandinavian Journal of Social Welfare*, 5(2): 62–8.

Kröger, T. (1999) 'Local historical case study: the unique and the general in the emergence of social care services in Finland', in S. Karvinen, T. Pösö and M. Satka (eds) *Finnish Reconstructions of Social Work Research*, Jyväskylä: University of Jyväskylä.

Kröger, T., Anttonen, A. and Sipilä, J. (2003) 'Social Care in Finland: Stronger and Weaker Forms of Universalism', in A. Anttonen, J. Baldock and J. Sipilä (eds) *The Young, the Old and the State. Social Care Systems in Five Industrial Nations* (Cheltenham: Edward Elgar), pp. 25–54.

Kuronen, M. (1993) *Lapsen hyväksi naisten kesken. Tutkimus äitiys- ja lastenneuvolan toimintakäytännöistä*. Tutkimuksia 35, Stakes, Helsinki, Gummerus.

Leira, A. (1992) *Welfare States and Working Mothers*, Cambridge: Cambridge University Press.

Lewis, J. (1992) 'Gender and the development of welfare regimes', *Journal of European Social Policy*, 2(3): 159–73.

Lewis, J. (2001) 'The decline of the male breadwinner model: implications for work and care', *Social Politics*, Summer: 154–69.

Lister, R. (1997) *Citizenship: Feminist Perspectives*, Basingstoke: Macmillan.

Markkola, P. (1990) 'Women in rural society in the 19th and 20th centuries', in M. Manninen and P. Setälä (eds) *The Lady with the Bow. The Story of Finnish Women*, Helsinki: Otava.

Marshall, T. H. (1950/1992) 'Citizenship and social class', in T. H. Marshall and T. Bottomore (eds) *Citizenship and Social Class*, London: Pluto Press, pp. 1–51.

Nätkin, R. (1997) *Kamppailu suomalaisesta äitiydestä*, Helsinki: Gaudeamus.

Pateman, C. (1988) *The Sexual Contract*, Stanford, CA: Stanford University Press.

Pfau-Effinger, B. (1998) 'Gender cultures and the gender arrangements. A theoretical framework for cross-national gender research', *Innovation* 11(2): 147–66.

Pulkkinen, T. (1987) 'Kansalaisyhteiskunta ja valtio', in R. Alapuro (ed.) *Kansa liikkeessä*, Kirjayhtymä: Helsinki.

Pulkkinen, T. (1998) *Postmoderni politiikan filosofia*, Helsinki: Gaudeamus.

Putnam, R. D. (2000) *Bowling Alone: The Collapse and Revival of American Community*, New York: Simon & Schuster.

Rostgaard, T. and Fridberg, T. (1998) Caring for Children and Older People: A Comparison of European Policies and Practices, Copenhagen: The Danish National Institute of Social Research.

Rothstein, B. (2000) 'The future of the universal welfare state: an institutional approach', in S. Kuhnle (ed.) Survival of the European Welfare State, London: Routledge, pp. 217–33.

Saarinen, A. (1992) 'Feminist Research – An Intellectual Adventure?' PhD thesis, University of Tampere, Centre for Women's Studies and Gender Relations.

Satka, M. (1994) 'Sosiaalinen työ peräänkatsojamiehestä hoivayrittäjäksi', in J. Jaakkola et al. (eds) Armeliaisuus, yhteisöapu, sosiaaliturva: suomalaisten sosiaalisen turvan historia, Helsinki: Sosiaaliturvan keskusliitto.

Satka, M. (1995) Making Social Citizenship. Conceptual Practices from the Finnish Poor Law to Professional Social Work, Publications on Social and Political Sciences and Philosophy, Jyväskylä: University of Jyväskylä.

Seligman, A. B. (1997) The Problem of Trust, Princeton, NJ: Princeton University Press.

Seligman, A. B. (2000) The Problem of Trust (Princeton, NJ: Princeton University Press).

Showstack Sassoon, A. (1997) 'Gender, Gramsci, and the debate about civil society', in A. Chirstensen, A. Ravn and I. Rittenhofer (eds) De Kønnede samfund, Aalborg: Aalborg Universitetsforlag.

Sihvola, J. (1996) 'Yksilö, yhteisö ja hyvä elämä. Aristotelismi ja suomalainen arvokeskustelu', in A. Hautamäki et al. (eds) Yksilö modernin murroksessa, Helsinki: Gaudeamus, pp. 63–116.

Siim, B. (1988) 'Towards a feminist rethinking of the welfare state', in K. Jones and A. Jonasdottir (eds) The Political Interests of Gender, Sage: London, pp. 160–86.

Sipilä, J. et al. (1997) 'A multitude of universal, public services. How and why did four Scandinavian countries get their social service model?', in J. Sipilä (ed.) Social Care Services: the Key to the Scandinavian Welfare Model, Aldershot: Avebury, pp. 27–50.

Stenius, H. (1997) 'Konformitetsideal blev universalitetsprincip', in G. Bexell and H. Stenius (eds) Värdetraditioner i nordiskt perspektiv, Lund: Lund University Press.

Sulkunen, I. (1987) 'Naisten järjestäytyminen ja kaksijakoinen kansalaisuus', in R. Alapuro (ed.) Kansa liikkeessä, Helsinki: Kirjayhtymä, pp. 157–72.

Sulkunen, I. (1990) 'The mobilization of women and the birth of civil society', in M. Manninen and P. Setälä (eds) The Lady with the Bow. The Story of Finnish Women, Helsinki: Otava.

Sulkunen, I. (1996) 'Finland – a pioneer in women's rights', Finfo 7: 9–16.

Szebehely, M. (2004) 'Nya trender, gamla traditioner. Svensk äldreomsorg i europeiskt perspektiv', in C. Florin and C. Bergqvist (eds) Framtiden i samtiden. Könsrelationer i förändring i Sverige och omvärlden, Stockholm: Institutet för framtidstudier, pp. 172–202.

Vattula, K. (1989) 'Lähtöviivallako? Naisten ammatissatoimivuudesta, tilastoista ja kotitaloudesta', in L. Laine and P. Markkola (eds) Tuntematon työläisnainen, Tampere: Vastapaino, pp. 13–38.

Williams, F. (2001) 'In and beyond New Labour: towards a new political ethics of care', Critical Social Policy, 21(4).

Wolfe, A. (1991) 'Welfare society and moral obligation. The case of Scandinavia', in *Forvitring eller fornyelse?* Rapport fra 6. nordiske sosialpolitiske forskerseminar. INAS-rapport 7, Oslo, pp. 89–113.

Young, I. M. (1990) *Justice and the Politics of Difference*, Princeton, NJ: Princeton University Press.

Yuval-Davis, N. (1997) *Gender and Nation* (London: Sage).

4
European Social Policies on Combining Work and Family Life: The Gap between Legislation and Practice

Inge Bleijenbergh

Public policy to support the combination of work and family life has been a claim of the women's movement across Europe since the 1960s. Danish grassroots women's organisations united in the Women's Liberation Movement and worked with female politicians in a successful bid to claim public care services and leave facilities (Siim, 2000). The French women's movement has been claiming money for better care facilities and for increasing women's presence in national politics (Fagnani, 1998: 62). In Italy and the United Kingdom (UK), women's organisations work at the local level in shaping social policies for children and the elderly (Bimbi, 1993: 165; Siim, 2000).

Some European Union (EU) member states introduced concrete policies on combining work and family life, including parental leave regulation, public child care services and tax support of private child care services. In the 1990s the EU also became involved in facilitating parents' care-giving tasks. In this period the EU adopted a series of Directives on maternity leave (or the protection of pregnant women at work, 1992), parental leave (1996) and part-time work (1997), and formulated common goals on stimulating care services in the Child Care Recommendation (1992). In 2002, EU member states formulated targets on provision of national child care services to be achieved by 2010 (Bleijenbergh, 2004a: 164). This chapter discusses the content of European social policies on combining work and family life and its effect on the combination of work and family responsibilities between men and women. Moreover, it explores what additional policies are needed to support fully the combination of work and family life in practice.

Table 4.1: EU policy on combining work and family life

Introduced	Policy measure
1992	Child Care Recommendation
1992	Maternity Leave Directive
1996	Parental Leave Directive
1997	Part-time Work Directive
2001	Child care target figures

Before looking at the present state of European care policies, theories on social care rights will be discussed. The second section will show how the issue of combining work and family life entered the European policy agenda. Following the theoretical distinction between rights to *time for care* and rights to *care services*, the third section explains the emergence of European rights to care services and the fourth section explains why European rights to time for care have been introduced and the extent to which they are implemented. The fifth section addresses present European policies on the division of care between men and women. The conclusion explores which additional policies are needed to support the combination of work and family life of men and women.

Including care in social citizenship

To describe and evaluate European social care rights, we need to address the theoretical debate on welfare state variety and gender equality. The development of the theoretical debate reflects the social and political call for public care-giving support in European countries. In the 1990s feminist scholars began to identify different types of care policies that could explain welfare state variety. The level of public care services and care leave was found to be important for explaining social inequalities in particular welfare states, just like the provision of public income support (Orloff, 1993; Anttonen and Sipilä, 1996; Sainsbury, 1999). Moreover, scholars have shown that variety in national care policies is reflected in the development of European social policy. They argue that opportunities for the development of European social care rights are restricted by the existence of national welfare states with low levels of public care-giving support (Ostner and Lewis, 1995; Plantenga, 1997).

The starting point of the theoretical debate on welfare state variety is Esping-Andersen's famous classification of West European welfare states (1990). He argues that it should not be automatically assumed that the welfare state creates a more egalitarian society. Instead, a welfare state is a system of social stratification in its own right. Historically, different systems of stratification have developed in Western Europe. In continental European countries such as Germany, France, Austria and Italy a corporatist model of welfare developed. Because benefits are based on social insurances, it consolidates rather than diminishes income differences. Anglo-Saxon countries guarantee universal flat-rate social rights, but with only very low minimum standards. Social assistance is means-tested, which means that the middle and upper classes have to compete (in the market) for their income. A more universalistic welfare model developed in Scandinavian countries, with earnings-related social insurance that are additional to flat-rate universal social rights. According to Esping-Andersen, the most egalitarian model for the redistribution of income is a combination of social insurance and universal flat-rate social assistance (Esping-Andersen, 1990: 21–6).

Feminist scholars criticised Esping-Andersen's welfare state classification, by arguing that his analysis of social inequality focuses on social security at the expense of the important role of services, such as care facilities for children and the elderly (Orloff, 1993; Anttonen and Sipilä, 1996). Anttonen and Sipilä argue that taking care services for children and the elderly into account helps explain patterns of social inequality, which cross right across Esping-Andersen's classification of welfare regimes. By incorporating services for children and the elderly in their analytical model for welfare state classification, Anttonen and Sipilä identify four groups of countries in Western Europe. First, they identify a Scandinavian 'model of public services', with services for children and the elderly widely available and women's participation outside the labour market higher than anywhere else in the world. Secondly, they identify a Southern European 'family care model' in countries such as Portugal, Spain, Greece and Italy, where very limited social care services are available and most care is provided by the informal sector, e.g. by grandparents. Thirdly, there is 'a model of abundant services for the elderly but scarce services for children', as found in the Netherlands, Norway and Great Britain. This model seems to traverse the mainstream division between Continental, Anglo-Saxon and Scandinavian countries. Fourthly, there is a model of countries with 'abundant services for children but scarce services for the elderly' in Continental countries such as Belgium and France (Anttonen and Sipilä, 1996). When provision of unpaid care or care services is considered, Continental Europe's countries are strongly divided.

Different types of care policies are also central in theories on European social policy-making. Ostner and Lewis predict the development of European social policy on the basis of a classification of national gender regimes. They view the United Kingdom, Ireland and Germany as strong male breadwinner regimes, where women have social rights as dependent wives. France and Germany have moderate male breadwinner regimes, since women have social protection as workers and as mothers. Denmark is categorised as a weak male breadwinner country because social policy primarily defines women as workers. They conclude that the European Union is unwilling to expand its territory from workers' rights to unpaid care because most European countries have strong breadwinner regimes (Ostner and Lewis, 1995: 185–93).

Unlike Ostner and Lewis, Plantenga argues that the male breadwinner ideology in corporatist welfare regimes is in decline. Taking the family as the smallest unit of the welfare state is no longer in keeping with the increasing pressure on women as well as men to participate in the formal economy. Moreover, the financial foundation for breadwinner facilities is endangered by continuing internationalisation. Nevertheless, Plantenga also feels that providing care will remain an individual responsibility as she argues that European social policy is most likely to converge on a liberal welfare model. She asserts that a Liberal welfare model, with formal gender equality but without material support for caring responsibilities, is best suited to an integration process towards a common market (Plantenga, 1997: 100–1).

The focus on care services in the analysis of European social policies has ultimately fashioned the definition of social citizenship. Knijn and Kremer formulate a definition of inclusive social citizenship that includes social care rights. They argue that social citizenship should cover care services for children and the elderly and social transfers for caring work such as paid leave facilities, which represent two possible ways for the state to take responsibility for the caring tasks traditionally performed by women. In terms of social rights, inclusive social citizenship consists of the right to time for care as well as the right to receive care (Knijn and Kremer, 1997: 332–3; Knijn, 1998: 73). Following Fraser and Sainsbury, I would add a third dimension to inclusive social citizenship, namely public support for a redivision of care-giving responsibilities between men and women. When men and women are individually supported in combining earning and caring, increasing women's labour market participation should be compensated by increasing men's caring activities. Herewith the gendered opposition between breadwinning and care-giving would be dismantled and is the most structural way to achieve gender equity (Fraser, 1994: 611; Sainsbury, 1999: 261).

So just as Esping-Andersen defines the redistribution of income as a condition for social equality, feminist scholars show that the provision of care, whether via care services, leave facilities or support for a redivision of care-giving, is a necessary condition as well. In keeping more or less with Marshall's (1950) classical definition of social citizenship, I define social citizenship as the right to a modicum of welfare, i.e. to a minimum level of economic welfare and a basic level of care. For decreasing gender inequality within the European Union, European social citizenship that redistributes income and care-giving is called for.

Combining work and family life on the European policy agenda

As we have seen, the EU developed social policy on combining work and family life in the 1990s. But how did the issue of combining work and family life enter the EU policy agenda? As in national member states, the issue was debated within European institutions long before concrete policies were introduced. The European Commission's (EC) Social Action Programme in 1974 was the first EU document articulating the policy goal of facilitating the reconciliation of family responsibilities with professional life. It argued that care facilities are needed to support the gradual attainment of gender equality on the European labour market (Commission of European Communities, 1974; Hantrais, 1995: 108). This reference to the need for care-giving support remained however free of correlative obligation: the European Commission then focused only on the development of the first three equal treatment Directives, on equal pay (1975), equal treatment at work (1976) and social security (1978). European involvement in the field of working conditions and social security in particular proved to be controversial enough for the EC explicitly to declare itself not to be concerned with 'family policies as such', leaving this to the member states for the time being (Hoskyns, 1996: 102).

In the 1980s the issue of reconciling work and family life reappeared on the European policy agenda. Two parties in particular were active in putting the issue back on the agenda, namely the European

Commission's Equal Opportunities Unit and the Committee for the Rights of Women of the European Parliament. As the official unit responsible for equality policies, the Equal Opportunities Unit prepared the first Action Programme on Equal Opportunities for women (1980), announcing the introduction of concrete European policies towards facilitating care-giving. However, EC proposals for Directives on part-time work (1981) and parental leave (1983 and 1984) failed to be adopted by the Council of Ministers, because member states, especially the UK, wanted to confine the issue to national competency. The Second Equal Opportunities Action Programme, which came out in 1985, more explicitly put the issue of social care rights on the policy agenda. Equal opportunities for men and women had to be achieved by 'the sharing of family and occupational opportunities and measures to achieve this' (Commission of the European Communities, 1985: 5). In order to improve women's opportunities on the labour market, the Action Programme aimed at developing European legislation on parental leave and increasing European involvement in child care services. Member states were called on to promote a more equal share of occupational and family responsibilities. At this stage, concrete action was restricted to setting up a Child Care Network, which was achieved in 1986. The Child Care Network was composed of national experts in the field, who were asked to coordinate research and advise on the direction of future policy.

In the same decade, the European Parliament also brought the issue of reconciling work and family onto the political agenda. At the beginning of the 1980s it formulated resolutions on parental leave and part-time work, calling for the development of European legislation on the provision of leave facilities and basic social protection of part-time workers in order better to distribute domestic and family responsibilities between men and women (Official Journal of the European Communities, 1982: 77–8; Rutherford, 1989). On the initiative of its Committee for the Rights of Women, the Parliament adopted a resolution on child care in 1986, calling on the Commission to draw up proposals for a Directive on equal access to child care (Official Journal of the European Communities, 1986: 22).

Although no concrete EU social care policies were adopted in the 1980s, the efforts of the EC and the European Parliament were not totally in vain. At the end of the decade, the combination of work and family life was recognised for the first time as a basic social right of all workers in the European Union. In 1989 the Council of Ministers adopted the Social Charter of the Fundamental Social Rights of Workers. Article 16 of the Charter states that equal treatment of men and women must be assured, which also means that 'measures should be developed enabling men and women to reconcile their occupation and family obligations' (Commission of European Communities, 1990). Although a measure of symbolic value, its incorporation in the Social Charter shows that in the Council of Ministers too, consensus had grown that something had to be done on the issue of care-giving support.

To conclude, feminist officials within the EC and female members of the European Parliament put the issue of facilitating care-giving on the European political agenda in the 1980s. The introduction of concrete policies on reconciling work and family life, however, had to wait until the 1990s, when economic and demographic changes called women to the European labour market.

A limited European right to care services: the Child Care Recommendation

The first European policy measure on combining work and family life was the 1992 Council Recommendation on child care. Unlike a directive, a recommendation is a statement of intent rather than a legal instrument. With the Child Care Recommendation, national governments showed their commitment to increasing the level of child care services in their national welfare states, to stimulate equal opportunities for women and men on the labour market and to address processes of demographic change (Official Journal of the European Communities, 1992). The Child Care Recommendation did not provide quality criteria or target figures, which raised fears that it would be a relatively meaningless document that would adopt the lowest common denominator (Randall, 2000: 356).

European pressure on national governments to invest in child care services, however, grew with the incorporation of equal opportunities policies in the 1997 Employment Strategy. Moreover, during its 2001 meeting in Barcelona, the Council of Ministers formulated concrete targets on child care provision. National governments made a commitment to provide child care for 90 per cent of the children from age 3 to compulsory school age and at least 33 per cent of the children in the age group from 0 to 3, by 2010. These figures were adopted in the European Employment Strategy of 2001. Similarly, the quality of child care provision has become a topic of common concern (European Commission, 2002). While access to child care services still is not a legal right at the European level, the Barcelona target figures constitute a binding commitment to increasing the level of public child care services for governments. Notwithstanding the variety of provisions in different welfare states, all countries have to meet the same basic standards. It seems that EU citizens can increasingly claim public care services for children, although access is not guaranteed. Why did this (limited) right to social care services emerge in the European Union? And to what extent has it been implemented on the national level?

As has been argued above, feminist officials and female politicians in the European Parliament and the European Commission put the issue of child care on the European policy agenda. They were outspoken on the need for child care services as a basic provision for all European citizens. The European Parliament formulated universal access to good quality and affordable child care as a condition for providing equal opportunities for children in disadvantaged positions (Official Journal of the European Communities, 1986: 22; Bleijenbergh, 2004a: 109). The EC's Child Care Network also pleaded for universal access to child care services, but shifted the perspective from individual children to the interest of society, by approaching children as a resource for the future health and prosperity of the Community. Like the European Parliament, it called for a Child Care Directive (Moss, 1988: 292).

For national governments in the Council of Ministers and especially the UK, this approach to child care as a basic European social right was very controversial. Room for agreement appeared only when the EC decided to propose the non-obligatory nature of a recommendation by opposition to a Directive. As Hedy D'Ancona, member of the Council of Ministers at the time explained:

> The transformation of the originally planned Child Care Directive into a less dangerous Recommendation was caused by the veto right the Thatcher government had in the Council of Ministers. Under the Thatcher government the United Kingdom was not prepared to pass any social policy measures at all. Since a Recommendation was free of obligations, everyone was ready to agree with it. (Interview with Hedy d'Ancona, Dutch former Minister of Welfare, Health and Culture, 16 June 1999)

Investing in social care rights was very controversial at a time of welfare state retrenchment. Most national governments aimed at cutting down rather than investing in social services. Moreover, the child care recommendation had to be acceptable by countries with very different traditions on combining work and family life. The Child Care Recommendation had to apply to countries with extensive public services like Denmark, countries with scarce child care services like the UK and the Netherlands and countries with a family care model like the South European countries. At the time of adoption of the Child Care Recommendation the use of services for children from 0 to 3 years in Denmark was 50 per cent, while in the UK it was only 2 per cent (Drew et al., 1998).

National governments committed to increasing the level of child care facilities by sharing the responsibility for providing services with European and local authorities, employers and trade unions, and private organisations. Child care was presented as an instrument for the improvement of women's participation in the labour market, which fitted member states' increased need for a female labour force in the context of ageing populations. The arguments on equal opportunities for men and women introduced by the EC helped to overcome member states' different approaches to care policies. The simultaneous emphasis on gender equality and free choice was acceptable to countries with both high and low levels of care services. References to child care as a workers' right replaced the far more controversial approach to child care as a basic right for all European citizens, as had been used by the EC's Child Care Network and the European Parliament at an earlier stage of policy-making.

In summary, the 1992 Child Care Recommendation was a weak translation of the feminist call for a Child Care Directive at the EC and the European Parliament. The Child Care Recommendation made employers and employees, private organisations and families respons-ible for child care, together with national governments and the EU. Access to child care became a right for workers rather than a right for all citizens. Public investment in child care services became a voluntary commitment rather than a legal obligation for national member states, even though the Barcelona targets emphasise national governments' responsibilities to increase their level of investment. Nevertheless there is evidence that the level of child care provision increased in most West European welfare states. For example, the percentage of chil-dren receiving public child care increased from 50 per cent of the 0–3 year-olds in 1993 to 64 per cent in 1998 in Denmark, but continued to be 6 per cent of 0–3 years old in Italy between 1993 and 1998. A general tendency towards increasing public involvement with child care can be noted (comparing Drew et al., 1998 with OECD, 2001: 144). This is not to say that the supply meets the demand. According to OECD figures, child care provision is still insufficient in most West European member states. This is not only the case for children younger than 3, but also for children between 3 and 6 years old (OECD, 2001: 144).

Table 4.2: Children in formal child care in 1998 (%)

	0–3 years	3–6 years
Austria	4	68
Belgium	30	97
Denmark	64	91
France	29	99
Germany	10	78
Finland	22	66
Greece	3	46
Ireland	38	56
Italy	6	95
Luxembourg	–	–
Netherlands	6	98
Portugal	12	75
Spain	5	84
Sweden	48	80
United Kingdom	38	56

(OECD, 2001: 144).

European rights to time for care: parental leave and part-time work

In 1992 the first Directive on time for care was adopted. With the maternity leave Directive, pregnant women in the EU were granted basic social protection with regard to health and safety at work and the duration of leave. In the mid-1990s it was followed by two other directives on facilitating the combination of work and family life. The 1996 Directive on Parental Leave grants fathers and mothers the right to three months' unpaid leave until their child reaches the age of 8. The 1997 Part-time Work Directive grants part-time workers in the EU the same working conditions and occupation social security as full-time workers.

Why did this series of European social rights to time for care emerge in the 1990s? And to what extent have they been implemented in practice? As we have seen, the issue was already on the European social policy agenda in the beginning of the 1980s, when the EC presented proposals for European legislation on part-time work and parental leave. They failed to be adopted due to the need for unanimous decision-making by the Council of Ministers. Both issues reappeared in the Council of Ministers at the beginning of the 1990s, but again a deadlock was reached (Rutherford, 1989; Hoskyns, 1996: 147; Bleijenbergh, 2004a: 133–4). The first European Directive on time for care to be adopted was the 1992 Directive on Maternity Leave. In contrast to earlier proposals on parental leave and part-time work a directive on maternity leave could be adopted by qualified majority voting because it was a health and safety measure. As there was no need for unanimity, the Council of Ministers was able to reach commitment on the issue relatively soon. In most member states, legislation on pregnancy and childbirth was already in place, but the adoption of the Directive on Maternity Leave improved the legal standard for working women in countries where such legislation was weak or absent, as in the UK (Hoskyns, 1996: 156–7; Guerrina, 2002: 56).

Commitment to facilitating time for care was again shown in the mid-1990s when, under new institutional conditions, the EC strategically brought back the social policy proposals of the 1980s and the early 1990s onto the policy agenda. With the adoption of the Social Protocol to the Maastricht Treaty in 1992, opportunities for social policy-making had increased. The proposal for the Social Protocol had been an ingenious trade-off between the EC and the European social partners, i.e. the European Trade Unions Confederation (ETUC), the European employers' organisations UNICE (Union of Industrial and Employers' Confedera-tions of Europe) and CEEP (European Centre of Enterprises with Public Participation). The EC had to consult with the European social partners on all social policy issues it wanted to develop. If both sides of industry decided to conclude a framework agreement on the issue, the EC would leave the initiative to them on the condition they reached agreement in a limited period. If not, the EC would send a proposal to the Council of Ministers. With the Maastricht Treaty, eleven of the then twelve member states had agreed to introduce qualified majority voting on social policy, thus improving their opportunities for common decision-making if the social partners should fail to reach an agreement. The European social partners now had formal precedence in social policy-making.

In 1995, the EC started consulting the European social partners on their willingness to engage with the issue of 'reconciliation of profes-sional and family life'. A general consensus had grown among European policy-makers that something needed to be done and European social partners felt considerable pressure to reach an agreement: the Inter-governmental Conference on the revision of the Maastricht Treaty was scheduled, during which the Social Protocol was to be rewritten or incor-porated into the Treaty (Falkner, 1998: 115). The social partners needed to prove that they were willing and able to assume their central role in European social policy-making.

After five months of negotiations, the European social partners reached a framework agreement on parental leave. Parental leave was presented as a way of combining work and family life and promoting equal opportunities for women and men. The agreement granted all working parents a minimum right to three months' leave, by imposing a few minimum requirements and leaving member states and national social partners the opportunity to define the conditions of access and modalities of application of the right (Falkner, 1998: 119–21; Bruning and Plantenga, 1999). The Council of Ministers translated the agreement into a binding directive in 1996. The right to parental leave was explicitly granted to mothers and fathers alike, and thus went further than the lowest common denominator earlier reached by the Council of Ministers in the early 1990s, when the UK only wanted to grant leave to women. The Directive explicitly stated that men should be encouraged to accept their share of family responsibilities (Official Journal of the European Communities, 1996: 4–9; Falkner, 1998: 115–21).

The issue of including women in the labour market was also debated during the negotiations of a second Social Agreement on Part-time Work. While the Parental Leave Directive was still being discussed, in 1995, the Commission already began consulting with the European social partners on the issue of atypical work, or 'flexibility in working hours and security for workers'. In line with its proposal in the early 1990s, the EC suggested equal treatment of part-time workers with regard to all kinds of work-related issues, including social security. This suggestion met with the approval of the ETUC, while employers wanted to exclude social security rights from the debate. In the end, employers and trade unions agreed to include occupation social security and to leave matters of statutory social security to member states (Falkner, 1998: 135–41; Bleijenbergh et al., 2004b: 319). The agreement was translated in a binding directive from the Council of Ministers in 1997. The Parental Leave Directive did not meet the standards the Commission had proposed, but was not worse than the lowest common denominator reached in the Council in the early 1990s.

What about the use of the European rights to time for care in practice? The Parental Leave Directive led to the adaptation of national legislations in line with the European standard. Parental leave provided a right to (unpaid) time for care for both fathers and mothers. Nevertheless, in practice, in EU member states parental leave is mainly taken up by women and only rarely by men. The situation is better only in Nordic countries where parental leave is often longer than the prescribed three months and paid almost in full. In Denmark 10 per cent of fathers and in Sweden 36 per cent of fathers take up parental leave (OECD, 2001: 145–6).

A comparable gender division can be observed with respect to the use of the other right to time for care, namely part-time work. Women make up a big proportion of part-time workers, especially in countries with low levels of care services for children, like the Netherlands and the UK. In these countries part-time work is a popular strategy for combining work and family life. In 1998 in the Netherlands 68 per cent of women on the labour market had a part-time appointment, compared to 44 per cent of women in the UK (European Commission, 1999). Part-time work increases the risk of being low paid and decreases career opportunities. In the UK especially, part-time jobs are often poorly paid, which creates a sizeable difference in the wages of full-time and part-time workers (Land and Lewis, 1998: 65; Walby, 2001: 224–30). In the Netherlands since 1993, part-time workers have a legal right to the same hourly wages rate and working conditions as full-time workers (Plantenga et al., 1999; Visser, 2002). As a result the gender pay gap between part-time and full-time workers is small in comparative perspective (Grimshaw and Rubery, 2001).

To conclude, why did social rights to time for care emerge in the EU in the 1990s? The Directives on Maternity Leave, Parental Leave and Part-time Work emerged as a result of common pressure from the EC, the Socialists in the European Parliament and ETUC for legislation to protect the increasingly significant group of employees with atypical employment contracts (e.g, part-time, fixed term, employment agency), combined with employers' willingness to give part-time workers minimum social rights in return for more flexible working arrangements. Feminist officials in European institutions had introduced part-time jobs as a way of combining work and family life, relying on arguments of equal opportunities for men and women. It made the introduction of a European right to time for care relatively attractive to all parties, as a way of granting the feminist (and socialist) call for social justice without harming the European market forces.

Combining in practice: the need for a re-division of care-giving between men and women

The need to re-divide care-giving tasks between men and women has been articulated in EU policy debates since the 1980s. The 1992 Child Care Recommendation was the first European policy measure to actively target male involvement in care-giving; the issue was brought back in the Parental Leave Directive and the Part-time Work Directive. To reach substantial equal opportunities between men and women, men need to perform their care-giving responsibilities to the same extent as women, as the latter are entering the labour market. What is the present European policy on the division of care-giving responsibilities between men and women? And to what extent have the goals been achieved?

The Child Care Network and the socialist political parties in the European Parliament were the first actors to state publicly that child care facilities should be mixed with paid leave facilities and the re-division of care-giving between men and women. Unsurprisingly, the Child Care Network approached paid work and unpaid care-giving as equivalent. It put forward that men's comparatively low involvement in care-giving, especially in comparison with women's participation in the labour market, should be a matter of European concern. In its 1990 report 'Child Care in the European Communities 1985–1990', the Child Care Network argued that a more equal sharing of responsibilities between men and women should be an explicit EC policy goal. Although the Network was quick to state that while there was no unique formula to sharing care-giving responsibilities, the advantages of men playing more of a role in care-giving were considerable and should be promoted:

Child care is a 'men's issue' as much as a 'women's issue'. No formula can be applied uniformly in all families – how responsibilities are shared may vary between families and, within the same family, may vary over time with one parent doing more at one stage and less at another. Having acknowledged this, there is still ample scope and an urgent need for a greater role by men in child care (particularly in families but also as workers in services), and for policies to encourage and support this process. (Commission of the European Communities, 1990: 3)

Some members of the European Parliament agreed with the Child Care Network's approach. In a debate on child care in April 1991, members of the Socialist Party supported a plea by the Committee for the Rights of Women to push forward men's care-giving. The Socialist Party argued that increasing men's care-giving was to the benefit of men, women and children. As Bowe, a male British member of the Socialist Party, noted:

I count myself very fortunate in that for three years I had the major responsibility for the care of my own young son and consequently can appreciate some of the difficulties and joys faced by the vast majority of women at some time in their lives. So I commend the report to Parliament, not just because it will liberate the lives of women and enrich the lives and experiences of young children, but because in the long run it is a step towards liberating the minds of many men in our society. (Debates of the European Parliament, 1991: 366)

Cunha de Oliveira, a Portuguese female member of the Socialist Party, introduced an item on the agenda on the need for measures to facilitate men's care-giving; the proposal was deemed to go too far for the Conservative and Christian Democrat members and was rejected (Debates of the European Parliament, 1991: 367). By then, there was a consensus within the European Parliament on the need for equal opportunities between women and men on the labour market; yet the need to increase men's engagement in care-giving was still too controversial to be formulated as a common goal.

The issue was finally brought back into the final text of the Child Care Recommendation. The original proposal suffered various modifications during the policy-making process, but overall survived. The Council of Ministers supported participation of women in the labour market rather than participation of men in care-giving, but it still paid lip-service to the need for care leaves and a re-division of care-giving between men and women. As article 6 of the Child Care Recommendation states:

As regards responsibilities arising from the care and upbringing of children, it is recommended that member states promote and encourage, with due respect for the freedom of the individual, increased participation by men in order to achieve a more equal sharing of parental responsibilities between men and women and enable women to play a more effective role on the labour market. (Official Journal of the European Communities 1992: 18)

The ideal of sharing of care-giving responsibilities between men and women was repeated in the Parental Leave Directive and the Part-time Work Directive. The Parental Leave Directive is especially explicit on the issue. By referring to awareness programmes, it proposes concrete policy instruments on increasing men's use of parental leave. As one of its general considerations notes, 'men should be encouraged to assume an equal share of family responsibilities, for example they should be encouraged to take parental leave means such as awareness programmes' (Official Journal of the European Communities, 1996: 6).

There is less emphasis on part-time work as a mean to increase men's involvement in care-giving. The Part-time Work Directive only mentions that 'access to part-time work for men and women ... would facilitate reconciling work and family life' (Official Journal of the European Communities, 1998: 13). In fact, stimulating men's part-time work proved to be very controversial within the ETUC. Southern European unions in the ETUC adopted a reserved stance on the issue because part-time jobs were rarely of a high quality and only rarely permitted a decent standard of living in their own countries. As a result, trade unions at the European level generally viewed reducing working hours as a better strategy for redistributing care-giving between men and women than stimulating part-time work. The ETUC was able to get past the differences by emphasising the importance of high quality part-time jobs (Bleijenbergh, 2004b: 322).

What about the re-division of care-giving responsibilities in practice? Recent Eurostat figures on the 25 EU countries show that women start to work less and men begin to work more once they have children. In 2003, the employment rate for women aged 20–49 without children was 75 per cent, compared to 60 per cent for those with children under 12. The opposite effect was observed for men. The male employment rate increase from 86 per cent to 91 per cent for men with children under 12. A comparable pattern can be found with regard to part-time work: working women tend to work part-time more once they have children, while it is the opposite for men. In 2003, 23 per cent of women aged 20–49 with children under 12 work part-time, compared to 2.6 per cent of men (Eurostat, 2005).

Notwithstanding implicit and explicit commitments towards the need for a re-division of care-giving responsibilities between sexes in European social policy, women still carry the main burden and enjoy the main pleasures of reconciling work and family life. Obviously men with children feel pressure to increase paid employment rather than unpaid care-giving tasks in comparison to men without children. A traditional division of gender roles is still the norm.

Conclusion

Feminist scholars have convincingly argued that social equality is not only connected to the redistribution of income, but also involves the redistribution of care. Welfare states and the EU shape gender (in)equality through their provision of time for care and care services and by stimulating a re-division of care-giving between women and men. As we have seen, the issue of reconciling work and family life indeed has been on the European policy agenda for 25 years. Since the 1990s concrete European policy measures were introduced on maternity leave, parental leave and part-time work and in a lesser extent on child care services.

Why did a limited right to care-giving services emerge in the EU and to what extent has it been used in practice? Feminists within the EC and the European Parliament brought the issue on the agenda in the 1970s and 1980s, but concrete policies were only introduced when economic and demographic developments called for more women on the European labour market. The 1992 Child Care Recommendation was a weak translation of the feminist call for a Child Care Directive, by making public and private actors responsible for child care, together with national governments and the EU. For national member states improving child care facilities is still a voluntary commitment rather than a legal obligation, although the adoption of concrete target figures in the European Employment Strategy in 2002 encourages national governments to improve their policies. In practice this seems to have led to a stabilisation or increase of child care services throughout the EU, although the demand for child care services still surpasses the supply. Moreover, the EU is increasingly becoming involved with formulating common quality criteria, but the exercise of quality control is still done at the national level.

Why did the series of European directives on rights to time for care emerge? The adoption of a Parental Leave Directive in 1996 was the result of a first successful collective bargaining between European social partners, which derived from social partners' need to show the secondary route for making social policy-making work, rather than the need for gender equality legislation. The adoption of a 1997 Part-time Work Directive was the second result of EU collective bargaining, deriving from social partners' need to show they deserved their place in European social policy-making rather than the need for gender equality legislation.

In practice parental leave is mostly taken by women. Only where parental leave is paid, as in the Nordic countries, are men taking it. To increase the use of leave facilities by fathers, the EU should introduce paid leave schemes. A comparable pattern can be observed on the issue of part-time work, with women working part-time more in countries with scarce care services for children, like the Netherlands and United Kingdom. Part-time work considerably increases the risk of being low paid and decreases career opportunities. The EU should invest in good quality part-time work to improve gender equality in this respect.

Feminist scholars have shown that men need to perform their care-giving duties to reach substantial equal opportunities between men and women. Although the need for a re-division of unpaid care work has been articulated at the European level, European social policies only pay lip-service to the issue. Research suggests that measures should be taken on very different levels to increase men's care-giving. Workplace culture should become more supportive for men to take parental and care leave and work part-time. Women's wages need to improve to allow a re-division of tasks within a household to be financially attractive. And women need to stimulate and support men's involvement in the household, which is traditionally considered their sphere (Eurostat, 2005: 145–6). Substantial European policies on supporting and stimulating a re-division of care-giving between men and women are needed to fill the gap between European legislation and practice.

Scholars have been arguing that the development of a European market system would be incompatible with the development of European care policies (Ostner and Lewis, 1995: 177–83; Plantenga, 1997: 100–1). Recent developments in the EU however show that, although limited, European rights to time for care and care services are emerging. The development of West European welfare states showed that different levels and models of care-giving support can coexist with a capitalist market economy. Moreover, the development of a common European market shows an intrinsic drive for developing public care giving support to allow the participation of women to the labour market. So far, European social care rights are rights for workers, rather than European citizenship rights (Bleijenbergh et al., 2004b: 323). Full social equality for women and men will be possible only when inclusive citizenship rights are fully realised at the European level.

References

Anttonen, A. and Sipilä, J. (1996) 'European social care services: Is it possible to identify models?' *Journal of European Social Policy*, 6(2): 87–100.

Bimbi, F. (1993) 'Gender, "gift relationship" and welfare state cultures in Italy', in J. Lewis (ed.) *Women and Social Policies in Europe*, Aldershot: Edward Elgar, pp. 138–69.

Bleijenbergh, I. (2004a) *Citizens who Care: European Social Citizenship in EU Debates on Child Care and Part-time Work*, Amsterdam: Dutch University Press.

Bleijenbergh, I., de Bruijn, J. and Bussemaker, M. (2004b) 'European social citizenship and gender: discussions on the Part-time Work Directive', *European Journal of Industrial Relations*, 10(3): 309–28.

Bruning, G. and Plantenga, J. (1999) 'Parental leave and equal opportunities: experiences in eight European countries', *Journal of European Social Policy*, 9(3): 195–209.

Commission of the European Communities (1990) *Child Care in the European Communities 1985–1990*, Brussels: Directorate-General on Information, Culture and Women's Information Service.

Commission of the European Communities (1974) *Sociaal Actieprogramma, Bulletin of the European Communities, supplement 2/74*. Available at: http://aei.pitt.edu/archive/00001253/01/social_action_program_COM_73_1600.pdf [accessed 30 May 2005].

Commission of the European Communities (1985) *Equal Opportunities for Women – Medium Term Community Programme 1986–1990* (COM (85) 801 final), Brussels.

Commission of the European Communities (1990) *Community Charter of the Fundamental Social Rights of Workers*, Luxembourg: Office for Official Publications of the European Communities.

Debates of the European Parliament (1991) *Debate on Childcare*, No. 3-411/362–367, 22 November.

Drew, E., Emerek, R. and Mahon, E. (eds) (1998) *Women, Work and the Family in Europe*, London and New York: Routledge.

Esping-Andersen, G. (1900) *The Three Worlds of Welfare Capitalism*, Oxford: Oxford University Press.

European Commission (2002) *Impact Evaluation of the EES – Equal Opportunities for Women and Men – Background Paper*. Available at: www.europa.eu.int/comm/employment_social/employment_strategie/eval/papers/equ_opp_en.pfd [accessed 13 May 2005].

European Commission (1999) *Employment in Europe*, Luxembourg: Office for Official Publications of the European Communities.

Eurostat (2005) *Gender Gaps in the Reconciliation between Work and Family Life*, Luxembourg: Eurostat.

Fagnani, J. (1998) 'Recent changes in family policy in France', in E. Drew, R. Emerek and E. Mahon (eds) *Work and the Family in Europe*, London and New York: Routledge, pp. 58–65.

Falkner, G. (1998) *EU Social Policy in the 1990s: Towards a Corporatist Policy Community*, London and New York: Routledge.

Fraser, N. (1994) 'After the family wage; gender equality and the welfare state', *Political Theory*, 22(4): 591–618.

Grimshaw, D. and Rubery, J. (2001) *The Gender Pay Gap: A Research Review*, Manchester: Equal Opportunities Commission.

Guerrina, R. (2002) 'Mothering in Europe; feminist critique of European policies on motherhood and employment', *European Journal of Women's Studies*, 9(1): 49–68.

Hantrais, L. (1995) *Social Policy in the European Union*, Basingstoke and London: Macmillan.

Hoskyns, C. (1996) *Integrating Gender: Women, Law and Politics in the European Union*, London: Verso.

Lewis, J. (ed.) (1993) *Women and Social Policies in Europe; Work, Family and the State*, Aldershot: Edward Elgar.

Knijn, T. (1998) 'Participation through care: the case of the Dutch housewife', in J. Bussemaker and R. Voet (eds.) *Participation and Citizenship in the Netherlands*, Aldershot: Ashgate.

Knijn, T. and Kremer, M. (1997) 'Gender and the caring dimension in welfare states: towards inclusive citizenship?' *Social Politics* 4(3): 328–62.

Land, H. and Lewis, J. (1998) 'Gender, care and the changing role of the state in the UK', in J. Lewis (ed.) *Gender, Social Care and Welfare State Restructuring in Europe*, Aldershot: Ashgate, pp. 51–84.

Marshall, T. H. (1950) 'Citizenship and social class', in T. H. Marshall, *Sociology at the Crossroads*, London: Heinemann, pp. 67–127.

Moss, P. (1988) *Child care and Equality of Opportunity. Consolidated Report to the European Commission*, Brussels: Child care Network.

OECD (2001) *Employment Outlook 2001*, Paris: OECD Publications Service.

Official Journal of the European Communities (1998) *Council Directive Concerning the Framework Agreement on Part-time Work Concluded by Unice, CEEP and ETUC*, No. L14/ 9–14, 20 January.

Official Journal of the European Communities (1996) *Council Directive on the Framework Agreement on Parental Leave concluded by Unice, CEEP and the ETUC* No. L 145/4–9, 10 June.

Official Journal of the European Communities (1992) *Council Recommendation of 31 March 1992 on Child care*, No. L 123/16–18, 8 May.

Official Journal of the European Communities (1986) *Resolution of Child Care Infrastructures*, No. C 88/21–24, 24 April.

Official Journal of the European Communities (1982) *Resolution No C267/77–79*, 11 April.

Orloff, A. S. (1993) 'Gender and the social rights of citizenship, the comparative analysis of gender relations and the welfare state', *American Sociological Review* 58(3): 303–28.

Ostner, I. and Lewis, J. (1995) 'Gender and the evolution of European social policies', in S. Leibfried and P. Pierson (eds) *European Social Policy*, Washington: The Brookings Institution, pp. 159–93.

Plantenga, J., Schippers, J. and Siegers, J. (1999) 'Towards an equal division of paid and unpaid work: the case of the Netherlands', *Journal of European Social Policy*, 9(2): 99–110.

Plantenga, J. (1997) 'European constants and national particularities: the position of women in the EU labour market', in A. Geske Dijkstra and J. Plantenga (eds) *Gender and Economics: A European Perspective*, New York: Routledge, pp. 86–103.

Randall, V. (2000) 'Child care policy in the European states: limits to convergence', *Journal of European Public Policy*, 7(3): 346–8.

Rutherford, F. (1989) 'Policy and politics: the proposal for a European Directive on Parental Leave: some reasons why it failed', *Policy and Politics*, 17(4): 301–10.

Sainsbury, D. (ed.) (1999) *Gender and Welfare State Regimes*, Oxford: Oxford University Press.

Siim, B. (2000) *Gender and Citizenship; Politics and Agency in France, Britain and Denmark*, Cambridge: Cambridge University Press.

Visser, J. (2002) 'The first part-time economy in the world: a model to be followed?' *Journal of European Social Policy*, 12(1): 23–42.

Walby, S. (2001) 'The case of the United Kingdom', in U. Behning and A. Serrano de Pascual (eds) *Gender Mainstreaming in the European Employment Strategy*, Brussels: ETUI, pp. 221–50.

5
The Adoption and Enforcement of Equal Opportunity Measures in Employment: The Case of France in Comparative Perspective

Nicky Le Feuvre

This chapter discusses some of the issues arising from the adoption and implementation of equal opportunity (EO) measures, particularly with regard to gender equality in employment in European Union (EU) member states. Since it is impossible to compare all EU member states, I have chosen to take the case of France as a starting point, with a view to illustrating the influence of societal contexts on the manner in which equal opportunity measures are defined, adopted and implemented in different national contexts. Although it draws on a number of secondary sources, the chapter also uses the results of a recently completed cross-national European research project entitled 'European Women's Studies Integration' (EWSI).[1]

The initial aim of this project was to provide comparative data on and analysis of the labour market opportunities for Women's/Gender Studies graduates in different EU members states or accession countries (Griffin, 2004, 2005). The project was based on the hypothesis that the employment expectations and experiences of Women's Studies students and graduates would provide a rich source of data on the degree to which equal opportunity policy measures were adopted and implemented in different national settings. The study included an analysis of the level of 'equal opportunity awareness' among this particular group of women and an analysis of the degree to which a university degree, or any other form of higher education training, in Women's Studies, was seen as a requirement or as a bonus for employment in the 'equal opportunities' field.

The EWSI project adopted a three-stage research design. First, each partner prepared a background report on the situation in her home country with regard to three issues: the institutionalisation of women's studies courses and degree programmes in higher education (HE); the nature and the degree of institutionalisation of equal opportunity policy measures in that country; and the recent history of women's labour market participation and care responsibilities (Griffin, 2002). Second, a standardised questionnaire was fielded to a group of approximately 120 past and present Women's Studies students in each partner country. Finally, a series of semi-structured biographical interviews were carried out with 30 Women's Studies students/graduates in each country (Hanmer, 2005).

One of the unexpected results of the project was to highlight the fact that, despite the adoption of a range of relatively similar policy measures with regard to equal opportunities in employment in most of the partner countries,[2] huge differences existed in the way these broad policy objectives were interpreted and implemented in each national context (Crompton and Le Feuvre, 2000). Differences also existed in the degree to which training in Women's/Gender Studies was related to employment in the equal opportunities field.

In the following sections of this chapter, I will illustrate these cross-national differences with regard to three sub-themes: the variations in the visibility and legitimacy of equal opportunity discourses and practices in different national contexts; the degree to which the enforcement of existing equal opportunity legislation rests on the 'good will' of the protagonists or on legally binding means of enforcement, control and policy evaluation, and, finally, the degree to which equal opportunities have been 'professionalised' (i.e. have given rise to a number of specialist jobs) in different national contexts and the role of Women's Studies in providing training for employment in the equal opportunities field. In conclusion, I will attempt to show that a lack of understanding of the impact of societal level gender relations on men's and women's employment experiences is one of the major barriers to more effective implementation of equal opportunity measures in many EU member states.

National variations in the visibility and legitimacy of equal opportunity measures

In a series of recent publications on equal opportunities in employment in Europe, much attention has been paid to the gap that exists in many countries between the relatively satisfactory level of formal equality policy measures that have been adopted, often under the direct influence of European policy directives, and the actual impact of such measures on reducing gender inequalities in the labour market. According to many authors, equal opportunity measures represent a perfect illustration of the concept of 'symbolic reforms' developed by Edelman (Edelman, 1985). According to this author, symbolic reforms correspond to 'political declarations that are followed by no administrative action and by no effect' (Edelman, cited by Mazur, 2004: 173).

Several authors have recently developed detailed analyses of the 'symbolic' nature of the equal opportunity measures adopted by successive European governments since the beginning of the 1970s (Mazur, 1995; Crompton and Le Feuvre, 2000; Laufer, 2003; Junter, 2004). According to Amy Mazur, despite the adoption of the relatively progressive Roudy Law in 1983 and of the 'Equality in Employment' law in 2001, the 'symbolic' nature of French equal opportunity measures can be identified along three lines.

First, she notes the under-representation of grass-roots women's rights groups in all stages of the policy elaboration and implementation process. In France, as in several other European countries, there are few direct contacts between feminist activists involved in providing support services for women and the so-called 'femocrats' of the bureaucratic institutions that are responsible for translating European policy recommendations into national action plans. As I have argued elsewhere (Andriocci and Le Feuvre, 2005), the lack of collaboration between these groups is partly related to the 'radical' (as opposed to 'reformist') nature of the second-wave Women's Liberation Movement in these countries (Picq, 1993; Fougeyrollas-Schwebel, 1997; Riot-Sarcey, 2002). In such a context, feminist activism was based on creating 'alternative' structures, along the line of women's self-help voluntary associations and at organising mass demonstrations as a means of exerting their influence on the policy elaboration process, rather than on direct involvement in policy reforms.

In France, for example, there is little or no history of feminist activists becoming directly involved in the equal opportunity institutions that were progressively set up throughout the late 1970s and 1980s. As Amy Mazur rightly suggests, the only exceptions to this rule are found in the academic profession, where Women's Studies specialists, often with direct contacts with Brussels through their research activities, have played an important role in convincing their national authorities of the need to introduce legislative measures in favour of equal opportunities, particularly with regard to direct or indirect discrimination in employment. However, because of the relatively low levels of Women's Studies institutionalisation in the Higher Education sector of these countries (Silius, 2002; Association nationale des études féministes [ANEF], 2004;), even this influence has been relatively weak and has produced little more than 'piece-meal reforms' (Mazur, 2004: 174).

The lack of grass-roots mobilisation in favour of gender equality measures in France can be explained by a number of 'contextual factors' (Mazur and Zwingel, 2003), that are also important indicators for understanding the varying degrees to which similar equal opportunity policy measures or tools give rise to a wide range of equal opportunity actions in different national contexts.

The first factor can be identified through the national attitudes to citizenship and equality issues in general. Several authors have stressed the difference between those democratic regimes based on a 'universalist' conception of citizenship, founded on an abstract 'equality of rights' and those based on the notion of 'specific needs' or 'equality of outcomes' (Delphy, 1995; Crompton and Le Feuvre, 2000). There seems to be little question that the French notion of 'republican universalism', which Amy Mazur calls 'sexist universalism' (Mazur and Zwingel, 2003: 178), leaves little conceptual room for the kind of 'positive actions' to promote equality in employment that are recommended by the European Union and successfully implemented in other national contexts. Under universalistic regimes, even when structural inequalities have been identified and named as such, social actors are at pains to envisage compensatory measures, even when these are explicitly written into the equal opportunity measures adopted (Laret-Bedel, 1999; Lanquetin, 2004). The somewhat conflicting relationship between universalist democratic principles and the effective implementation of equal opportunity measures in employment was evident in the data from the EWSI project in several partner countries. Thus, for example, Harriet Silius and Salla Tuori argue that the Finnish tradition of 'equal treatment' of all adults in the labour market can act as a barrier to the promotion of equal opportunity measures, since these may often be founded on the principle of 'special treatment' of some groups, as a means of combating the discriminatory effects of apparently 'neutral' principles adopted in the past:

> There seems to be a dominant discourse on equality in Finnish society, which emphasises gender neutrality, a balance or equilibrium between the two sexes and non-conflict between men and women. Equality, which is the term used, is more conceived of as equity or parity than as emancipation of women.... Power differences are often denied or disguised in a gender-neutral rhetoric. Gender neutrality has, for example, been introduced into official language, by

erasing all words referring only to one sex (for example, parent instead of mother). When something is organised for women, there is a demand for something similar for men as well. (Silius and Tuori, 2004: 171)

The second 'contextual' influence on the efficacy of equal opportunity measures refers to the degree of mobilisation and support for such measures in civil society in general. We have already noted that the legacies of the 1970s second-wave women's movements vary considerably between countries. In some cases, there would seem to exist a strong coalition between the historical feminist activists and the current 'grass-roots' women's organisations, the 'intellectual arm' of the movement that led to the creation of Women's/Gender Studies training programmes within the HE sector, and women's groups within the leading political parties and/or trade union organisations. This would seem to be the case in Germany (Achin, 2003; Gerhard et al., 2004) and, to a lesser extent, in the UK (Griffin and Hanmer, 2002), the Netherlands (Van der Sanden and Waaldijk, 2002) and the Nordic countries. In these cases, the battle for the adoption and effective implementation of equal opportunity measures has benefited from a fairly high media profile and from concerted pressures from a variety of social groups, including trade union organisations. In many other EU countries, equal opportunity measures have received the support of only a small minority of 'femocrats', working inside government agencies, but who have been deprived of a wider support base (Mazur, 2003). Combined with low levels of institutionalisation of Women's/Gender Studies courses in the national HE institutions, this has led to the isolation of the main equal opportunity protagonists in many countries. Although direct pressure from the European Union may have helped the adoption of relatively progressive equal opportunity measures, the lack of collective mobilisation and the limited power resources of the 'femocrats' have been particularly prejudicial to the effective implementation of such measures in practice.

Indeed, in order to engage actively in the promotion of equal opportunities in employment, the nature of the existing legislation needs to be widely publicised and understood. However, the EWSI questionnaire and interview data indicate that a significant proportion of Women's Studies students in many EU countries have only a vague understanding of the notion of 'equal opportunities'. This was a somewhat surprising result of the project, which was based on the hypothesis that training in Women's Studies could provide the expertise base needed for the successful implementation of policies in this field. In their discussion of equal opportunities in cross-European perspective, Isabel Carrera Suarez and Laura Vinuela Suarez offer the following comments on the differences between Women's Studies students in Spain and Germany:

> The lack of specific equal opportunities knowledge among Spanish interviewees seems surprising in a country we had found to have a medium degree of institutionalisation of equal opportunities. Yet most interviewees admitted that they had never paid much attention to the issue of equal opportunities or reflected on the term. In many cases, it was obvious from the answers that students were talking about equal opportunities explicitly for the first time during the interview. . . . While we must keep in mind that most [Spanish] interviewees were PhD students, as this is where Women's Studies tends to be located in Spain, and that such curricula are not job-oriented, it still seems to reflect an obvious gap in disseminating policies, even to 'naturally' interested recipients. Among the German interviewees we found the opposite case. Not only were they fully aware of the term equal opportunities; they were also able to engage in a discussion of details. Thus, they distinguished between the terms 'promotion of women', 'equal rights' and 'mainstreaming' and problematized their meanings. The high degree of understanding and knowledge demonstrated by German students seemed to be a result of several factors: the presence of related issues in the media (an Equality Act had been discussed in Parliament, although unsuccessfully), the presence of equal opportunities in the university, the important role of the Commissioners for Women's Affairs and, of course, the personal interest of the students interviewed. However, it must be said that some of these elements also exist in other countries where the knowledge of equal opportunities was less thorough, so that the German case seems to show particularly effective dissemination of policies. (Carrera Suarez and Vinuela Suarez, 2005: 70–1).

There are, therefore, huge discrepancies between countries in the degree to which equal opportunity rhetoric is present in every-day life, even among those groups with an active interest in gender issues. In some countries, there is clearly a lack of knowledge about the equal opportunity measures that exist. Here, we can cite the example of a Women's Studies graduate who had been directly involved in the attempts to introduce gender awareness courses in teacher training institutions in France, in the wake of the February 2000 Action Plan for

Equality in Education. She insisted on the lack of impact of this legislation on the gender awareness levels in French universities:

> I don't believe that the whole equal opportunities thing has really
> been taken on board. In universities, for example, there are loads
> of people who really have no idea about gender relations, equality
> between the sexes, who have never even heard about the February
> 2000 Action Plan for Equality, so the effects can't be very positive
> (EWSI interview FRP17: 19).[3] (Le Feuvre and Andriocci, 2004b)

In other countries, there was undoubtedly a sense that equal opportunities had been taken on board by the vast majority of employers,
or at least that organisations and institutions had to be seen to take
the equal opportunities issue seriously. This was evident, for example,
in the number of job offers bearing the standard phrase 'X is an equal
opportunity employer'. Thus, although Women's Studies students often
have reservations about the degree to which many institutions paid 'lip-
service' to equal opportunity objectives and measures, these were very
much part of the 'societal ethos'.

Furthermore, there were considerable differences in the degree to
which equal opportunities policies are associated with feminism and
with the women's movement in general. Somewhat paradoxically, in
those countries where equal opportunity policies have so far failed to
muster widespread grass-roots support, they were more likely to be
branded as 'feminist' and to receive negative reactions than in countries where they were more developed and more visible. According to
the EWSI interviewees in several EU member states, the term 'equal
opportunities' is still associated with the Women's Movement of the
mid-1970s, although few of the activists from this period have actually
been involved in promoting such measures. Any mention of equality
measures in employment tends to lead to the student being branded
as a 'raving feminist' – a particularly derogatory label in many countries: '[When you mention equality] it's as if you were immediately
labelled, whatever you have to say will take on extremist connota-
tions and will be brushed away so that people can just carry on
saying what they were saying before you chipped in' (EWSI interview FRP2: 16). Most of the French EWSI interviewees admitted,
for example, that they often give up on any conversation on the
question of gender equality in employment because they encounter
such ferocious resistance from the vast majority of their friends and
acquaintances.

In conclusion to this section, I would argue that one of the most important conditions for reducing the 'symbolic' nature of much equal opportunity legislation lies in the ability to mobilise a wide range of grass-roots support for the principles and practices of equal opportunities within a given national context. However, the effectiveness of this condition also depends on the kinds of sanctions that exist in the case of non-compliance with the existing legislation.

From persuasion to coercion: the philosophy behind the implementation of equal opportunity policies in different national contexts

Most of the Women's Studies students interviewed in the course of the EWSI project had some work experience before or during their time at university. They were often employed part-time, on fixed-term contracts and worked in the most highly feminised and least well-paid sectors of the labour market. The interviews thus provide a wealth of knowledge about the kind of discriminatory practices that abound in many EU countries, despite the existence of quite progressive equal opportunity legislation. The following citations are drawn from the French interviews, but similar experiences were recounted in every national case study:

> I was working as a newspaper journalist and the Chief Editor was this really awful guy, fat and ugly, with a beer gut, who used to try and charm his way round all the young women working there, including me. I'll always remember the way he harassed me, right up until the day I hit back. After that, he gave up on me, but he didn't give me any more assignments either. So you really got to understand how things worked there quite quickly. That guy oppressed me. He thought that he was going to sleep with me and 'in exchange' give me more work assignments. That's how I analyse the situation today, but even at the time, I knew that it wasn't right for him to dominate me like that with his body and his power, I was sure of that. (EWSI interview FRP14: 6).

This first-hand account of blatant sexual harassment at the workplace did not lead to any legal action being taken against the perpetrators and clearly illustrates the lack of knowledge and awareness of existing equal opportunities legislation on the part of the female workforce. Even when they are qualified to do a job, women still face discrimination at the point of recruitment. This French Women's Studies student took a postgraduate diploma in transport management, before applying for a middle-management position with a large travel firm:

> There are only about 18 per cent women in the field I work in. When I went for the interview, the guy who has since became my line manager came out with a sentence like: 'I'm going to be perfectly frank with you, I'm not too keen on employing a woman for this position, because it involves a lot of contact with the coach drivers and, as I'm sure you are aware, coach drivers are a terribly macho lot.' (EWSI interview FRP2: 6).

Although almost all our interviewees mentioned several examples of discriminatory practices in employment, most of the cases cited of women's more limited career progression did not concern the Women's Studies students themselves, but rather friends or colleagues. This is partly because our sample was made up of women who were still in the early stages of their career, most of whom had not yet had children and/or who had only recently gained the qualifications that would enable them to develop a 'career', rather than to occupy a job. This graduate from a Women's Studies vocational course in France gave an example of the unfavourable promotion experiences and pay conditions of women engineers:

> My husband has [female] colleagues who are engineers in the same firm as him, in the same team. I was talking to one of them the other day and she said that she did manage to get away from work at around 6 pm but, well, her career has suffered. My husband has progressed really, really quickly; he has already got to grade 3A [upper management level]. She has been working for a bit longer than he has and she still hasn't made it to 3A grade. There are plenty of really objective differences. For example, my husband was saying just the other day that he had been given a package of stock options, whereas none of the women in his team had had any. (EWSI interview FRP10: 3)

One of the difficulties of identifying the 'glass ceiling' that limits women's career prospects lies in the fact that an apparently equal position on paper can in fact cover very different experiences in practice. This is particularly important in a country like France, where the highly regulated labour market apparently leaves relatively little room for direct discrimination, but where various forms of 'individualised' rewards (like access to company stock options) may create large pay disparities between male and female employees on the same grade in the same company (Le Feuvre and Andriocci, 2004a).

These empirical examples serve to illustrate the second aspect of the 'symbolic' nature of equal opportunity measures identified by Mazur. By the time they are approved by Parliament, the few equal opportunities measures that are adopted are usually 'deprived of any real degree of coercion' (Mazur, 2004: 174). Thus, contrary to the situation in other EU member states, in several countries, including France, 'there is still no central organisation armed with the appropriate coercive means to help victims of discrimination to bring court actions against their employers, to identify cases of inequality or discrimination or to control the different tools elaborated to promote equality in employment' (Mazur, 2004: 174). Contrary to the Equal Opportunities Commission in the UK, for example, the institutions created to support the equal opportunity policy objectives in many other EU countries are generally devoid of the autonomy and resources necessary to guarantee the effective enforcement of the policies adopted by Parliament. Thus, despite the progressive development of an 'equal opportunity rhetoric' within the main political parties and some trade unions (CFDT Cadres, 2004), there is little evidence of this rhetoric filtering down to the day-to-day practices in the labour market. One of the most paradoxical consequences of this situation is to create the illusion that the existing policy measures are sufficient to produce a 'level playing field', since the absence of cases of discrimination brought before the courts is interpreted as proof of the absence of discriminatory practices.

A third aspect of the 'symbolic' nature of equal opportunity measures in some countries, which is directly related to the two preceding points (Mazur, 2004: 175), relates to the degree to which the enforcement of the legal obligations rests on the voluntary actions of employers and trade unions alike. Thus, although considerable lip-service is paid to the question of equal opportunities during the different phases of collective bargaining, the resolution of existing inequalities is rarely seen as a central preoccupation. As Catherine Laret-Bedel has stressed, although the 1983 Equality in Employment Law required private companies employing 50 or more staff in France to return annual 'comparative gender equality reports' on the relative situation of their male and female employees, with regard to recruitment, training, promotion and working conditions, the results of such initiatives have been extremely disappointing to date (Laret-Bedel, 1999).

First, a significant minority of companies simply failed to return their reports, and generally incurred no sanctions for doing so (Laret-Bedel, 1999). Second, the vast majority of the companies that did return a report, which inevitably revealed significant inequalities between the sexes, failed to make any concrete proposals concerning the actions that would be undertaken to correct such inequalities in the future (Laufer, 2003). Indeed, there would seem to be an overriding belief that the inequalities that can be measured at the level of an individual firm are largely due to 'external factors', over which neither the employer nor the trade union representatives are liable to exert any influence. Thus, the persistence of inequalities in employment (Commission européenne, 2002; INSEE, 2004) tends to lead to the call for new public policy measures, rather than to 'attempts to improve the efficiency of existing measures' (Mazur, 2004: 175).

As Catherine Laret-Bedel has stressed for the French case, the implementation of equal opportunity measures often rests primarily on the principle of negotiation and, therefore, on the 'good will' of the social partners to undertake negotiations. According to Christina Lunghi, the disappointing results of existing legislation in countries like France can be explained by five factors:

1. Lack of awareness/knowledge about existing equal opportunity measures, on the part of employers, trade unions and employees alike, but also a lack of pressure on social partners to address the equal opportunity issues.
2. Lack of awareness/knowledge about the issues under-lying equal opportunity aims and objectives.
3. Lack of effective measures to encourage social partners to negotiate on equal opportunity issues.
4. Lack of sanctions in the face of discrimination (few cases brought to the courts) and/or in the face of failure to implement existing equal opportunity measures.
5. Lack of women amongst the representatives of the social partners on whom responsibility lies for implementing the law (Lunghi, 2003).

Indeed, one of the aims of the 2001 Equality in Employment Law adopted in France was precisely to make annual negotiations on equal opportunity issues an obligatory part of labour relations, both within individual firms and at branch level (Laufer, 2003). Furthermore, companies with more than 300 employees are legally bound to set up an internal 'gender equality in employment commission', which is supposed to advise the social partners on measures to combat discrimination and reduce existing gender inequalities. Unfortunately, few systematic empirical studies have been carried out to date on the impact of the 2001 equality in employment legislation. One could argue that the lack of policy evaluation studies is in itself indicative of the 'symbolic' nature of such measures in many EU countries. The results of a series of qualitative studies on this topic in France make for depressing reading. In two separate regional case studies, Annie Dussuet and Frédéric Joly identified very similar barriers to the effective implementation of existing equal opportunity measures (Dussuet, 1997; Joly, 2004). Not only were the return rates of the 'comparative reports' by companies extremely low, these were generally very scant in content – often little more than a single page of quantitative data on pay differentials, for example – and were almost systematically devoid of any proposals to reduce the gender inequalities they revealed. Indeed, in the rare cases where the data provided were analysed in any way, the comments tended to illustrate the very limited understanding of 'equal opportunities' as a concept among the social partners responsible for the implementation of existing measures. Thus, to cite a single example amongst many, one of the reports returned to the work inspectors in the Dordogne region of France states: 'There is no professional inequality between the men and the women employed by our company, because they do not occupy the same jobs' (cited Joly, 2004: 27).

These examples provide ample evidence of the pitfalls that abound when responsibility for the implementation of equal opportunities is confided in social partners who have received no training whatsoever on this issue. This is compounded by the arguments that are used in countries where policy implementation rests solely on the shoulders of the (untrained) social partners, in order to encourage them to engage in negotiations. As Annie Junter has suggested, there is a tendency in many countries, and sometimes in the discourse of the EU itself, to promote equality between the sexes in employment as a means to an end, rather than as an objective in itself (Junter, 2004). The 'problem' with equal opportunities is posed in somewhat misleading terms. First, there exists a deep-rooted belief within the institutions responsible for promoting equality that the social partners need to be 'convinced' about the importance of equal opportunities in employment. Secondly, in order to convince them on this point, equal opportunity measures are explicitly 'marketed' on the basis of the fact that they are really 'in the best interests' of individual companies or of national economic vitality more generally. Thus, the first paragraph of the preamble to the national agreement on equality between men and women in employment, adopted in France on 1 March 2004, reads as follows:

> Women's employment contributes to social dynamics and to economic growth. Society needs the pool of abilities and talents which women possess. Equal opportunity and equal treatment at all stages of professional life is a form of social investment, which is equally important for the respect of people's dignity as it is for economic development. (cited Junter, 2004: 198)

As Annie Junter rightly observes, this kind of equal opportunity rhetoric tends to reproduce at least two stereotypical ideas about women that are at the heart of gender inequalities in the labour market: 1) that women represent a 'reserve army of labour', which can be called on in times of economic growth and relegated to the home in times of recession; 2) that all women are endowed with 'specific talents', which seem to come as naturally to them as childbirth (Junter, 2004: 199). Not only is this kind of equal opportunity promotion rhetoric infused with gender stereotypes, it also serves to minimise the legal obligations associated with the implementation of measures to combat discrimination and fight against inequalities. Thus, strategies to encourage private firms to adopt 'best practices' with regard to women's recruitment, training, promotion, etc., often act as a substitute for the effective implementation of the law (Junter, 2004: 198). It is worth noting that, in many other fields of public policy, the objective of 'educating' the population in accordance with the general rules adopted in Parliament is often accompanied by the imposition of sanctions in the case of non-compliance. For example, it is obviously 'in the best interests' of all members of society that the number of road accidents be reduced. In order to 'market' the idea of reduced speed limits as a means to this end, the state usually combines a mix of road safety education campaigns with tightened law enforcement measures (increased fines for speeding, for example) for those who fail to comply with the law. In the case of equal opportunities, however, a consensus would seem to exist in most countries around the idea that equal opportunity measures need to be adopted on a purely voluntary basis; they cannot or indeed should not be 'enforced' in any way, since any degree of coercion would be 'counter-productive'. Why this belief persists is something of a mystery. It is nevertheless clear that it seriously undermines the effectiveness of much existing legislation in many EU countries. As Annie Junter has argued:

> The main aim of equal opportunity policies should not be to improve the human resource management of the female workforce, to optimise the use of women's 'human capital', to help companies solve their recruitment problems, to foster economic growth or local development. [Rather], equal rights and equal opportunities should be considered as a fundamental right to equality between women and men, an in-dissociable part of human rights in the economic and social spheres of society. (Junter, 2004: 201)

If such were the case, there would be no need to 'convince' social actors of the need to adopt more progressive equal opportunity legislation or to 'gently persuade' them to implement existing measures (with the aid of government subsidies, cash prizes or 'quality labels' for those employers who actually do comply with the existing legislation), since this fundamental human right would simply be defended by law and compliance would be obtained through direct sanctions. Examples from other EU countries show quite clearly that the courts have a central role to play in increasing the visibility and social legitimacy of equal opportunities as a principle rather than as an option (Crompton and Le Feuvre, 1992, 2000).

Thus, in conclusion to this section, I would insist on the fact that the effective implementation of equal opportunity policies not only requires the mobilisation of a wide range of social actors. For equal opportunities to be seen as an integral part of human rights (Junter, 2004) rather than as an optional human resource management tool, the obligatory nature of policy initiatives also needs to be fully understood. With regard to both these issues, the professionalisation of the equal opportunities field and the development of equal opportunities training modules are obviously of vital importance.

The professionalisation of equal opportunities policy implementation

The EWSI study of the employment expectations and experiences of Women's Studies graduates once again revealed significant differences between countries as far as the professionalisation of equal opportunities was concerned (Silius, 2005). In some countries (the UK, Germany, the Netherlands and, to a lesser extent, Spain and Finland), there is a clear 'equal opportunities' labour market niche, with jobs available, primarily in local government and the voluntary sector, but also in some multinational private companies, with the specific aim of elaborating, implementing and evaluating measures to promote equality in employment or in other spheres (health, housing, etc.). In other countries (Hungary, Slovenia and, to a lesser extent, France and Italy), there is little trace of an equal opportunities labour market. In France, for example, the job title of 'equal opportunity officer' was only introduced into the national repertory of job titles in 2001 and none of the Women's Studies students we interviewed had ever seem a job advertisement from a local government agency or from a private company requiring expertise in gender (or indeed ethnic) equality issues (Le Feuvre and Andriocci, 2004b: 23).

In the course of the EWSI project, we also discovered similarities between countries with regard to the relationship (or lack of relationship) between HE training in Women's Studies and access to employment in the equal opportunities field.

First, even in those countries where there was a clearly identifiable equal opportunities labour market niche, the students we interviewed did not see any direct link between the topic of their degree courses and jobs with an equal opportunity brief. In some cases (the Netherlands and Germany, for example), this was generally because the HE system is clearly divided between 'academic' and 'vocational' institutions. Since Women's Studies courses tend to be offered more frequently in universities than in technical HE institutions, students were more likely to state that they had chosen to study Women's Studies out of academic or personal interest, rather than as a direct route to the labour market (Van der Sanden, 2004: 151).

Second, in those countries where the number of jobs with a specific equal opportunities focus was more limited, the students we interviewed stressed that an academic record in Women's Studies could even represent a handicap for working in equal opportunities. This was notably the case in France, where the local equality officers (one in each of the 25 administrative regions and at least one – sometimes part-time – in each of the 95 administrative departments) are almost all civil servants on temporary assignment from their administrations or are local political party activists, who have generally received no prior training in gender issues (Le Feuvre and Andriocci, 2004b: 22). French Women's Studies graduates thus doubt the 'market value' of their gender expertise. For example, a French Women's Studies graduate described how one of the rare Regional Councils to have created an 'equal opportunity officer' position had decided to exclude all Women's Studies graduates from their short-list. This decision was explained by the fact that, because the decision to create this position had met with much resistance within the organisation, it was felt that the person recruited should be as 'neutral' (i.e. non-feminist) as possible. Those applicants with an academic record in Women's Studies were thus excluded on the basis of their supposedly 'ideological' attitude towards equality. In the end, the Council recruited a regional equal opportunity officer with a Masters degree in psychology, who had never taken a single Women's Studies course in her life. The lack of academic training in gender theory and practice thus became a bonus for working in the equal opportunities field! The same fear of 'rocking the boat' by recruiting people with basic knowledge about gender relations in general and some expertise in equality issues seems to have been at the root of the decision taken by the same French Regional Council to subcontract a study of women's regional employment patterns:

> They gave the contract to this private company, mostly sociologists with no training in Women's Studies or in gender issues, they were specialised in employment programmes. I said to the woman in charge that [not using someone with Women's Studies expertise], was like trying to build a house without using an architect, but they went ahead anyway. (EWSI interview FRP16: 6)

Because of the barriers to their recruitment by local government agencies or private companies, many Women's Studies graduates who decide to work in an area related to women's rights and equality often turned to the voluntary sector and to grass-roots women's organisation rather than to institutional settings. With the recent possibilities to secure funding for concrete equal opportunities initiatives – notably under sections 8 and 9 of the European Social Fund programme – there is some evidence of a slight improvement of the employment opportunities in this area in some EU member states. However, in countries where the links between grass-roots organisations and the political 'femocrats' are weak, the concentration of women with an academic background in Women's Studies in jobs with no direct impact on the adoption and implementation of equal opportunity policies in private companies and public sector jobs only serves to reduce further the chances for concerted action in favour of equality on the basis of existing policy measures.

Despite only medium levels of equal opportunities institutionalisation in many of the EWSI project partner countries, a large minority of the Women's Studies graduates surveyed claimed to have worked in an equal opportunities-related job. This apparent contradiction is explained by the fact that the students adopted a fairly broad definition of 'working in equal opportunities'. Although their job titles did not explicitly mention an equal opportunity brief, they tended to consider themselves to be working in this area as long as they had the possibility to introduce women's or gender equality issues in their workplace. Thus, for example, a French graduate working for a public opinion company stated that she was involved in promoting equality because she always paid attention to the gender composition of the samples used by her company – a fairly 'minimalist' notion of 'equal opportunities', to say the least! (Le Feuvre and Andriocci, 2004b).

Or course, we also identified a sub-group of Women's Studies graduates in each country, who adopted a much narrower definition of 'working in equal opportunities'. These were the students who have been recruited specifically on the basis of their Women's Studies training and qualifications, to work on projects or in organisations that develop an explicit gender equality agenda. Thus, for example, a French graduate was working for a voluntary association on projects to help unemployed women back onto the labour market. She had previously spent a year working for an association that encouraged women's entrepreneurship. The accounts of these students are particularly interesting, since they confirm the relatively low levels of recognition given to Women's Studies graduates in many EU countries, even in jobs that involve working to improve the position of women in society:

> The [women's rights association] was going through a time of change, the person who has taken over as Director at the national level is a feminist and she is trying to push for a more feminist approach at the local level, so there is quite a lot of movement going on. It just so happens that the new director of the branch in [Town] is in favour of this feminist orientation. When we first met, she told me that most of the members of her Board – the President, the General Secretary and the Treasurer – were not really in favour of recruiting someone with a Women's Studies background, they would have preferred someone who had previous experience in an employment agency or something like that. But for the director, it was clear that they needed someone with a Women's Studies background and so that's how I came to get the job. (EWSI interview FRP4: 13)

It is thus quite astounding to note that, in some EU countries, even the most 'natural' partners in the equal opportunity policy implementation process continue to believe that equal rights are best promoted by people who possess no theoretical tools for understanding the mechanisms behind gender inequalities in the labour market and no personal commitment to changing the current pattern of gendered power relations in society.

Conclusions

Since the mid-1970s almost all EU governments have set up a political and/or administrative structure responsible for women's rights and, more recently, for promoting gender equality in employment, although the size and resources of these agencies varies considerably from country to country and over time within a particular national setting. Under pressure from the EU, most member states have adopted fairly extensive equal opportunities programmes. However, despite similar broad tendencies on the formal policy adoption level, there is ample proof of the fact that, in many countries, the principles of equal opportunities have not yet filtered down to the level of regional and local government, nor have they been widely adopted in private companies and public sector organisations, including academia. To a certain extent, the notion of 'mainstreaming' remains an alien concept in many national cultures, since the responsibility for gender inequalities is rarely seen to lie in the hands of those parties who are formally charged with implementing equal opportunity policies, often on a 'voluntary' basis.

Despite very different levels of institutionalisation of Women's Studies within the HE systems of different countries, academic training in gender issues is rarely seen as having any particular impact on the graduates' access to the labour market (Silius, 2005). However, Women's Studies graduates in all the EWSI partner countries insisted on the multiple ways in which their Women's Studies training had influenced the kind of work they had sought and the ways in which they carry out their jobs. Whether they are working directly in 'women's rights' or 'equal opportunities' jobs, the students insisted on their increased awareness of gender equality issues following their training and on their ability to become 'actors of social change' in their immediate work and home environments. They are more sensitive to the different aspects of sex discrimination and more likely to intervene directly to transform the reality of the people they work with (Gerhard et al., 2004; Griffin, 2004; Le Feuvre and Andriocci, 2004b).

However, overall estimates of the number of Women's Studies graduates working in equal opportunities should be treated with some caution. Given the low levels of equal opportunities institutionalisation in many countries, the students tend to adopt a very broad definition of what 'working in equal opportunities' might mean. There is nevertheless evidence to suggest that, with increasing opportunities to fund equal opportunity actions with EU support, the number of jobs in the equal opportunities field is currently rising in most EU member states. In many cases, graduates with Women's Studies expertise are attempting to create their own labour market niches by developing training and research activities in the equal opportunities field. It must nevertheless be stressed that, in those countries where equal opportunity policies operate on an essentially 'symbolic' level, such initiatives are often short-lived and imply high levels of professional uncertainty and low levels of remuneration for the women concerned.

In conclusion, it would seem that Women's Studies training raises students' awareness of gender-based inequalities and leads to a greater level of personal involvement with equal opportunity issues. This may translate into jobs with a specific equal opportunities or women's rights brief, but may also be restricted to the fight for more equality in their personal lives (Griffin, 2005). Whatever the case, Women's Studies graduates in Europe possess detailed knowledge about the social mechanisms that create gender inequalities in employment and are generally committed to the fight against direct and indirect forms of discrimination. As such, they represent potential 'agents of social change' in many areas of society. However, their expertise has been under-utilised in many countries to date. This situation may be partly due to the increasingly abstract content of many Women's Studies degree courses in some EU member states (Griffin, 2004), but it is also related to the widely held belief that the implementation of existing equal opportunity legislation requires no particular training or expertise in gender issues. Given the disappointing record of the existing equal opportunities legislation in reducing inequalities in the labour market in many EU countries to date, the development of Women's Studies degree programmes and of more systematic gender awareness training for those groups who are supposed to implement existing policy measures 'voluntarily' would seem to offer a promising solution to the relatively 'symbolic' effect of public policy initiatives in this field.

Notes

1. EWSI – Employment and Women's Studies: The Impact of Women's Studies Training on Women's Employment in Europe, HPSE-CT2001-00082, DGXII (Research), European Commission, 2001–2003. The project, coordinated by Professor Gabriele Griffin, of Hull University, brought together partners from nine EU member states: Finland, France, Germany, Hungary, Italy, Netherlands, Slovenia, Spain and the UK. For full project results, see www.hull.ac.uk.ewsi.
2. Similarities that were obviously related to the influence of EU directives with regard to such issues as equal pay, discrimination, the reconciliation of work and family life, etc.
3. In all the EWSI partner projects, the interviews were coded according to a standard pattern. The codes refer first to the country (FR = France), to the status of the students (P = past; C = current), then to the number code of the interview, followed by the page number of the citation.

References

Achin, C. (2003). 'Le mystère de la Chambre basse. Comparaison des processus d'entrée des femmes au Parlement, France, Allemagne, 1945–2000', PhD thesis, Université de Grenoble II.

Andriocci, M. and Le Feuvre, N. (2005) 'Les enjeux sociaux de l'institutionnalisation des 'études féministes' à l'Université', in C. Solar and E. Ollagnier (eds) *Parcours de femmes à l'Université*, Paris: l'Harmattan.

Association nationale des études féministes [ANEF] (2004), *Premier recensement national des enseignements et des recherches sur le genre en France*, Toulouse: Rapport au Ministère des affaires sociales, du travail et de la solidarité et au Service des droits des femmes et de l'égalité.

Carrera Suarez, I. and Vinuela Suarez, L. (2005) 'Equal opportunities in cross-European perspective', in G. Griffin (ed.) *Doing Women's Studies: Employment Opportunities, Personal Impacts and Social Consequences*, London: Zed Books: pp. 64–88.

CFDT Cadres (2004) *Inégalités professionnelles. CFDT Cadres*, Paris: CFDT.

Commission européenne (2002), *La Vie des femmes et des hommes en Europe. Un portrait statistique. Données 1980-2000*, Bruxelles: Commission européenne.

Crompton, R. and Le Feuvre, N. (1992) 'Gender and bureaucracy: women in finance in Britain and France', in M. Savage and A. Witz (eds) *Gender and Bureaucracy*, London: Basil Blackwell, Sociological Review Monograph, pp. 94–123.

Crompton, R. and Le Feuvre, N. (2000) 'Gender, family and employment in comparative perspective: the realities and representations of equal opportunities in Britain and France', *Journal of European Social Policy*, 10: 334–48.

Delphy, C. (1995) Egalité, équivalence et équité: la position de l'Etat français au regard du droit international, *Nouvelles questions féministes*, 16(1): 5–58.

Dussuet, A. (1997) *Sur l'égalité professionnelle entre les hommes et les femmes*, Nantes: Rapport à la Direction régionale du travail de l'emploi et de la formation professionnelle des Pays-de-la-Loire.

Edelman, M. (1985) *The Symbolic Uses of Politics*. Urbana: University of Illinois Press.

102   *Nicky Le Feuvre*

Fougeyrollas-Schwebel, D. (1997) 'Le féminisme des années 1970', in C. Fauré (ed.) *Encyclopédie politique et historique des femmes*, Paris: Presses universitaires de France, pp. 729–70.

Gerhard, U., Schmidbaur, M. and Wischermann, U. (2004) 'A little bit wiser . . . ' The impact of women's studies on students' experiences and expectations in Germany', in G. Griffin (ed.) *Employment, Equal Opportunities and Women's Studies. Women's Experiences in Seven European Countries*, Köenigstein: Helmer Verlag, pp. 52–76.

Griffin, G. (2002) *Women's Employment, Women's Studies and Equal Opportunities, 1945-2001. Reports from Nine European Countries*, Hull: The University of Hull.

Griffin, G. (2004) *Employment, Equal Opportunities and Women's Studies. Women's Experiences in Seven European Countries*, Königstein: Helmer Verlag.

Griffin, G. (2005) *Doing Women's Studies: Employment Opportunities, Personal Impacts and Social Consequences*, London: Zed Books.

Griffin, G. and Hanmer, J. (2002) 'Women's employment, women's studies and equal opportunities in the UK, 1945–2001', in G. Griffin (ed.) *Women's Employment, Women's Studies and Equal Opportunities, 1945–2001. Reports from Nine European Countries*, Hull: The University of Hull, pp. 1–68.

Hanmer, J. (2005) 'Comparative research in Europe', in G. Griffin (ed.) *Doing Women's Studies: Employment Opportunities, Personal Impacts and Social Consequences*, London: Zed Books, pp. 213–35.

INSEE (2004) *Femmes et hommes : regards sur la parité 2004*, Paris: INSEE.

Joly, F. (2004) *De l'égalité professionnelle au pays de l'Homme*. Toulouse: Rapport de stage du DESS 'Politiques sociales et rapports sociaux hommes-femmes'.

Junter, A. (2004) 'L'égalité professionnelle entre les femmes et les hommes: une exigence politique au cœur du droit des femmes', *Travail, genre et sociétés*, 12: 191–202.

Lanquetin, M. T. (2004) 'Une loi inappliquée', *Travail, genre et sociétés*, 12: 182–90.

Laret-Bedel, C. (1999) 'Bilan de l'application de la loi du 13 juillet relative à l'égalité professionnelle entre les femmes et les hommes', in B. Majnoni d'Intagnano (ed.) *Egalité entre hommes et femmes: aspects économiques*, Paris: La Documentation française, pp. 185–96.

Laufer, J. (2003) 'Equal employment policy in France: symbolic support and a mixed record', *Review of Policy Research*, 20: 423–42.

Le Feuvre, N. and Andriocci, M. (2004a) 'Employment opportunities for women in Europe', in G. Griffin (ed.) *Doing Women's Studies: Equal Opportunities, Personal Impacts and Social Consequences*, London: Zed Books, pp. 13–63.

Le Feuvre, N. and Andriocci, M. (2004b) 'The impact of women's studies on women's employment opportunities and expectations in France', in G. Griffin (ed.) *Employment, Equal Opportunities and Women's Studies. Women's Experiences in Seven European Countries*, Köenigstein: Helmer Verlag, pp. 16–51.

Lunghi, C. (2003) *L'Egalité professionnelle en pratique*, Paris: Editions d'organisation.

Mazur, A. G. (1995) *Gender Bias and the State: Symbolic Reform at Work in Fifth Republic France*, Pittsburgh: University of Pittsburgh Press.

Mazur, A. G. (2003) 'Drawing comparative lessons from France and Germany', *Review of Policy Research*, 20: 491–523.

Mazur, A. G. (2004) 'La France est-elle toujours le pays des réformes symboliques?' *Travail, genre et sociétés*, 12: 173–81.

Mazur, A. G. and Zwingel, S. (2003) 'Comparing feminist policy in politics and at work in France and Germany: shared European Union setting, divergent national contexts', *Review of Policy Research*, 20: 365–85.

Picq, F. (1993) *Libération des femmes: les années mouvement*, Paris: Seuil.

Riot-Sarcey, M. (2002) *Histoire du féminisme*, Paris: La Découverte.

Silius, H. (2002) 'Women's employment, equal opportunities and women's studies in nine European countries: a comparative summary', in G. Griffin (ed.) *Women's Employment, Women's Studies and Equal Opportunities, 1945–2001. Reports from Nine European Countries*, Hull: The University of Hull, pp. 470–514.

Silius, H. (2005) 'The professionalization of women's studies students in Europe: expectations and experiences', in G. Griffin (ed.) *Doing Women's Studies: Employment Opportunities, Personal Impacts and Social Consequences*, London: Zed Books, pp. 111–40.

Silius, H. and Tuori, S. (2004) 'Gender-neutral Finland? Women's Studies students as gender experts in Finland', in G. Griffin (ed.) *Employment, Equal Opportunities and Women's Studies. Women's Experiences in Seven European Countries*, Köenigstein: Helmer Verlag, pp. 163–86.

Van der Sanden, J. (2004) 'The impact of women's studies training on women's employment in the Netherlands', in G. Griffin (ed.) *Employment, Equal Opportunities and Women's Studies. Women's Experiences in Seven European Countries*, Köenigstein: Helmer Verlag, pp. 139–62.

Van der Sanden, J. and Waaldijk, B. (2002) 'Women's employment, women's studies and equal opportunities in the Netherlands, 1945–2001', in G. Griffin (ed.) *Women's Employment, Women's Studies and Equal Opportunities, 1945–2001. Reports from Nine European Countries*, Hull: The University of Hull, pp. 122–76.

6
The Risk of Poverty among Women in Europe

Morag Gillespie

Women are at greater risk of poverty than men and the feminisation of poverty is well documented in the literature (Goldberg and Kremen, 1990; Glendinning and Millar, 1992; Orloff, 2002). However, the risk of poverty is not universal for women who are not a homogeneous group and a range of factors can increase or reduce the likelihood of poverty, including nationality, ethnic origin and citizenship status, marital status, age, disability and health. These factors are all crucial in determining the risk of poverty for individual women. The way that different welfare states' regimes operate in relation to care, work and promoting collective welfare is complex and diverse (Daly and Rake, 2003). However, assessing the causes and understanding the nature of women's poverty involves exploring a host of social, institutional and economic relationships that impact on the well-being of women. The aim of this chapter is to identify the issues that may increase the risk of poverty for women living and working in Europe, including the impact of recent developments in terms of European Union (EU) expansion.

Measurement and definition of what poverty is and what it means for groups in society remain contested issues. In relation to women's poverty, analysis can be hampered by measurement that takes the household as the unit of analysis and it has been argued that women and men experience poverty differently, even when they live in the same household (Ruspini, 2000; Millar and Ridge, 2001). Such differences arise mainly because unpaid care work is still unequally shared between women and men. Women and men do not occupy the same social or/and economic situations, and as a consequence their needs, and the resources available to them in meeting those needs, can differ significantly. These differences can affect the way in which women and men access everything from the formal labour market to a whole range of public services.

Women who are lone parents or single pensioners, from minority ethnic backgrounds, refugees, asylum seekers, migrant workers and disabled people form a disproportionate number of people living in poverty across Europe. However, relationships between the state, the family and the labour market are complex and are not uniform across countries in Europe. Lone parents in Sweden, for example, are far less likely to experience poverty than those living in the UK or Germany (Kilkey and Bradsaw, 1999). Both direct and indirect discrimination serve to restrict many women's access to the labour market and a range of services such as health, education and housing. It is clear then that a multidimensional analysis is necessary for an understanding of the causes of poverty. There is, as Williams has argued (2001a: 132), a need 'to be aware of the variety of structured divisions that affect both people's lives and the development of welfare provisions', at the same time as recognising that social difference and identity as well as power differences change over time.

This chapter begins by discussing the 'feminisation' of poverty in Europe, including consideration of the specific context of transitional economies in Central and Eastern Europe (CEE), which have recently joined the EU. The next section outlines key issues affecting the risk of poverty among women. Nationality and migration are considered first, followed by a discussion of welfare state regimes, the labour market, skills and education, and caring roles, the relationships between which are significant for women. Some specific characteristics that increase the risk of poverty for women are then considered, including lone parenthood, old age, disability and ill health. These are followed by concluding comments that highlight the interaction of gender with a wide range of other factors that need to be considered more fully in moving towards a gender-sensitive analysis and policy development.

The feminisation of poverty

Although women and children have always been over-represented among people in poverty, the 'feminisation' of poverty became a focus of feminist writers during the 1990s for two reasons. First, for reasons 'arising from the increase in families headed by single women – either unmarried or divorced – and the overrepresentation of women among the elderly and especially the very old' (Sainsbury, 2001: 120). The causes of female poverty and its visibility have changed. Large surveys tend to use the household as the main level of analysis and confirm the view that female-headed households are generally poorer and more deprived

(Oxley et al., 2000; European Foundation for Living and Working Conditions, 2004a). However, although a growing proportion of families living below the official poverty line are headed by women alone, Chant argues that policy responses have focused too strongly on female headed households and face the risk of:

> generalising about women's poverty, and of engaging in superficial dualistic comparisons between male- and female-headed households within, as well as across, cultures. Even if it continues to be impossible to pin down the fine detail of exactly how many women are poor, which women are poor, and how they become and/or remain poor, unpacking the 'feminisation of poverty', and problematising some of its conventional wisdoms (not least that women-headed households are the worst afflicted), broadens prospects for change insofar as it demands tackling gender inequalities in a number of arenas. (Chant, 2003: 46)

Although much emphasis is placed on female-headed households in discussions of feminisation of poverty, there is also the argument that women, as a group, experience a greater risk of poverty due to the entrenched male breadwinner model of family relationships. To reach a greater understanding of women's poverty, it is therefore necessary to take account of gender differences in social and economic relationships. For instance, as Elson (2000) argues, a whole range of social and economic policies rely heavily on the amount of unpaid work that people do as well as paid work, and

> unpaid care work is still unequally shared between women and men in most countries and this is one of the major obstacles to equality in paid work and to the full development of the talents of both women and men. (Elson, 2000: 6)

Women's poverty in the European Union

In the EU member states prior to enlargement in 2004, the four key strands of welfare capitalism – Scandinavian liberal, Anglo-Saxon, Bismarckian or Rhineland, and southern European/civil society – have been under pressure for a considerable period and have been influenced by an increasingly powerful neoliberal agenda. In the UK, there has been a 'profound shift from universalism and strong political commitment to market-oriented reform', but the strains are also evident in other EU member states (Hudson and Williams, 2001: 43). In response to growing unemployment and the rising costs of social assistance and unemployment compensation systems, governments have embarked on radical reforms aimed at creating 'work-based' welfare systems. The shared aim of what are increasingly described as these 'welfare to work' strategies is to create new, active benefit regimes which improve employability, reinforce work incentives and reduce costs and welfare dependency (Finn, 2000: 43).

While there is an increasing focus on employment in EU economic and social policy, the commitment to addressing gender inequality would appear to be weakening. The European Commission's Social Agenda included a Community Framework Strategy for Gender Equality that is due to end in 2005. The lack of political commitment to a new Framework Strategy has been criticised by the European Women's Lobby, which expressed concerns about the failure to address gender mainstreaming in the EU properly (European Women's Lobby, 2005).

The addition of ten new member states in 2004, including several CEE countries witnessing the transition from a centrally planned to a market economy, marks a significant development in EU social and economic policy. With reference to women's poverty, Baden argues that women are likely to be more vulnerable than men to increased poverty or insecurity in periods of economic transition:

> While job losses may affect men and women, women may find it harder than men to regain employment or become self-employed, due to relative lack of education and skills, lifecycle issues (employers may favour younger women) and lack of independent access to capital. Poor women are more likely to have no other adult earners in the household and to have a higher dependency ratio and may be especially vulnerable to the removal of subsidies and increasing charges for services and rising prices, leaving them in deepening poverty. (Baden, 1997: 8)

Schnepf (2004: 23) uses analysis of subjective data to argue that women were already at greater risk of poverty than men before the transition and there is 'little evidence of a consistent regional pattern that women fared worse during the transition process than men'. However, other studies suggest that the process of transition has major implications for women, including an increased risk of poverty as a consequence of the lower value of benefits and a drop in female labour force participation (Grootaert and Braithwaite, 1998).

The Luxembourg Income Study has been used by a number of researchers to explore women's poverty and economic gender inequality. These studies confirm the income disadvantage of women, mothers and female-headed households (Gornick, 2004). The European Commission used Eurostat estimates to suggest that the income disparities between states have 'widened considerably' with enlargement to 25 member states (2004a: 11). However, using a relative poverty threshold within countries, based on 60 per cent of equivalised[1] national median income, they suggest that a similar proportion of populations in the new member states was at risk of poverty in 2001 when compared with the existing EU member states. They note that 'despite a trend over the last decade towards a higher risk of poverty, the New Member States, mainly thanks to historical circumstances, still tend to score comparatively well on this indicator' (ibid.: 12). The average proportion considered to be at risk of poverty is 15 per cent but, in most member states, the risk of poverty is estimated to be higher for women than men (ibid.: 40). Data from the World Bank also suggests that, in selected countries in the CEE, women are at greater risk of poverty than men, and lone parents at greater risk compared with other households with children (Schnepf, 2004). Thus, very significant changes are taking place in the CEE and these are have an impact on the risk of poverty for women, but it is important to recognise that, as with Western and Southern Europe, the new member states are not homogeneous.

Factors affecting the risk of poverty

Complex factors contribute to different outcomes and risks for women and different groups of women, many of which are highly relevant to the social agenda in Europe. They contribute to understanding which groups of women risk living in poverty and why. Labour market participation, skills and qualifications are central to strategies within the EU for improving social cohesion and reducing the risk of poverty. Existing welfare regimes and the way they interact with contemporary labour markets often fail to account adequately for the unpaid caring work that is carried out predominantly by women and, as a result, increase the risk of poverty for women. However, other factors interact with work, care and welfare considerations to create a more complex picture of disadvantage.

What is provided below is not a statistical profile, nor is it a comprehensive analysis of poverty among women in Europe, not least because the data available are limited. Reference is made to a variety of research projects and data, but strengths and limitations of methodologies used are not discussed, although it is recognised that measurement of poverty and exclusion is complex and different methodologies can produce different results and emphases (Tsakloglou and Papadopoulos, 2002a). However, each of the sections summarises the relevance of key factors for understanding the risk to women of living in poverty and provides examples from across the EU that serve to illustrate the true nature of women's risk of poverty which may not be transparent in large statistical data sets.

Nationality and migration

The over-representation of ethnic minority groups, migrants and refugees in poverty has been apparent from poverty studies for some time. Research by the European Industrial Relations Observatory and the European Foundation for Living and Working Conditions (2004b: 13) suggests that, in some of the new CEE member states, 'gender equality per se is regarded as less of a problem than the integration of minority ethnic groups and migrant workers'. Hudson and Williams (2001) argue that there is consistent evidence that culturally or racially different migrants have been subject to social exclusion that manifests itself in several ways, including poverty and economic exclusion, significant immigrant labour market segmentation and increasing polarisation of international migrants in terms of their skills, incomes and positions in class structures.

There are an estimated 15 million immigrants in Europe who are foreigners in their countries of residence. Residency or citizenship status and the rights they confer on such individuals are less clearly defined and less intrinsically linked than in the past. This is attributed to factors such as the growing significance of universal human rights and the 'emergence of multi-level polities', such as the development of the EU, that confer 'rights that are not necessarily located in a bounded nation state' (Soysal, 2001: 67). Social exclusion, formal citizenship and conditions of residence can generate different forms of exclusion with specific gendered effects and there is a 'growing divergence between the rights of EU migrants and those from third world countries' (Kofman and Sales, 2001: 108). For Kofman, 'the discussion about gendered welfare states and the crisis of care seems to have entirely ignored migrant women, despite the crucial role they have played' (2004: 13). She stresses that many formal rights and entitlements that are taken for granted by citizens of the European Union may be legally withheld, subject to conditionality and discretion for migrants. There are fewer women in more privileged migrant groups and skilled female spouses face accreditation problems that create barriers to professional integration, while less skilled women face great difficulty in maintaining legal status:

> Both women who enter as labour migrants and family members are thus more likely to be forced into the informal sector and undertake poorly paid and undervalued work with little social protection. (Kofman, 2004: 24)

One example from Austria concerns child care allowance which is considered to be below the social assistance level and most carers doing long-term care receive only token payments, which serve to 'increase inequalities more than they improve the situation of carers, because of the inherent trend to get "cheap" informal care and care services... especially from migrants' (Kreimer, 2005: 8). However, although there has been a strong focus on domestic labour, there are numerous other sectors in which flexible contracts and informal work in low-skilled jobs prevail (Kofman, 2004).

In the CEE, the situation of the Roma population, who comprise the largest cross-national group, has been identified as a particular concern in relation to poverty and health, and improvement in the economic and social position of Roma is a precondition of EU accession for Bulgaria and Romania (Feliciano et al., 2004). Feliciano et al. show that in Bulgaria in 1996, 74 per cent of Roma, 32 per cent of ethnic Turks were unemployed compared to only 12 per cent of Bulgarians. Overall, 90 per cent of self-identified Roma were defined in the research as poor at both stages of their fieldwork in 1999/2000 and 2001. Roma also face significant disadvantage in some of the new EU member states, including Hungary, Slovakia and the Czech Republic. In Hungary, unemployment among the Roma population has increased over the years and is thought to be 3–4 times higher than in the majority population (Social Innovation Foundation, 2003). Feliciano et al. suggest that absolute poverty rates among the Roma population have increased dramatically in contrast to relative stability for the wider population in Hungary. However, Feliciano et al. also suggest that the 'Roma label is a fluid one' and that being poor opens the door to being classified as Roma (2004: 10), which they link to the Brazilian saying, 'money whitens'. In their research, they identified differences in self-identification and classification by researchers of individuals as Roma (4 per cent and 6 per cent respectively). They suggest that 'Roma' should refer to 'an extremely heterogeneous and fluid ethnicity, considered a unitary group only by outsiders' who are comprised of multiple groups with different languages, religions and cultural heritages. However, their classification as Roma, whether by individuals themselves or researchers, means they 'may experience discrimination that makes it difficult to escape poverty' (ibid., 2004: 28). Roma women are likely to bear the brunt of such disadvantage and discrimination in the complex interaction of factors involved in their situation:

> In general, class, gender and race can be seen as the most salient social divisions in twentieth century industrialised societies, but their constitution and significance vary... they are mutually constitutive: the effects of race, class and gender divisions are interrelated and multifaceted – one element compounds or modifies the other. (Williams, 2001a: 132)

Welfare states

There is a significant interrelationship between 'systems of income maintenance, taxation, public provision of services, and the labour market in structuring and transforming gender relations' (Sainsbury, 1999: 9). Sainsbury identifies five principles of entitlement that are central to the construction of welfare state policies covering maintenance, care need, work, performance and citizenship/residence. She highlights that, although welfare regimes can be categorised into different types, these are theoretical or ideal regime types that are not fully reflected in the real world in which politics and policies can contribute to differences that are 'significant in structuring gender relations' (1999: 260).

Given the current economic conditions in most EU member states, welfare states have been increasingly characterised by greater use of means-tested benefits and targeting. This implies less generous benefits and an erosion of the notion of rights to minimum income guarantees and a range of related services. Given that women rely more heavily on state welfare arrangements, current developments indicate that a limited range of resources are available to them. While the welfare reform agenda has evolved in recent years to take account of the need to address gender difference (Esping Andersen et al., 2002), to date welfare regimes remain highly gendered in terms of their outcomes. Sainsbury highlights that:

> Gender differentiation in entitlements occurs when claims to benefits are based on the traditional division of labour between sexes. Men receive benefits as family providers and workers, while women claim benefits as wives and mothers. Benefits tied to participation in the workforce are usually more generous than benefits claimed on the basis of wifely or motherly labour. (Sainsbury, 1999: 3)

Although there is a greater recognition of the need to incorporate gender in welfare systems, the welfare-to-work agenda has come to dominate welfare reform debates and has subsequently been prioritised over issues relating to gender inequality in recent years. This strategy has an underlying assumption that the world of paid work is the main mechanism for delivering economic and social welfare to all citizens of the EU. However, the operation of contemporary labour markets is characterised by highly unequal gender outcomes.

Work

Survey data indicate that during the 1990s overall, employment in the EU rose, but fell in the CEE new member states (European Commission, 2004a). In Hungary, for example, there has been a substantial decline in female employment among both working age women and those over the retirement age: at the beginning of the transition process 85.7 per cent of women (aged 15–54) were active earners compared to only 69.7 per cent by 2001 (Koncz, 2005: 2).

Despite the overall increase in women's employment in recent decades, significant gender inequalities remain in the labour market, including the extent of engagement in paid employment. The proportion of women in employment in 2002 in EU member states ranged from 38 per cent in Greece, Italy and Spain to about 48 per cent in Denmark, Finland and Sweden (European Commission, 2004b). The EU Quarterly Labour Force Survey shows the 2004 male employment rate as being 70.7 per cent on average compared with 55.7 per cent for women. However, the growth of women's employment is due in large part to increasing numbers working part time – 7 per cent of men work part-time compared with 31.3 per cent of women, averaging just over 20 hours a week. The extent of part-time work also varies greatly between countries and is highest in the Netherlands and the UK. With the exception of the Netherlands, male part-time employment is consistently below

12 per cent and it is women who account for the fluctuation in part-time work – while 74.8 per cent of women work part-time in the Netherlands, only 4 per cent do so in Slovakia. Women are marginally more likely to have temporary contracts and are more likely to be unemployed (9.8 per cent) than men (8.3 per cent) (Harðarson and Romans, 2005).

The nature of employment is important and, although part-time work may be viewed as beneficial for women wishing to combine paid work with unpaid care-work, such dual roles come at a price: 'other things being equal, any departure from full-time employment increases the risk of social exclusion', while unemployment and precarious employment are the main factors to increase 'significantly and substantially the risk of social exclusion in most countries' (Tsakloglou and Papadopolous, 2002b: 220). In another study, Bardasi and Gornick (2000) analyse part-time employment in five countries including three in the EU, and conclude that there are wage penalties associated with part-time employment, even after different characteristics of workers and occupations are taken into account.

However, in addition to the greater likelihood of women being unemployed or in part-time or temporary employment, occupational gender segregation contributes to a greater risk of low pay for women which makes them more vulnerable to poverty both during their working lives and in later life. Occupational segregation is a feature of labour markets across Europe. In 2000, almost half of women in employment in the EU worked in only four main areas of activity: healthcare and social services, education, public administration and retailing.

> In child care, eldercare and domestic cleaning, the percentage of women remains at 90% and often reaches 98–100% (e.g. among nursery teachers in Portugal; child care generally in the UK, and home helps in France and Finland). (European Foundation for Living and Working Conditions, 2004b: 11)

Occupational segregation has been described as economically inefficient as well as being detrimental to women, negatively affecting their status and income and contributing to poverty and income inequality (Anker, 2001). In addition, there are significant pay gaps between women and men in equivalent occupations, the UK, Cyprus, Estonia and Finland being notable in this regard (Robinson, 2001). In former Soviet Union countries, wage differentials were found to be low by international standards and, 'despite labour market upheavals gender pay gaps appear relatively stable', but occupational segregation, as elsewhere in Europe, is high (Pascall and Manning, 2000: 248).

Skills and education

Skills and education are generally identified as being crucial to strategies for improving access to better paid employment and reducing the risk of poverty and low pay. Among young people in Europe there are substantial differences in access to employment (Hudson and Williams, 2001). Middleton (2002) identifies diverging trends: on the one hand more young people are staying longer in education which is positive in so far as educational achievement is linked to (better paid) employment; while, on the other hand, youth unemployment is higher than general unemployment rates. The inability to secure employment in the labour market and the lack of financial autonomy for young people in terms of access to social security and benefits are factors that that help to explain why young people live at home with their parents 'until well into their twenties' (Middleton, 2002: 78). However, there are gender differences in the age that young people leave home – in the five Western European countries Middleton studied, women left home earlier than men. One factor affecting this is that young women form relationships or marry earlier, while young men spend longer in education and form relationships later than women.

Differences in education and experience perpetuate labour market segmentation and occupational gender segregation plays a role in perpetuating labour market discrimination into the next generation 'because women are generally discriminated against, they are likely to obtain less education than men and to pursue careers that reinforce the current segregation' (Anker, 2001: 139). Research in the UK suggests that women returning to the labour market are more likely to have fewer qualifications than women who have continuous employment and, consequently, are likely to remain financially disadvantaged in the labour market unless they can improve their qualifications. This is particularly significant for families with pre-school children and for lone mothers (Millar and Ridge, 2001; Rake, 2001).

However, gaining new skills or qualifications does not necessarily remove all disadvantages: some research suggests that skills and qualifications make more of a difference for men than women. In Germany, for example, young women have to invest more in terms of qualifications and time required to enable them 'to realize comparable employment outcomes to men but the gender differences here are far less striking as compared to those seen for the likelihood of leaving unemployment' (Trappe, 2005: 24). Although women in Slovakia are marginally more likely to complete secondary or university education, their earnings are lower across education levels (Bitusikova, 2003). Similarly, women's greater likelihood of having a higher educational qualification in Hungary 'does not readily translate into skilled or professional occupational attainments and economic security for Hungarian women' (Koncz, 2005: 8). In view of women's economic disadvantage despite higher qualification levels, a future risk lies in the fact that governments are now:

> seeking to contain the costs of providing extended education by restricting financial support for students. It is too soon to assess the impact of such retrenchment on future education patterns, but it is clear that in some countries acquiring third level educational qualifications will become significantly more expensive. (Middleton, 2002: 77)

Care

The unpaid work that women do and the caring roles they undertake are also significant contributory factors in explaining women's disadvantage in the labour market and their greater risk of poverty. Care is an increasingly significant issue in political terms across a range of different policy areas, including community care, looking after children, parenting, care of the elderly, work–life balance policies and the development of a mixed economy of care (Williams, 2001b). Taking care into account when addressing social policies is not straightforward because of the complex nature of care-giving and receiving, its relationship to poverty, the need to consider differences among women and families in possible models of work/care arrangements and the way in which these interact with income and labour market inequalities between groups of women (Innes and Scott, 2002). In European welfare states, the interaction of care and social, economic and political processes is a central consideration, particularly in a context where:

> the state is not just some passive monolith adjusting and adapting as its environment dictates. When one starts from the position of social care, the state assumes a central role but shares the limelight as (just) one agent of change. For if care is becoming increasingly problematic given that the demand for it is growing at a time when the supply is diminishing, welfare states play a crucial role in mediating the

dilemmas just as care creates new dilemmas for welfare states. (Daly and Lewis, 2000: 296)

In the UK, the model that informs policy has been criticised as being over-simplified; where women are seen as taking 'time out' to care for young children and returning, after a period of readjustment and training, to the labour market, which fails to take sufficient account of:

> the complexity of social and personal factors involved; as in relation to substitutability of care, the social realities are oversimplified and the experience of and constraints on low-income families insufficiently recognised. (Innes and Scott, 2002: 61)

Research using the Luxembourg Income Study shows that 'motherhood is a consequential factor nearly everywhere; while parenthood typically has little effect (or a positive effect) on men's employment rate and earnings, it weakens women's everywhere' (Gornick, 2004: 1). In her research, Gornick found that married women's caring responsibilities, as indicated by the presence of young children in the home:

> sharpen the overall gender inequality seen in all countries, dramatically so in some countries. These findings indicate that married women with young children are, for the most part, economically dependent on their husbands. In none of these fifteen countries – including the three with the highest level of gender equality on the composite measure, that is, Denmark, Finland, and Sweden – do women directly claim more than approximately one-third of the earnings taken home by parents. Remarkably, in five countries – Germany, Luxembourg, Netherlands, Spain, and the UK – mothers command less than one-fifth of all parental earnings. (Gornick, 1999: 32)

In the UK, a range of measures has been introduced to reduce child poverty, and the package of child benefits

> now looks more generous in international context, particularly for lower-earning families. Yet in-work poverty remains high, especially for lone parent families. Other countries such as Denmark and Finland, have much lower poverty rates among working households with children than might be expected on the basis of the level of child support. The relationship between working poverty and the generosity of the social transfer system is clearly far from perfect, drawing

our attention back to the importance of market wage inequality as a factor driving in-work poverty. (Stewart, 2005: 311)

There are different stages of development across countries in terms of attitudes to women's roles outside of the family (Sjöberg, 2004). Several studies suggest that the (re)organisation of care work contributes to explaining women's disadvantage, both in terms of reconciling caring and working roles and in the conditions of care work that continue to be heavily gender-segregated. For example, in a study of employment patterns in five industrialised countries, Bardasi and Gornick (2000) identify that, although variations were found across countries in the effects of having young children, child-related factors generally are important to women's employment outcomes and being a mother decreases the likelihood of full-time work in preference for part-time work or not working. Ungerson (2000) argues that, in the UK, disadvantages for women are intensified in the development of a mixed economy of care that locks lower paid workers, most of whom are women, into a marginalised and exploited form of dependency as both care producers and care providers. Research also suggests that women may experience more severe poverty than other family members because they deny themselves basic needs in order to protect children or partners from the worst effects of poverty (Rosenblatt and Rake, 2003).

Researchers from Hungary and the Czech Republic have argued that family policy has placed too much emphasis on offering parents the alternative of staying at home for long periods of child care, in preference to developing child care institutions, and this results in negative attitudes among employers with regard to employment of women (Marksova-Tominova, 2003; Ferge and Juhász, 2004). However, there is also evidence of reluctance among women to use employment-based rights to family benefits (Steinhilber, 2004a). Women are under pressure to take less leave than they are entitled to because of job insecurity, reduced maternity benefits and family sickness support, inflation and a decline in real wage rates. The consequent reduction in the value of benefits means that employment becomes more necessary for mothers while the systems that support them are under strain (Pascall and Manning, 2000).

Evidence suggests that there was a reduction of social support for health and education in former Soviet countries between 1989 and 1997 that is most strongly represented in falling nursery enrolments, while kindergarten attendance has been sustained in most CEE countries. However, the real value of state financial support for children has declined in many countries (Poland being the main exception), which suggests a cost for women. For Pascall and Manning, the overall situation is:

> Familializing the work of health and education and it is certainly increasing women's care work. It is also likely to be familializing women, intensifying their need for family connections to survive the losses of social support. (Pascall and Manning, 2000: 257)

Lone parents

Women account for 'the vast majority – 80–90 per cent' of lone parents everywhere and thus are a key group for analysis of the relationship between poverty and gender (Millar, 2002: 79). For the purposes of this chapter, lone parents are assumed to include never-married people and those who are separated, divorced or widowed, all of whom generally face a higher risk of poverty than other members of society.

In a study using the European Community Household Panel, lone parents were found to run a higher risk of poverty, non-monetary material deprivation and multidimensional disadvantage than the average population member across Austria, Germany, Greece, Portugal and the UK (Tsakloglou and Papadopoulos, 2002a). Sainsbury and Morrissens (2002) point to significant variation in poverty rates to argue that the high risk of poverty is not inevitable: among the European countries they studied, the highest rates of poverty were in Germany, the UK and Italy, whereas low poverty rates were found in the Czech Republic, Sweden, Finland and Denmark. They concluded that generous means-tested benefits were important in reducing poverty in Nordic countries. Italy presents a contrasting situation where lone mothers are more likely to work than other mothers. This has been linked to the 'lack of solid social protection', which is particularly limited for those who are separated or divorced. In comparison, unmarried or widowed mothers enjoy more support which 'presumably comes form the extended family to enable these women to work, generally full-time'. (Trifiletti, 1999: 60–1) There may also be:

> a difference between rhetoric and reality with respect to enabling policies, for example, in whether child care provision is affordable and adequate to meet demand, and whether the measures for balancing work and life are, in practice, available to all working parents. (Himmelweit, 2004: 238)

One example of this tension is provided by Kreimer's (2005) analysis of lone mothers in Austria. Kreimer refers to a high level of formal employment among lone mothers in an environment where child care services are limited and not affordable for many, which means that they are forced into, rather than supported towards, paid work. There are wide variations in the extent of support in relation to child care through service provision of publicly funded places or subsidies that support the financing of care services. France has a highly developed system of child care and Norway has good quality care, 'whereas the Netherlands and the UK have only recently stated to invest in child care provision and subsidies and supply is much lower' (Rowlingson and Millar, 2002: 209).

Sainsbury and Morrissens (2002) identified that the risk of poverty among lone parents in three transitional countries (Hungary, Czech Republic and Poland) had increased significantly between the early and mid-1990s. In the Czech Republic, for example, although the rate of poverty overall has remained relatively low (Potůček, 2004), a growing number of children now live in lone-parent families and, while lone parenthood is generally accepted in Czech society, lone parents are subjected to a higher risk of poverty than are two-parent families (Marksova-Tominova, 2003). In relation to former Soviet Union countries, overall, there have been limited policy responses to the needs of children in lone-parent families with few special provisions for lone parents.

> Living outside marriage – even to escape violence – is not in general a realistic option. It is possible that women's labour market status enhances their position within family relationships but is not strong enough to support life outside family relationships. (Pascall and Manning, 2000: 249)

Older women

Age is an important source of social inequality. Gunnarson (2002: 713) highlights that at every stage of life, 'the conditions of the individual are affected by such structuring dimensions as gender, class and ethnicity'. Hudson and Williams describe the better-paid 'insider' jobs in the European labour market as being 'not only the preserve of men, but of men aged between the mid-twenties and the mid-fifties' (2001: 55).

An area of significant change in the age profile across Europe in the last 50 years is the growth of the population over 65 which has been accompanied by an increase in the proportion aged 75 or more, particularly in Southern Europe where state welfare provision is weaker (Hudson and Wiliams, 2001). The domestic division of labour, including caring commitments of motherhood and adult care, levels of employment and low wage rates are important factors explaining women's risk of poverty throughout their lives (Arber and Ginn, 1991; Gunnarson, 2002; Harðarson and Ginn, 2004; Romans, 2005). As a consequence, women are more vulnerable to poverty in later life because of their reliance on systems of social protection.

> Women are often poor throughout their life times as a result of the caring work they have done for others at various stages in their lives, and by the time they reach retirement age are likely to be entitled to a lower independent pension than a man despite having a longer life expectancy. State pension provision is therefore particularly important for women and likely to remain so well beyond the considerable change in gender roles that would be necessary to rectify this inequality. (Himmelweit, 2001: 10)

The risk of poverty among older people has decreased in recent years but remains high. There is a greater risk of poverty for single elderly households including, in some countries, a higher risk for women (Grootaert and Braithwaite, 1998; Sainsbury and Morrisens, 2002b). Smeeding and Williamson's (2001) analysis of eight countries, including UK, Netherlands, France Sweden, and (West) Germany, showed that, with the exception of the Netherlands, older people in or at risk of poverty are overwhelmingly women, regardless of the level of poverty within a nation. Older women living alone make up 28–38 percent of the elderly population, but 49–59 percent of the poor. In other words, 'to be old and poor is disproportionately to be a woman in general, and a single woman in particular' (Smeeding and Williamson, 2001: 14). Schnepf (2004) adds that the poverty risk for female-headed households rises with age, whereas elderly males have a lower likelihood of being poor.

Although there are differences in pension schemes across the world, a feature of many recent reforms has been privatisation. However, gender equality has been absent from much mainstream pension policy debates and fails to take account of pension reform that may have a detrimental effect on women, for example in closer links between contributions and benefits:

> gender inequalities in the larger environment, namely the labor market, have a substantial impact on pension rights and the future level of benefits. A lower retirement age for women further exacerbates the problem of women's shorter tenure. A pension system based

on the individual accumulation of pension rights thus exacerbates gender inequality in the labor market. (Steinhilber, 2004b: 11)

In her analysis of pension reform in three countries (Poland, Hungary and Czech Republic), Steinhilber (2004b) summarises changes in pension provision. These include partial privatisation in two countries to create two-tier systems involving state and private provision and reform to the existing pension scheme in the Czech Republic. Although the empirical picture is complex, projections show that in Poland both men and women will have lower replacement rates from reforms, but the gender gap in replacement rates will widen: Steinhilber ascribes half the difference to different retirement ages and the other half to wage differences between women and men linked to the unequal division of caring roles.

The importance of the precise nature of pension reforms and systems of means-tested benefits look set to remain central to the risk of poverty for older women, particularly given all the other evidence which suggests women's disadvantage in the labour market remains substantial and many older women 'will find their later lives to be persistently constricted by poverty or near poverty' (Gunnarson, 2002: 726). Steinhilber (2004a) identifies a retreat from redistributive pension schemes throughout CEE that is detrimental to women and will leave them with lower pensions. According to Ginn (2004), the scenario of benign pension privatisation is unlikely for several reasons: the economic effects of large pension funds, public costs through tax relief, transitional cost, reduced motivation to defend declining state pensions and the aim of 'most OECD governments to contain state pension spending'. While such changes will allow some individuals to compensate for diminishing state pensions, they leave others – mainly women, manual workers and ethnic minorities – to face the 'indignities of means testing or the uncertainties of relying on family members for support' (Ginn, 2004: 132). Poverty among older women looks set to remain an enduring challenge across Europe.

Disability and health

The links between poverty and ill health, impairment and disability are well documented: poor people are more likely to be affected by ill health and disability; disabled people and those with poor health are more likely to live in poverty; and women, children and older people are particularly disadvantaged (Priestly, 2001; World Health Organisation, 2001). Poverty is a major determinant of poor health, but it may also be an effect of ill health. It can also be argued that good health and well-being are resources that contribute to enabling individuals to reduce the risk of poverty and that they are enhanced by many of the factors discussed in this chapter, such as education, employment, a decent income, social networks and access to resources. In their study of five countries (Austria, Germany, Greece, Portugal and the UK) using the European Community Household Panel, Tsakloglou and Papado-poulos (2002a) found that, like lone parents, sick or disabled people run a greater risk of poverty, non-monetary material deprivation and multidimensional disadvantage than populations as a whole. Their data were not gender disaggregated, but they acknowledge the potential for sub-groups to face particularly high or low risks of poverty or depriva-tion. Using the same data source, Heady (2002) emphasises the reliance on family in relation to care for disabled people and that the burden of care mainly falls on women, which in turn affects their ability to work and build up their own benefit entitlements.

Legal provisions to address discrimination against disabled people are limited and, where they do exist, 'such provisions tend to lack teeth or are not reinforced' (Heady, 2002: 104). The extent of access to paid work and the nature of the work that disabled people do mean that, even when they do find work, disabled people are under-represented in professions and management and over-represented in low-skilled, low-paid, less secure jobs, and there is evidence of 'horizontal segregation, with disabled people (or particular impairment groups) over-represented in specific occupations or congregated in sheltered workshops' (Barnes and Mercer, 2003: 47).

Several studies have identified that benefit systems can act as barriers to disabled people taking employment because of the conditions for benefit receipt (Simons, 1998; Wilson et al., 2000; Heady, 2002; Gillespie and Scott, 2004). Although disability benefits may result in higher levels of state financial support in some countries in comparison with other groups, women's employment patterns can be a disadvantage if that support involves contributory benefits. For example, high levels of part-time work among women in the Netherlands mean that their disability benefits are lower: 'an increasing proportion of women among disability entrants, therefore, implies lower benefits, other things equal' (de Jong, 2003: 55). Studies also suggest that benefit provision combined with high unemployment among older workers can lead to states using disab-ility 'as a substitute for early retirement' which serves to conceal the true level of unemployment (Heady, 2002: 106): in Finland, for example, disability is the most common reason for retirement (Aro, 2003).

The World Health Organisation (WHO) considers that maternal mortality is associated with poverty and that there is 'clear evidence' that poverty affects reproductive health, particularly in women:

> This is true for all countries in the European Region, not just those that have recently undergone, or are still in a period of, economic transition: it also applies to poor populations of socially disadvantaged people, migrants or refugees in rich western European countries. (WHO, 2001: 7)

Domestic violence is another significant concern in relation to women's health and well-being. Pascall and Manning (2000) highlight that, in CEE countries, despite the legislation to support equal relationships in marriage, 'the inequality of marriage in practice is illustrated by the extent of domestic violence and the domestic division of labour'. Research in the UK suggests that lone parents show a higher incidence of having poor health themselves or having children with health problems compared with other family groups (Marsh and Rowlingson, 2002), some of which can be accounted for by the experience of long-term poverty and the consequences of domestic violence in an earlier relationship (Land, 2001). Domestic violence is a significant cause of marital breakdown and this can have a significant impact on the risk of poverty for women. In one UK study among white working-class women, poverty emerged from difficulties arising from unmanageable debt, including debt incurred during the violent relationship and in which it was 'difficult, if not impossible, to deny their former male partners money which had been budgeted for household items or food, since the outcome would frequently be violent' (Wilcox, 2000: 179). Women faced additional costs in setting up a new home, getting children into new schools and replacing essential documentation, and had to deal with health issues arising from years of violence and abuse and the stress and isolation of setting up home in a new community.

Conclusions

In this chapter, it has been highlighted that gender interacts with a wide range of other factors to reduce or limit women's social entitlements. These factors need to be better integrated into analysis and policy responses. Existing data sources do not provide a comprehensive picture of poverty and disadvantage amongst women. Gaining a better

understanding of how different and often multiple forms of discrimination interact throws up many additional opportunities and challenges
for ensuring better representation of women in all their diversity when
welfare solutions are proposed (Fawcett Society, 2003). There remains an
urgent need to develop gender-sensitive methodologies for analysis of
poverty, including methods for opening 'the family "black box" in order
to understand to what extent women's poverty is masked' (Ruspini,
2000: 128). Analysis of multidimensional disadvantage is necessary for
a greater understanding of critical factors in 'the complexity of social
divisions that have a bearing on peoples' lives and their needs, experiences and demands for welfare provision: class, gender, race/ethnicity,
disability, age sexuality and religion' (Williams, 2001a: 131).

Clearly the welfare reform agenda and the emphasis on paid work,
which is the key driver for economic and social policy in Europe, have
the potential to improve the position of some women, but to exacerbate
further the risk of poverty for others. Failure to take adequate account
of gender when designing social policy, implementation and evaluation
processes may conceal the relative disadvantage faced by women or
particular groups of women, but does not make their risk of poverty
any less real or urgent. Women bear much of the burden of an implicit
reliance on family welfare: unless they are moving into work, too many
women remain in a situation of caring without support, caring for adults
as well as children. Meanwhile, women moving into work too often
face low-paid and insecure employment that does not guarantee a route
out of poverty, but forces them to juggle formal and informal care
responsibilities to make paid work possible.

Instead of its current diminishing significance in the European policy
agenda, gender must remain a central and long-term policy concern.
Welfare reform debates need to incorporate a foundation of social entitlements that has broad public support and that acknowledges the differences for women and men and different groups of women and men.
Crucially, within that debate there is a task of winning hearts and minds
to build a consensus that recognises and values the significant role of
unpaid and care work that is carried out disproportionately by women
and the importance to wider society of securing equal economic and
social rights for all women.

Note

1. 'Equivalisation' involves adjustment of household income to account for variation in household size and composition.

References

Anker, R. (2001) 'Theories of occupational segregation by sex', in M. Loufti (ed.) *Women Gender and Work: What is Equality and How Do We Get There?* Geneva: International Labour Organisation, pp. 129–56.

Arber, S. and Ginn, J. (1991) *Gender and Later Life: A Sociological Analysis of Resources and Constraints*, London: Sage.

Aro, T. (2003) 'Work ability and functional capacity – the Finnish point of view', in R. Gould. and S. Laitinen-Kuikka (eds) *Current Trends in Disability Pensions in Europe, Proceedings from a Seminar held in Helsinki on 8 April 2003*, 87–94, Helsinki: Hakapaino Oy. Available at: http://www.etk.fi/Dynagen_attachments/Att17209/17209.pdf [accessed 25 February 2005].

Baden, S. (1997) *Economic Reform and Poverty: A Gender Analysis. Bridge Report no. 50*, Brighton: Institute of Development Studies. Available at: http://www.bridge.ids.ac.uk/reports/re50.pdf [accessed 25 February 2005].

Bardasi, E. and Gornick, J. (2000) *Women and Part-Time Employment: Workers' 'Choices' and Wage Penalties in Five Industrialized Countries. Luxembourg Income Study Working Paper No. 223*, New York: Syracuse University. Available at: http://www.lisproject.org/publications/liswps/223.pdf [accessed 25 February 2005].

Barnes, C. and Mercer, G. (2003) *Disability*, Cambridge: Polity Press.

Bitusikova, A. (2003) 'Women's social entitlements in Slovakia', paper presented at the 1st NEWR workshop on social entitlements, Panteion University, Athens, 9–11 October.

Chant, S. (2003) 'Female household headship and the feminisation of poverty: facts, fictions and forward strategies', *Gender Institute New Working Paper series 9*. Available at: http://www.lse.ac.uk/collections/genderInstitute/pdf/femaleHouseholdHeadship.pdf [accessed 25 February 2005].

Daly, M. and Lewis, J. (2000) 'The concept of social care and the analysis of contemporary welfare states',*British Journal of Sociology*, 51(2): 281–98.

Daly, M. and Rake, K. (2003) *Gender and the Welfare State*, Cambridge: Polity.

De Jong, P. (2003) 'New directions in disability (benefit) policy: the Dutch experience', in R. Gould. and S. Laitinen-Kuikka (eds) *Current Trends in Disability Pensions in Europe, Proceedings from a seminar held in Helsinki on 8 April 2003*, 87–94, Helsinki: Hakapaino Oy. Available at: http://www.etk.fi/Dynagen_attachments/Att17209/17209.pdf [accessed 25 February 2005].

Elson, D. (2000) 'Gender budget initiatives as an aid to gender mainstreaming', paper presented at the Ministerial Conference on Gender Mainstreaming, Competitiveness and Growth, Paris: OECD, 23–24 November.

Esping-Andersen, et al. (2002) *Why We Need a Welfare State*, Oxford: Oxford University Press.

European Commission (2004a) *The Social Situation in the European Union: 2004 Overview*, Available at: http://europa.eu.int/comm/employment_social/news/2004/oct/socsit_2004_en.pdf [accessed 11 February 2005].

European Commission (2004b) *Work and Health I the EU: A Statistical Portrait*, Luxembourg: Office for the Official Publications of the European Communities.

European Foundation for the Improvement of Living and Working Conditions (2004a) *Quality of Life in Europe: First Results of a New pan-European Survey. Foundation Paper No. 6,* Luxembourg: Office for the Official Publications of the European Communities. Available at: http://www.eurofound.eu.int/publications/EF04105.htm [accessed 24 February 2005].

126 *Morag Gillespie*

European Foundation for the Improvement of Living and Working Conditions (2004b) *Equal Opportunities for Women and Men in Services of General Interest*, Luxembourg: Office for the Official Publications of the European Communities. Available from: http://www.eurofound.eu.int/publications/EF04128.htm [accessed 24 February 2005].

European Women's Lobby (2005) *Women are Disheartened as the Commission Rips out the Heart of Social Europe*, Available at: http://www.womenlobby.org/Document.asp?DocID=840&tod=12722 [accessed 24 February 2005].

Fawcett Society (2003) *Many Women, Multiple Identities*, London: Fawcett Society.

Feliciano, C., Cook, D. and Emigh, R. (2004) *Changes in Poverty in Post-Socialist Europe: The Role of Ethnicity and State Transfers*, Los Angeles: California Center for Population Research. Available at: http://www.ccpr.ucla.edu/ccprwpseries/ccpr_010_04.pdf [accessed 25 February 2005].

Ferge, Z. and Juhász, G. (2004) 'Accession and social policy: the case of Hungary', *Journal of European Social Policy*, 14(3): 233–51.

Finn, D. (2000) 'Welfare to work: the local dimension', *Journal of European Social Policy*, 10(1): 43–57.

Gillespie, M. and Scott, G. (2004) *Advice Services and Transitions to Work for Disadvantaged Groups: A Literature Review*, Glasgow: Scottish Poverty Information Unit. Available at: www.equal-access-scotland.org.uk [accessed 25 February 2005].

Ginn, J. (2004) 'European pension provision: taking account of gender', *Social Policy and Society*, 3(2): 123–34.

Glendinning, C. and Millar, J. (1992) *Women and Poverty in Britain: the 1990s*, Hemel Hempstead: Harvester Wheatsheaf.

Goldberg, G. S. and Kremen, E. (1990) 'The feminisation of poverty: discovered in America', in G. S. Goldberg and E. Kremen (eds), *The Feminisation of Poverty – Only in America*, New York: Greenwood Press, pp. 1–15.

Gornick, J. (2004) 'Women's economic outcomes, gender inequality and public policy: finding from the Luxembourg Income Study', *Socio-Economic Review*, 2: 213–38.

Gornick, J. (1999) *Gender Equality in the Labour Market: Women's Employment and Earnings, Luxembourg Income Study Working Paper No. 206*, New York: Syracuse University. Available at: http://www.lisproject.org/publications/liswps/206.pdf [accessed 25 February 2005].

Grootaert, C. and Braithwaite, J. (1998) *Poverty Correlates and Indicator-Based Targeting in Eastern Europe and the Former Soviet Union*, Available at: http://www.worldbank.org/html/dec/Publications/Workpapers/WPS1900series/wps1942/wps1942.pdf [accessed 25 February 2005].

Gunnarson, E. (2002) 'The vulnerable life course: poverty and social assistance among middle aged and older women', *Ageing and Society*, 22: 709–28.

Harðarson, O. and Romans, F. (2005) 'Labour market latest trends: 2nd quarter 2004 data', *Statistics in Focus: Population and Social Conditions*, Eurostat, 1. Available at: http://www.eustatistics.gov.uk/statistics_in_focus/downloads/KS-NK-05-001-EN.pdf [accessed 23 March 2005].

Heady, C. (2002) 'Sickness and disability', in M. Barnes et al. (eds) *Poverty and Social Exclusion in Europe*, Cheltenham: Edward Elgar, pp. 101–22.

Himmelweit, S. (2001) 'Tools for budget impact analysis: taxes and benefits', paper presented at *UNIFEM-OECD-Nordic Council-Government of Belgium High Level Conference: Towards Gender Budgeting*, Brussels, 16–17 October.

Himmelweit, S. (2004) 'Lone mothers: what is to be done?' *Feminist Economics* 10(2): 237–64.

Hudson, R. and Williams, A. (2001) 'Reshaping Europe: the challenge of new divisions within a homogenized political-economic space', in J. Fink, G. Lewis and J. Clarke (eds) *Rethinking European Welfare*, London: Sage Publications, pp. 33–64.

Innes, S. and Scott, G. (2002) *Families, Care and Women's Transition to Paid Work. Rosemount Lifelong Learning Research Report 1*, Glasgow: Scottish Poverty Information Unit.

Kilkey, M. and Bradsaw, J. (1999) 'Lone mothers, economic well being and policies', in D. Sainsbury (ed.) *Gender and Welfare State Regimes*, Oxford: Oxford University Press.

Kofman, E. (2004) 'Female migrants and refugees in European welfare regimes: employment and entitlements', paper presented at the 2nd NEWR workshop on social entitlements, University of Latvia, Riga, 14–15 May.

Kofman, E. and Sales, R. (2001) 'Migrant women and exclusion in Europe', in J. Fink, G. Lewis and J. Clarke (eds) *Rethinking European Welfare*, London: Sage Publications, pp. 33–64.

Koncz, K. (2005) 'Labour market characteristics of female employment in Hungary in comparison with tendencies are taking part in the European Union', paper presented at the IAFFE-Europe Conference 'Central and Eastern Europe: A feminist economic dialogue on transition and EU-enlargement', Budapest, 21–22 January.

Kreimer, M. (2005) 'Economic restructuring and welfare reforms in Austria: caregiving parity and/or transitional labour markets?', paper presented at the IAFFE-Europe Conference 'Central and Eastern Europe: A feminist economic dialogue on transition and EU-enlargement', Budapest, 21–22 January.

Land, H. (2001) 'Lone mothers, employment and child care', in J. Millar and K. Rowlingson (eds) *Lone Parents, Employment and Social Policy*, Bristol: Policy Press.

Marksova-Tominova, M. (2003) 'Social Services and Women's Employment In The Czech Republic', paper presented at the 1st NEWR workshop on social entitlements, Panteion University, Athens, 9–11 October.

Marsh, A. and Rowlingston, K. (2002) *Low/Moderate Income Families in Britain: Change in 1999 and 2000*. DWP Research Report No. 181, Leeds: CDS.

Middleton, S. (2002) 'Transitions from youth to adulthood', in M. Barnes et al. (eds) *Poverty and Social Exclusion in Europe*, Cheltenham: Edward Elgar, pp. 53–78.

Millar, J. (2002) 'Lone parenthood', in M. Barnes et al. (eds) *Poverty and Social Exclusion in Europe*, Cheltenham: Edward Elgar, pp. 79–100.

Millar, J. and Ridge, T. (2001) *Families, Poverty, Work and Care: A Review of the Literature on Lone Parents and Low Income Couple Families*. Research Report No. 153, Leeds: CDS.

Orloff, A.S. (2002) 'Women's employment and welfare regimes', Social Policy and Development Programme Paper No. 12, Geneva: United Nations Research Institute for Social Development.

Oxley, H., Dang, T.T. and Antolin P. (2000) *Poverty Dynamic in Six OECD Countries*, Available at: http://www.oecd.org/dataoecd/31/31/2732278.pdf [accessed 11 February 2004].

Pascall, G. and Manning, N. (2000) 'Gender and social policy: comparing welfare states in Central and Eastern Europe and the former Soviet Union', Journal of European Social Policy, 10(3): 240–66.

Potůček, M. (2004) 'Accession and social policy: the case of the Czech Republic', *Journal of European Social Policy*, 14 (3): 253–66.

Priestley, M. (2001) 'Thinking global: challenges to disability studies', paper presented at the Society for Disability Studies' 14th annual meeting, 'Democracy, Diversity and Disability', Winnipeg Convention Centre, Winnipeg, 21 June.

Rake, K. (2001) 'Gender and New Labour's social policies', *Journal of Social Policy*, 30(2): 209–32.

Robinson, D. (2001) 'Differences in occupational earnings by sex', in M. Loufti (ed.) *Women Gender and Work: What is Equality and How Do We Get There?* Geneva: International Labour Organization, pp. 157–88.

Rosenblatt, G. and Rake, K. (2003) *Gender and Poverty*, London: Fawcett Society.

Rowlingson K. and Millar J. (2002) 'Lone parents, poverty and work: policy approaches and lessons from abroad', *Benefits*, 10(3): 207–13.

Ruspini, E. (2000) 'Women and poverty: a new research methodology', in D. Gordon and P. Townsend (eds) *Breadline Europe: The Measurement of Poverty*, Bristol: Policy Press, pp. 107–39.

Sainsbury, D. (2001) 'Gendering dimensions of welfare states', in J. Fink, G. Lewis and J. Clarke (eds) *Rethinking European Welfare*, London: Sage, pp. 115–30.

Sainsbury, D. (1999) 'Gender policy regimes and politics', in D. Sainsbury (ed.) *Gender and Welfare State Regimes*, Oxford: Oxford University Press, pp. 245–75.

Sainsbury, D. and Morrisens, A. (2002) 'Poverty in Europe in the 1990s: the effectiveness of means-tested benefits', *Journal of European Social Policy*, 12(4): 307–27.

Schnepf, S. V. (2004) 'The feminisation of poverty in transitions countries: evidence from subjective data', paper presented at the IAFFE-Europe Conference 'Central and Eastern Europe: A feminist economic dialogue on transition and EU-enlargement', conference venue, Budapest, 21–22 January.

Simons, K. (1998) *Supported Living and Supported Employment: Opening up Opportunities to People with Learning Difficulties*, Available at: http://www.jrf.org.uk/knowledge/findings/foundations/SCR728.asp [accessed 10 July 2003].

Sjöberg, O. (2004) 'The role of family policy institutions in explaining gender-role attitudes: a comparative multilevel analysis of thirteen industrialized countries', *Journal of European Social Policy*, 14(2): 107–23.

Smeeding, T. and Williamson, J. (2001) *Income Maintenance in Old Age: What Can be Learned from Cross-national Comparisons*, Luxembourg Income Study Working Paper No. 263, New York: Syracuse University.

Social Innovation Foundation (2003) *Gender Assessment of the Impact of EU Accession on the Status of Women in the Labour Market in CEE, National Study: Hungary*, Budapest: Social Innovation Foundation.

Soysal, Y. (2001) 'Changing citizenship in Europe: remarks on postnational membership and the national state', in J. Fink, G. Lewis and J. Clarke J. (eds) *Rethinking European Welfare,* London: Sage Publications, pp. 65–76.

Steinhilber, S. (2004a) 'Gender dimensions of social security reforms in transition economies', paper presented at the Regional Symposium on Mainstreaming Gender into Economic Policies, Geneva: Palais des Nations, 28–30 January.

Steinhilber, S. (2004b) 'The gender implications of pension reforms. General remarks and evidence from selected countries', paper presented at the IAFFE-Europe 'Central and Eastern Europe: A feminist economic dialogue on transition and EU-enlargement', Budapest, 21–22 January.

Stewart, K. (2005) 'Changes in poverty and inequality in the UK in international context', in J. Hills and K. Stewart (eds) New Labour, Poverty, Inequality and Exclusion, Bristol: Policy Press, pp. 297–321.

Trappe, H. (2005) 'Gender inequality in the East German labor market seen through a generational lens', paper presented at the IAFFE-Europe 'Central and Eastern Europe: A feminist economic dialogue on transition and EU-enlargement', Budapest, 21–22 January.

Trifiletti, R. (1999) 'Southern European welfare regimes and the worsening position of women', Journal of European Social Policy, 9(1): 49–64.

Tsakloglou, P. and Papadopoulos, F. (2002a) 'Poverty, material deprivation and multi-dimensional disadvantage during four life stages: evidence from the ECHP', in M. Barnes et al. (eds) Poverty and Social Exclusion in Europe, Cheltenham: Edward Elgar, pp. 24–52.

Tsakloglou, P. and Papadopoulos, F. (2002b) 'Aggregate level and determining factors of social exclusion in twelve European countries', Journal of European Social Policy, 12(3): 211–25.

Ungerson, C. (2000) 'Thinking about the production and consumption of long-term care in Britain: does gender still matter?' Journal of Social Policy, 29(4): 623–43.

Wilcox, P. (2000) 'Lone motherhood: the impact on living standards of leaving a violent relationship', Social Policy and Administration, 34(2): 176–90.

Williams, F. (2001a) 'Race/ethnicity, gender and class', in J. Fink, G. Lewis and J. Clarke (eds) Rethinking European Welfare, London: The Open University, pp. 131–61.

Williams, F. (2001b) 'In and beyond New Labour: towards a new political ethics of care', Critical Social Policy, 21(4): 467–93.

Wilson, A., Riddell, S. and Barron, S. (2000) 'Welfare for those who can? The impact of the quasi-market on the lives of people with learning Difficulties', Critical Social Policy, 20 (4): 479–502.

World Health Organisation (2001) Poverty and Health – Evidence and Action in WHO's European Region, Regional Committee for Europe, Copenhagen: World Health Organization Regional Office For Europe. Available at: http://www.euro.who.int/Document/RC51/edoc8.pdf [accessed 23 March 2005].

7
Migration, Ethnicity and Entitlements in European Welfare Regimes

Eleonore Kofman

In the past few years a number of theoretical and empirical studies have highlighted the pivotal role of migrant women in global chains of care and the globalisation of social reproduction. Hence their livelihoods should be seen as maintaining welfare regimes. At the same time their labour market positions within changing welfare regimes as well as their immigration status determine their rights and entitlements.

In the NEWR (2003) background paper on social entitlements, the concept of entitlements was based on Sen's definition as 'the commodities over which a person can establish her ownership and command', but this could be broadened to include resources of different kinds (material, emotional and symbolic) and social networks. While the concept of rights may seem too narrow, we should note that many formal rights and claims to entitlements are taken for granted by citizens of the European Union; for migrants, these rights may be legally withheld, subject to conditionality and discretion. Migrants' relationship to entitlements is more problematic. On the one hand, it is constrained by lack of rights; on the other, by the imposition of additional obligations. It is therefore not just a matter of their inability to exercise their rights, but of formal exclusion, which is sanctioned by immigration, residence and employment regulations.

Some of the key areas differentiating citizens and migrants are: the right to enter, conditions of residence and unlawful presence in the territory, security from deportation, the rights and conditions of family life, employment, including access to the public sector, self-employment and the liberal professions, access to citizenship and the ability to make the transition from one migration, residence and employment status to another. Formal dependency may be sanctioned through immigration legislation, a situation which particularly affects migrant women. They may be bound as family members by a probationary period in most European states and in a few cases, as in Germany, not permitted to enter the official labour market in the first few years. Thus for an increasing number of migrants, their lives are constrained by a tenuous status and limited claims to welfare entitlements.

The chapter focuses on the livelihoods and differential rights and entitlements of Third Country women, i.e. non-EU nationalities who enter on their own for work and education, as family migrants or as asylum seekers and refugees. It is primarily restricted to first-generation migrants, that is those who were born in another country. In many European countries the term migrant is both narrower and more extensive – narrower in the sense that too often a 'migrant' is someone from a Third World country with value systems different to prevailing European norms. Frequently, the migrant woman, especially if she is Muslim, quintessentially exemplifies the weight of tradition. At the same time, 'migrant' may, in states such as Austria, Germany and Switzerland, be applied to all non-nationals, many of whom have been born and educated in the country.[1] In this case it is difficult to distinguish those of migrant origin from recent arrivals.

The analysis is limited to the EU before its enlargement in May 2004 when eight Eastern and Central European and two Mediterranean states were added. In terms of migration, the enlargement has been contentious and politically exploited. Discourses of welfare scroungers by the right-wing tabloid press pushed the UK government to withdraw its initial willingness to open up labour mobility. Instead, it adopted a more restrictive policy requiring registration and delayed access to a range of benefits (Nationality and Immigration Directorate, 2004). Apart from Ireland, Sweden and the UK, a transitional period of up to seven years for full mobility has been imposed. However, even though without the right to reside permanently or work, many migrants from Eastern European countries had developed strategies to accumulate resources from short-term and rotational stays in what Mirjana Morokvasic (2003) depicts as a pattern of 'settled in mobility'.

The first section outlines different routes of entry (labour, family and asylum) and gendered patterns of immigration. The second explores some key forms of employment in changing welfare regimes and particularly those sectors linked with the globalisation of care and social reproduction. The third turns to rights and entitlements arising from immigration policies which have generated complex systems of stratification based on the interplay of routes of entry and labour market position. Several countries have been selected to exemplify the role of migrant women in welfare regimes and their intersection with immigration regimes. The typology of welfare regimes is largely drawn from the influential model proposed by Gøsta Esping-Andersen (1990) and modified to take account of their recent trajectory in the 1990s. Sweden has a social democratic welfare regime and has mainly received family reunion migrants and large numbers of asylum seekers since the halt to labour migration in 1972. Germany is a conservative corporatist welfare regime which originally drew its migrants from the Mediterranean as guest workers, based on an ethnic and exclusionary model of incorporation. Following the end of the bipolar world, its migrants have increasingly come from Eastern Europe, while the numbers applying for asylum have on average been the highest in Europe. France, also a conservative corporatist welfare regime, has a long history of waves of immigration, from both neighbouring states and its colonies in North and West Africa and South East Asia. Spain could also be said to have become a conservative Southern rim welfare regime. Its immigration history is more recent and diversified than countries in Northern Europe. Colonial links too play a part in migratory patterns, though its proximity to North Africa and the opening up of Eastern Europe have shaped its recent migratory patterns. Lastly, the UK, a welfare regime which has been in the vanguard of neoliberal measures, has been profoundly marked by its colonial ties in its migratory patterns and policies. Its deregulated labour markets have also offered migrants employment unwanted by home state labour. The UK sees itself positioned as a global player eager to compete in the market for skilled labour.

Gender patterns of immigration

Given the diversification of migratory categories, histories and policies of immigration and integration, there are inevitably major variations between countries in relation to different types of flows, participation in the labour market and in particular sectors, the size and citizenship of second and subsequent generations, and degrees of racial and sexual discrimination confronted by migrant women. Though Southern European states have also become societies of long-term settlement of migrants, substantial differences remain compared to Northern states in the proportion of female migrants (see Table 7.1), composition of migrant populations and settlement policies.

Migrant women have entered the European Union under different immigration categories and for different purposes. Until the stoppage of mass labour migration in the mid-1970s (earlier in the UK), female

Table 7.1: Proportion of women in immigration flows in selected EEA countries, (1999, unless otherwise indicated)[2]

	Proportion of women in immigration flows, % of total	Average annual growth since 1990[3]
Austria (1998)	46.5	–
Belgium	50.7	0.9
Denmark (1998)	49.7	0.4
Finland	50.3	1.4
France[4]	52.8	0.4
Germany	41.3	−0.1
Greece (1998)	56.8	0.3
Luxembourg	46.4	−1.1
Netherlands	49.1	1.7
Norway (1998)	50.1	0.1
Portugal[5]	48.6	4.3
Spain (1998)	50.1	0.4
Sweden	51.6	0.9
Switzerland	49.8	1.2
UK	50.6	0.2

Sources: Eurostat (New Cronos database); Office des migrations internationales (France).

migrants constituted a significant minority of labour migrants but often entered without children. In many instances, their participation rate in the labour market was higher than home state women at a time when many of the latter did not work. Following the halt of mass labour, family reunion became the main route of legal entry into the European Union and was predominantly female. By the 1990s, refugee flows with variable gender balances began to increase. Quota refugees, such as the Bosnians, often had a more equitable gender balance (Kofman, 2002). From the 1980s Southern European countries clearly shifted from being countries of emigration to countries of immigration, including a strong demand for female labour. Since the 1990s, the opening up of Eastern Europe and its economic transformation resulted in loss of employment for women and the search for new possibilities in European Union countries. In particular new forms of transient labour migration, often based on a rotational system, have led to women undertaking domestic work, care, cleaning and trading and combining this with familial responsibilities in their home countries (Morokvasic, 1996). Others have gone into prostitution, a number of them having been trafficked.

In the following sections I outline the different modes of entry. Though not directly entering through labour channels, those entering family reunification and asylum will in many cases eventually join the labour market. Their entitlements are derived both from their entry status and their labour market position.

Labour migration

It is argued that new and alternative global gendered circuits of servicing (Sassen, 2000) and care (Ehrenreich and Hochschild, 2003) explain the transfer of female labour from poorer to richer countries. Men and women circulate differently in the new global economy. Men occupy an elite space of flows (Castells, 1996) in a masculinised high-tech world of global finance, production and technology, the commanding heights of the knowledge economy, while women provide the services largely associated with a wife's traditional role – care of children and the elderly, homemaking and sex (Ehrenreich and Hochschild, 2003). For Sassen (2001) migrant women fill the devalued, marginalised and flexible sectors of production and services in increasingly polarised global cities. On the other hand, Ehrenreich and Hochschild (2003) emphasise the production of care in its material and emotional dimensions, enabling economic expansion in the First World to take place under neoliberal conditions of welfare restrictions and flexible labour. Globalisation has led to the marketisation of various services, including care, which is now brought into global care chains. These are defined 'as a series of personal links between people across the globe based on the paid or unpaid work of caring' (Hochschild, 2000: 131). The chains may vary in their number and connective strength, combining internal and international caring links.

In the European context, the development of such chains of care has to be understood in relation to analyses of welfare state change and resettlement (Williams, 2003), models for dealing with a care deficit and the role of migrant women in providing care for the elderly, children, the disabled and people with mental health problems in paid, unpaid, formal or informal capacity. The development of care in the home, as we shall see, is not just a function of changes in gender divisions of labour and family structures but is also due to the shift from direct provision of services to a variety of forms of privatisation and informalisation of care. In Southern Europe the shortage of labour has been recognised in several less skilled sectors (agriculture, construction, hotels and restaurants and the household) and this has led to the development of quotas, albeit totally inadequate to meet the real shortages. And throughout Europe as elsewhere, migrant women underpin the globalisation of care and social reproduction (Hill Maher, 2004); yet except for the most skilled in the education and health sectors, the role of migrants is undervalued.

Thus migrants are not just recipients of entitlements but providers of care in a variety of settings (Kofman et al., 2000). In general, an increasing proportion of female migrants are engaged in biological and social reproduction in the household, the community, the private sector and the state. The over-representation of Third Country women in devalued sectors of the economy, both as legal and undocumented migrants, has profound consequences for their entitlements compared to home state women. Work in the domestic sphere (cleaning and care) has risen sharply in the 1990s, especially in Southern Europe but also in Northern countries (Cancedda, 2001; Cox, 2000). Traditionally domestic service was the major employer of women until after the Second World War and this historical process is partly being recreated (Friese, 1995), especially in Southern Europe, where it is the main source of employment for migrant women. The participation of home state women in the labour force is both dependent on and creates demand for domestic work, which is heavily supplied by women of migrant origin, though in some countries by established migrants and by home state labour as in France and the UK (Anderson, 2000).

There are, of course, differences between countries and nationalities. Southern European countries recognise the domestic sector as an area of employment. Spain, which recognised it as salaried work in 1985, establishes an annual quota, while in Italy legislation enacted in 2002 specifically allowed for the regularisation of domestic workers, who are seen to be less threatening and of strategic importance for the Italian economy (Fasano and Zucchini, 2002). In some Northern countries, for example Germany, it has become possible since February 2002 for citizens of accession countries to work legally for up to three years in households that are taking care of a relative, i.e. elderly care, and are receiving benefits from the statutory long-term care insurance system (European Industrial Relations Observatory, 2003; Menz, 2002). Though legally employed and paid at German rates, the state has in effect sanctioned deskilling in stipulating that these carers cannot compete against German-trained nurses and home care employees and must be given a household assistant work permit so that 'untrained foreign workers' do not put those they care for at risk. This represents a somewhat different resolution of labour shortages compared to information technology workers, who are employed at the same grades as Germans. In the UK, domestic worker quotas were phased out at the end of the 1970s and only admitted as a concession to foreign employers; workers did not have their own permit or the right to change employers. Over the years numerous cases of abuse and exploitation were reported, and after years of campaigning by Kalayaan, led to a change in immigration regulations in 1997 and the special right of regularisation for those who remained in the country undocumented (Anderson, 2000).

Since the 1990s Eastern European women have joined the stock of domestic workers, especially in Austria and Germany. They often circulate for short periods (Morokvasic, 1996), rotating a job between several people. While they had right of residence for up to three months, others from Latin America and South East Asia were likely to be undocumented. Au pairs from Eastern Europe too are a form of hidden domestic labour which enables them to build up contacts and overstay as undocumented domestic workers (Cox, 2000; Hess and Puckhaber, 2004; Williams and Balaz, 2004). Stratification by nationality, religion, race and language skills leads to different conditions and pay. Filipinas are generally viewed as the most valuable domestic workers, being Christian, English-speaking and well educated. On the other hand, Albanians in Greece or Moroccans in Spain are considered less valuable and have less negotiating power with their employers, often doing less rewarding work and receiving lower wages (Anthias and Lazardis, 2000). What seems to be emerging is a differential valuation between tasks, which can be seen in the way that the care of the elderly is more likely to result in work permits (Germany) and regularisation (Italy) than for child care.

Writing on gendered migrations allocates women lowly occupations 'as exotic, subservient or victimised, or relegated to playing supporting roles' (Pratt and Yeoh, 2003) as homemakers. All too often female migration is associated with domestic labour and sex work (Campani, 2000; Ehrenreich and Hochschild, 2003), with little research being undertaken into their presence in other areas such as industrial cleaning, retailing, hotel and catering and tourism. Such a perspective precludes a more accurate analysis of the implications of diversification and gendered stratification (Kofman, 2002, 2004b) resulting from the differential conditions of immigration, employment and possibilities of settlement and citizenship. However, women have used their skills to develop a niche in the community and inter-cultural sector in advocacy, mediation, translation and general community tasks (Federal Institute for Vocational Training, 2000). Some have sought autonomy and greater satisfaction through self-employment. Finally, a significant and growing number of migrant women from First and Third World countries are filling severe shortages in skilled sectors such as health, especially nursing, and education which can also be analysed in terms of social reproduction and global chains of care (Yeates, 2004). Their rights are different from those working in less skilled sectors and in the household (Kofman et al., 2005).

UK work permit data for 2000 (Dobson et al., 2001) show that sectors with high proportions of female staff constituted some of the fastest growing sectors of migrant employment. Nursing and other health and medical occupations as well as teachers formed the overwhelming majority of applications for work permits since the late 1990s (Kofman et al., 2005). Recourse to foreign nurses in response to severe short-ages has constituted a truly global labour market, especially in the UK and Ireland. Other countries have recruited primarily in neigh-bouring regions (Kingma, 2001; Buchan et al., 2003). Above all, it is the Philippines which supplies the overwhelming number.

Family-linked migration

Family-linked migration remains the main source of permanent migra-tion (estimated at about 65 per cent of permanent immigration in the European Union), and has been particularly dominant in France and Sweden, which have low levels of labour migration. In Southern European states, family reunification immigration is on the increase. In Italy, for example, 26.4 per cent (366,122) of residence permits in 2000 were for family reunification (Caritas, 2001).

The 'family' in the context of family migration into the European Union is defined by the state; migrants cannot determine for them-selves the persons who constitute their family. It includes spouses and dependent children usually under the age of 18 years (16 in Germany). Though ways of living together have altered radically in European states, migrants must still conform to traditional marriage patterns as the basis of entry into most European states. Only a few countries, for example in Scandinavia, the Netherlands and more recently the UK (Home Office, 2002), allow the entry of cohabiting or same-sex couples if they form 'relationships akin to a family' in the receiving society (Simmons, 2004). The 'family of choice' is still some way off (Weeks et al., 2001). Parents are generally permitted to join their families only if they are dependent (Denmark, Spain and over 65 years in the UK), for humanitarian reasons (Germany) or if they are in serious difficulties (Netherlands). Thus the generally limited conceptualisation of the family leaves little consideration for problems generated by caring at a distance (Ackers, 1998; Baldassar and Baldock, 2000), cultural differences in familial relationships, and the role of grandparents or other collateral relations in providing nurturing and support for different members of the family.

Today, the survival of the household in the country of origin increasingly depends on the livelihood of migrant women (Sassen, 2000) who are creating a nexus between the formal and the informal sectors in circuits of counter-globalisation. In Italy, Filipinas, though only the fourth largest group in 2000, remitted by far the largest amount of money (Caritas di Roma, 2002). Separated families, transnational mothering and parenting, and care at a distance have once again become more important due to the nature of employment that is available for female migrants, often in personal services and initially without a residence permit. Women migrating from Eastern and Central Europe within a rotational system (Morokvasic-Muller, 2002) and those moving independently, for example from the Philippines, often leave their families behind for many years (Zontini, 2002). At the same time family members, at least for the first few years, are not permitted recourse to public expenditure, i.e. those who enter as family members cannot make claims against benefits that others take for granted.

Despite the significance of this form of migration in Europe, it receives little attention, though this is beginning to change (special issue of *Journal of Ethnic and Migration Studies* 2004, no. 2). In part this is due to its association with female migration and dependency rather than work and autonomy. The assumption is that (female) family migrants do not enter the labour force or are not concerned about employment (Kofman et al., 2000); it is merely a secondary issue. Little is known of the professional aspirations of female family migrants, whether they enter under family reunification regulations or as partners of skilled spouses. With the expansion in skilled migration and marriage migration (Ackers, 1998; Riano, 2003), there is an increasing number of educated women who are blocked in their career paths.

Asylum seekers and refugees

Little is known about the gender breakdown of asylum seekers in the European Union (389,500 in 2000), though coverage is beginning to improve. Norwegian statistics (Hauge Byberg, 2002) by type of entry show that the gender balance has become more equitable since 1990. In terms of principal applicants in 2000, women formed 34 per cent of asylum seekers, 38 per cent of resettlement refugees pre-selected from camps, and 50 per cent of those from the war zones of former Yugoslavia.

One of the key subjects of debate is the extent to which women have access as asylum seekers to West European countries and are subsequently able to gain recognition as Geneva Convention refugees, a secondary status or even less secure humanitarian protection. In relation to access it is clear that women are less able to reach European countries as principal applicants due to their lesser resources. In the UK, the vast majority of principal asylum applicants making claims were men (74 per cent in 2002, 69 per cent in 2003), but higher proportions of women are now being granted refugee status (Kofman et al., 2005). However, recognition as a refugee raises quite complex issues concerning whether their political activities and specific forms of gender persecution, such as sexual violence or behaviour and dress in public, are recognised in the asylum determination process (Wetten et al., 2001). Some argue that women's political activities, which are often located in the private sphere or involve sustaining dissidents, do not conform to the prototypical male refugee (Crawley, 2001); others contend that women do not fare worse in the determination process (Bhabha, 2002). Some European states (Denmark, Germany, Ireland, Norway, Sweden and the UK) have developed guidelines for gender persecution in their asylum determination process along the lines implemented in Australia, Canada and the USA (Crawley, 2001).

Another set of problems relating to settlement and integration confronts refugee women who face particularly severe problems in accessing entitlements of training, employment and language classes, especially those with children (Sargeant et al., 1999; Kofman, Lloyd and Sales, 2002). Qualified refugees are beginning to receive greater support to retrain, as have those with health qualifications in the UK (Dumper, 2002).

Welfare regimes, employment and migration

As noted in the previous section, the livelihoods offered to female migrants in Europe are increasingly, though by no means exclusively, in sectors connected with care and more widely social reproduction. Following Esping-Andersen's (1990) influential work on comparative welfare regimes, a wide-ranging analysis has ensued (Sainsbury, 1999; Daly and Lewis, 2000) on care and changing welfare regimes across gender and generations. Daly and Lewis (2000: 285) defined social care 'as the activities and relations involved in meeting the physical and emotional requirements of dependent adults and children, and the normative, economic and social frameworks within which these are assigned and carried out'. In analysing the changing context (demo-graphic, economic, social) of care in different welfare states, they raise issues of the division and infrastructure (cash, services) of care between state, market, family and community, and the trajectories of change between them. The boundaries between sectors of care and individuals and families have shifted as welfare states have experienced crises of care in the past decade arising from decreasing supply and increasing demand. They point out that much existing work on care has concentrated on the complexity of the everyday and neglected its role in the dynamic political economy of the welfare state.

However, the discussion about gendered welfare states and the crisis of care seems to have almost entirely ignored migrant women, despite the crucial role they have played. Part of the reason is that the analysis of the globalisation of social reproduction (Anderson, 2000; Hill Maher, 2004) has been conducted separately from comparative welfare state studies. Similarly the social reproduction literature tends to assume that transnationalism is primarily due to the combination of women's increasing participation in formal employment and relatively unchanging gender relations in the household. Within this framework, market forces bring First and Third World women together. Only a few authors (Kofman et al., 2000; Williams, 2003) have considered, in the context of the welfare state analyses, the extent to which migrant women have supplied the care underpinning welfare provision in the home, the community, the private sector and the state. Not only are migrant women 'partial citizens' (Parrenas, 2001), but through their labour they enable citizen women to access child and elderly care to combine care and work, participate more fully in the labour force (Friese, 1995), and have time for other activities. And in addition, migrant labour leaves undisturbed prevailing gender norms in the household (Williams, 2003). The dependence of particular welfare configurations on migrant women's employment varies substantially; it is a complex issue which will be explored in relation to a number of developments: home state women's employment, the relationship between the state, market, community and family in the provision of services, and the economic incorporation of migrants in specific sectors (see Table 7.2 for welfare and migration regimes).

The increased *labour force participation* of home state women in the past decade has characterised all EU countries except Finland and Sweden where it has decreased and Denmark where it increased very slightly. This higher participation has increasingly replaced the breadwinner model with an adult worker model where both partners work.

Table 7.2: Typology of welfare regimes, female employment and migration

Country	Welfare regime	Service provision	Home state women employment[6]	Female migrant employment[7]
Sweden	Social Democratic	Abundant child and elderly	Very high employment Medium p/t High children	Insignificant domestic High social
Germany	Conservative Northern	Limited young Elderly	High employment High p/t Low child	Low domestic Low social
France	Conservative	Abundant child Limited elderly	High employment Medium p/t High children	Medium domestic Low social
Spain	Conservative Southern	Limited young And elderly	All low rates	High domestic Low social
UK	Liberal with Social Dem	Poor young Abundant elderly	High employment High p/t Low children	Low domestic High social

Table 7.3: Migration regimes

Country	Postwar	Current
Sweden	Regional and European Labour	High family and asylum, low labour
Germany	Guest worker	High asylum and labour, medium family
France	Colonial and European Labour	High family, medium asylum, low labour
Spain	Emigration	High labour, low family, Low asylum
UK	Colonial	High labour, high asylum, Medium family

In Scandinavian countries and in France female participation is very high or high with medium to low levels of part-time work. What distinguishes this group is the high full-time participation rate of women with young children, reflecting the provision of services either through the public sector, as in Sweden, or a combination of public and house-hold (registered childminders) services as in France. The market plays a much bigger role in the provision of care for the elderly. Intensi-fied domestication of these caring services has led to the employment of migrant women in France, particularly more recent arrivals such as African women. In a second group, female employment has substantially expanded in the past two decades, though this has been through women working part-time, often for relatively few hours. In the absence of public or affordable market services a low percentage of women with young children are able to work full-time. This applies to both the continental corporate countries such as Germany and the more liberal system in the UK. The high percentage of part-time employment means that the use of migrant women for care remains low. The third grouping covers the southern rim, with the exception of Portugal, where the employment rate of women in general, including part-time, is low, as is the propor-tion of women with young children working full-time. Thus in Southern countries the proportion of migrants employed in households to make good the deficiencies of public, community or market services is high and represents the major source of employment for female migrants.

The second aspect which requires consideration is the relationship between the state, the market and the family in the provision of care and the reconfiguration of welfare delivery. This needs to take account of services for children, the elderly and the disabled. While feminists addressed the patchwork quilt of caring, particularly of child care in the early 1990s, they devoted less attention to care for the elderly and those with special needs, where public intervention had been far more limited in most European states. Trends in child care across EU states are more coherent than for the elderly and are moving towards the acceptance of public subsidisation of private (parental) caring (Daly and Lewis, 2000: 293). For the elderly, changes are particularly complex and shaped by different sources and forms of privatisation (Trydegard, 2003). De-institutionalisation, application of management and market principles (separation of the purchaser and provider and the creation of internal markets) and more systematic targeting of recipients of care have all played their part in shaping a more privatised, managerialist and informalised economy of care.

It is only very recently that research on care has begun to take up the issue of employment as opposed to the gendered redistributive implica-tions of welfare regimes (Ungerson and Yeandle, 2003; Cameron, 2002). While the employment of female migrants in states with low levels of subsidies for family and care may be clear, there is a whole series of changes which are likely to make the presence of migrant women in the household more significant as a result of the new mixed economy of care. In a highly labour-intensive sector, this shift to a more diversified supply in effect produces an intensification of the domestic economy in which services are supplied by a plurality of providers: international and national companies, the voluntary sector (secular and religious), local authorities, national agencies and individuals hired by households. The attempt by the state to balance supply and demand and by companies to work within low profit margins encourages the expansion of low-paid, part-time and flexible employment.[8] In addition, the introduction of cash for care policies, as has happened in elder care in a number of countries, such as the Netherlands, Italy, France, the UK and Austria, has commodified, to varying degrees, previously informal and unpaid care arrangements by which households are able to employ domestic workers (migrants and members of their own family) privately (Yeandle and Ungerson, 2002).

The extent of the domestication is not picked up statistically through the category of household services since those employed by companies will not be treated as employees of the private household. Hence in Sweden, the percentage of migrants employed in households is insignificant. Yet, at the same time, the number of migrants employed in the health sector (covering all skill levels) has increased dramatically and at 19.2 per cent in 2001–2 is the highest after Norway. Furthermore, the focus on the domestic sector by many researchers misses out the substantial use of new and established migrant labour in social reproduction in other sites such as schools, hospitals, and residential homes.

The stratification generated by welfare regimes is also of considerable relevance for understanding employment patterns of migrant women. Conservative regimes have been defined in terms of their stratified rights, especially the secure tenure and generous benefits enjoyed by civil servants, from which non-EU citizens are excluded. Furthermore, the boundaries of the civil service are drawn very broadly to include professions such as teachers. Liberal professions (doctors, lawyers, vets) also operate in an exclusionary corporatist manner and are often barred to non-EU citizens who are more likely to be employed in these occupations as assistants on less secure and les lucrative contracts. On the other hand, liberal/social democratic states tend to have much lower barriers to public employment, usually demanding legal residence as the prerequisite for employment in most areas. In addition, in these regimes the older regional and colonial links continue to influence the sources of skilled labour. In Sweden, three out of the four major female nationalities in the labour market are from the Nordic region (Finland, Norway, Denmark), constituting in total 42 per cent of the stock of foreign labour (SOPEMI, 2004: 370). In the UK, female Commonwealth citizens are prominent in professions of social reproduction, both as permanent and temporary labour. At the skilled end, employment is eased through the recognition of professional training, as in medical diplomas (Raghuram and Kofman, 2002) and for less skilled and temporary work through the Working Holiday Makers Scheme which, until recently, was available only to citizens of the Old Commonwealth.

Scandinavian countries and the UK have the highest percentages of migrant women employed in social and welfare sectors of education and health. In Sweden these two sectors accounted for 27.4 per cent of migrant employment in 2001–2, in Finland 22.3 per cent and in the UK 21.7 per cent. In continental corporate regimes, especially those in Southern rim, the percentages are far lower – 8.3 per cent in France, 9.7 per cent in Germany 5.1 per cent in Spain.

Thus, to summarise, employment opportunities have opened up well beyond the narrower preoccupation with social reproduction within the household. Reproduction encompasses the whole array of activities and relationships involved in maintaining people, whether they are undertaken by the market, the community, the state or the household, or the interaction between them. It should also be noted that migrants do not only provide material and emotional care for home state populations but also for other migrants, often through migrant community organisations. Access to entitlements by migrant women depends, as we have noted, on their entry and residence status and labour market position.

Immigration policies and stratified rights and entitlements

In many states of immigration,[9] a succession of legislative changes and regularisations has refashioned migratory regimes and citizenship regulations. In countries where the Right, with or without a Far Right component, has gained power in recent elections, as in Denmark, France, Italy and the Netherlands, one of the first policy areas to be addressed was immigration control and the introduction or reinforcement of obligatory integration measures. In a number of European states, especially those with high proportions of family reunification migrants, compulsory integration programmes have also been implemented (Denmark, France, Germany). Failure to comply with compulsory integration schemes, which are directed not just at those applying for citizenship but also long-term residence permits, may have serious consequences. Within an increasingly assimilationist framework in France (Zappi, 2003), failure in the programme can result in withdrawal of entitlements (Ahmad and Sheriff, 1999), while success may be rewarded with a reduction in the number of years required for naturalisation, as in Denmark (European Industrial Relations Observatory, 2003).

General regularisation programmes have also been significant in legalising large numbers of migrants in many European states, particularly in Southern Europe but also in Belgium and France. Each round draws in larger numbers with the last one in Italy in 2002 receiving 700,000 applications, of which 350,000 were from those in domestic work (SOPEMI, 2004). In Northern European states, amnesties have tended to be granted for small numbers on humanitarian grounds or to clear an asylum backlog, as in the UK. Ever more restrictive measures have meant that a growing number of migrants in the European Union fall into the category of the undocumented, with EU estimates that 500,000 migrants enter illegally every year while many more enter legally but become undocumented.

Since the Tampere conference in 1999, the EU has put forward a spate of directives with the aim of establishing a harmonised legislative framework covering the rights of resident Third Country nationals, discrimination, integration, family reunification, illegal migration and asylum. While encouraging a more realistic and managed system of immigration, the EU nevertheless would leave it to states to decide what level of immigration they deem appropriate (EC, 2003). A key principle of access to entitlements is that the level of rights would be derived from length of residence, with a recommendation that European civic citizenship is attained at the end of five years' legal residence on condition that the migrant was willing to integrate. Civic citizenship constitutes the bundle of rights almost equivalent to the rights of nationals, except for full political rights. The pattern that has generally emerged in European states is, on the one hand, an improvement of entitlements for the legally settled, in exchange for the acceptance of obligations and responsibilities, and, on the other hand, the withdrawal of basic economic and social rights for the most precarious, that is asylum seekers and the undocumented, who more than ever risk deportation.

Some of the crucial axes demarcating the bundle of entitlements are those between the skilled and the lesser skilled, and the legal compared to the undocumented. A sharper distinction has been drawn between the skilled and the lesser skilled, whose numbers are to be controlled and entitlements limited. The two are connected since the lesser skilled are far more likely to enter illegally and become undocumented. In turn, a migrant's position in relation to these axes influences access to the entitlement of family reunification, which though in principle stems from the right to family life, is in reality limited by a series of conditionalities. So too are asylum seekers graded in terms of their level of protection. Although policies governing the different categories are expressed in gender-neutral terms, in reality, they affect women and men very differently due to gendered economic and social power and, as we have seen, the gender composition of particular migratory flows.

Skilled migrants are welcomed; they are represented as unproblematic, easily assimilated and, of course, beneficial to the economy. So in order to attract them, many countries have offered easier entry, the right to be accompanied by one's family, family members' right to work, permanent residence permit and citizenship (Kofman, 2002; Morris, 2002). Thus a distinguishing characteristic of skilled migration is its possibility of settlement and family reunification. Nurses in the UK are able to decide whether they want to bring in family members or not (Allan and Aggergaard Larsen, 2003). Many do not because work commitments preclude it. It may also be easier for the skilled to bring in family members other than spouses or dependent children e.g. parents, which is treated as largely discretionary. Furthermore, female spouses of the skilled migrants are allowed to work, though not in sectors reserved for nationals or EU citizens.

The lesser skilled generally enter as contract labour, or a revived guest worker system, without the possibility of transition to a more secure settlement status or the right to bring in family members. Gender, of course, structures the entry of the lesser skilled for although, as we have seen in the section on labour migration, opportunities for female labour have expanded throughout Europe, it is in sectors that are socially devalued and often unrecognised for purposes of official work permits. Even where quotas for domestic labour have been agreed, they are insufficient to meet demand and are forcing female migrants to reside as undocumented migrants.

Being undocumented not only leaves one without access to basic entitlements (such as education and health), which is a right of citizens incorporated in many constitutions, but also renders eventual acquisition of citizenship difficult. Acquiring resident permits through regularisation programmes, and hence being able to return to one's home country, become eligible for family reunification, and access to welfare services and benefits, has often proved more difficult for women than men. It may also be more difficult for those in informal work and domestic labour who have to supply proof of employment (Anderson,

2000). It is virtually impossible for those in the sex trade (Lazaridis, 2001).

Family migration, though underpinned by human rights conventions enshrining the right to family life, in reality has been closely regulated by a set of criteria based on resources (such as income, housing and the ability to maintain members without recourse to public funds). The conditionality has applied not just to the right to live a family life in the receiving country but also the obligations with which new members must comply. Success in applying for family reunification may be lower for migrant women due to their labour market position and greater difficulty in accumulating the necessary resources (income and access to housing). Their work as live-in domestics in Southern European countries presents an obstacle for female migrants to bring in male spouses and children. So what offers advantages for women in the beginning may present as obstacles once they are more established. Being undocumented and working within the confines of the household makes it difficult to benefit from family reunification procedures.

A major issue concerns the dependency and autonomy of spouses (Kofman et al., 2000), whose residence permits are linked to those of the primary migrant and the continuation of their marriage. Although some countries have reduced the probationary period, as in Germany where it was decreased from four to two years in 2001, others have lengthened it from one to two years in the UK, on the grounds of the need to deter marriages of convenience. There have been some improvements in the interpretation of the probationary period in that domestic violence, if reported to public authorities, has increasingly been taken into account in deciding the residence status of the spouse. Moreover, women marrying men from Third World countries are often viewed with suspicion (de Hart, 1999).

Some of the most severe disentitlements (such as employment, welfare, family reunification, and security) occur among asylum seekers and refugees. Increasingly asylum seekers have been criminalised, withdrawn from mainstream society and entitlements and the right to work. Nor do they have the right to choose where they live, for many states pursue policies of dispersal. Failed asylum seekers or those who have exhausted their ration of welfare, and do not officially have the right to work,[10] can be compared to the diminishing number of Geneva Convention refugees who have full rights. Only Convention refugees are able to bring their families in immediately without meeting the normal criteria of income and housing. It is, however, difficult to ascertain the gendered outcomes of recent changes in asylum policies.

Entitlements, racism and cultural differences

An understanding of stratified rights needs to take into account more than formal entitlements based on entry and residence and legal statuses. Actual access to rights or substantive rights are deeply affected by processes of racialisation and differential representation of groups. Some of these aspects have been raised in the examination of livelihoods and migration. It is a major issue that cannot be explored more fully in this chapter. However, one aspect has become much more prominent in the past few years and that is discrimination against Muslims. The current targeting of Muslim women raises a number of human rights challenges. Anti-discrimination legislation will have to counter the heightened racism against Muslims since 11 September 2001, especially against those who visibly affirm their religious affiliation, as with veiled women in the workplace and in schools (Ahmad, 2003). France, for example, banned the wearing of religious symbols in state public spaces, especially in schools, in February 2004 (Freedman, 2004); in Germany, several right-wing states have prohibited the employment of Muslim women wearing headscarves as teachers. Thus the strengthening of Islamophobia (Runnymede Trust, 1997) and emphasis on cultural practices (such as headscarves, arranged marriages and honour killings) associated with Islam focuses attention more than ever on Muslim women oppressed by patriarchal systems (Dietz and El-Sohoumi, 2002). Even before the Gulf War, the link of Islam with terrorism and the oppression and the expulsion of women from the public sphere in Afghanistan, the headscarf affair in France in 1989 had propelled Muslim girls into the limelight (Dayan-Herzbrun, 2000). Apart from the veiling of Muslim women in public places, two extreme practices – forced marriages and honour killings – have captured much media attention which has often portrayed Muslim women as unrelentingly oppressed by dogma and without any religious autonomy.

Conclusion

The proliferation and polarisation of statuses affect both men and women migrants and refugees, but its impact on women is different from that of men due to the channels through which they enter and the gendered division of labour. One of the key divisions is that between the skilled and the lesser skilled. Fewer women are to be found in the more privileged groups (as skilled migrants or Geneva Convention refugees). Among skilled migrants, whose entry, rights and access to citizenship are being facilitated, the areas of shortage still operate in men's favour. Caring, healing and educating people are undertaken by highly regulated professions (doctors, nurses, teachers and social workers) unlike IT, a new and far less regulated occupation. And for skilled female spouses, the barriers to professional integration remain very strong due to problems of accreditation, lack of local experience and closure of public sector employment to non-citizens. The latter hits women hardest since the feminised professions in many European countries fall under the umbrella of civil service employment. National variations in the size of the civil service public sector are considerable, for example, between the low levels of the UK and the high levels in France. Conservative welfare regimes are likely to present the most difficult barriers to entry. Thus many women, who have entered as family migrants, or who marry after entering as students or tourists, find their careers and professional aspirations blocked. The control over their environment and their right to seek employment on an equal basis is thus severely compromised.

At the less skilled end of the employment spectrum, women face great difficulties in maintaining a legal status. Failure to acknowledge the economic and social value of women's work means that although their labour is in demand, it is not matched by official recognition in the form of work permits and proper employment contracts. Both women who enter as labour migrants and family members are thus more likely to be forced into the informal sector and to undertake poorly paid and undervalued work with little social protection. While domestic labour has captured much of the attention, numerous other sectors employ less skilled labour on flexible contracts or informally, including industrial cleaning, hospitality, agriculture, tourism and care outside the home.

Even more vulnerable, insecure and unprotected are migrant women who are employed in the sex trade, which has grown rapidly since the 1990s. The drive against trafficking and illegal migration has not led to the protection of the person being trafficked or the pursuit of a human rights approach (UNICEF/UNHCR/OSCE, 2003). At best the victim gains a temporary respite in return for information against the trafficker. Protection is complicated by the fact that the sex trade in many European countries is either a criminal or public order offence.

The impoverishment of women's entitlements and the lack of protection within the workplace, especially within the confines of the home, limit a number of the key capabilities outlined by Martha Nussbaum (2002) – bodily integrity, control over one's environment, practical reason enabling one to plan one's life and affiliation. These capabilities seem to be particularly appropriate in charting degrees of autonomy and dependency experienced by migrant women. Inevitably these capabilities are far more difficult to achieve for some migrants than for others. As has been highlighted throughout this chapter, skill, nationality, legal status and channels of entry determine migrant women's rights, access to entitlements and capabilities. In seeking to overcome the difficulties of starting a new life and overcoming exclusions and restrictions, migrants depend on the material and social resources of networks (such as friends, family, and institutions) in order to access entitlements and empower themselves (Boyd, 1989). These networks enable women, probably more than men, to find employment, leave degrading and exploitative work situations, help each other out in emergencies, find housing and get information, among other things (Mozère, 2002). They are especially important in certain sectors, such as domestic work, as well as for the undocumented. Nevertheless, despite the relative lack of entitlements and social status in the receiving state, many women deploy the resources they accumulate to maintain their own and their families' social and class position in the country of origin.

Notes

1. These states have until recently followed the principle of *jus sanguinis* where citizenship follows kin lines and naturalisation is lengthy and costly. In Germany since the 1990s there have been changes to naturalisation and citizenship laws which have facilitated the take-up of German citizenship.
2. Data refer to people (excluding nationals for France, Greece and Portugal) who wish to settle permanently in the country.
3. 1992 for Portugal; 1994 for Luxembourg
4. Data relate only to entries of foreigners (excluding refugees and people who benefited from the regularisation programme).
5. Data relate only to entries of foreigners (excluding returns of nationals).
6. The three indicators refer to rate of employment, part-time employment (p/t) and full-time employment of women with children under ten.
7. Domestic refers to employment in households and social to employment in education, health and other community services.
8. In Sweden, these companies are forcing employees into part-time contracts (personal communication, Jane Lethbridge, Public Sector International).
9. New legislation was passed in 2002/3 in Denmark, France, Greece, Italy, Netherlands, Portugal and the UK.
10. France had already withdrawn the right to work in 1991 but in the UK it was permitted for the principal applicant after six months, but discretionary for other members. Inevitably the outcome was unfavourable to women. However, since July 2003 this right has been withdrawn for everyone in an attempt to dissuade asylum seekers.

References

Ackers, L. (1998) *Shifting Spaces. Women, Migration and Citizenship within the European Union*, Bristol: Policy Press.

Ahmad, F. (2003) 'Still "in progress?" – methodological dilemmas, tensions and contradictions in theorizing South Asian Muslim women', in N. Puwar and P. Raghuram (eds) *South Asian Women in the Diaspora*, London: Routledge.

Ahmad, F. and S. Sheriff (1999) 'Muslim women of Europe: welfare needs and responses' *Social Work in Europe*, Vol. 8(1): 2–10.

Allan, H. and J. Aggergaard L. (2003) *'We Need Respect': Experiences of Internationally Recruited Nurses in the UK*, London: Royal College of Nurses.

Anderson, B. (2000) *Doing the Dirty Work*, London: Zed Press.

Anthias, F. (2000) 'Migration, gender and self-employment: opportunity and education', paper presented at Self-Employment, Gender and Migration, San Feliu de Guixols, 28 October–2 November.

Anthias, F. and Lazaridis. G. (eds) (2000) *Gender and Migration in Southern Europe. Women on the Move*, Oxford: Berghan.

Baldassar, L. and Baldock, C. (2000) 'Linking migration and family studies: transnational migrants and the care of aging parents', in B. Agozino (ed.) *Theoretical and Methodological Issues in Migration Research*, Aldershot: Ashgate.

Bhabha, J. (2002) 'More or less vulnerable? Women, children and the asylum paradox', paper presented at 43rd Annual Studies Association Convention, International Studies Association, Challenges to the Liberal paradox and root cause theory: differential treatment of asylum seekers in the USA and the European Union, New Orleans, 23–27 March.

Boyd, M. (1989) 'Family and personal networks in international migration: recent developments and new agendas', *International Migration Review*, 23: 638–70.

Buchan, J., Parkin T. and Sochalski J. (2003) *International Nurse Mobility: Trends and Policy Implications*, available at: www.rcn.org.uk/downloads/InternationalNurseMobility [accessed 30 March 2004].

Campani, G. (2000) 'Immigrant women in Southern Europe: social exclusion, domestic work and prostitution in Italy', in R. King, G. Lazaridis and C. Tzardanidis (eds) *Eldorado or Fortress? Migration in Southern Europe*, London: Macmillan.

Cameron, C. (2002) 'Care work in Europe: future needs', paper presented at Careworkers: matching supply and demand. Employment Issues in the Care of Children and Older People Living at Home, Sheffield Hallam University, 20–21 June.

Cancedda, L. (2001) *Employment in Household Services*, Dublin: European Foundation for the Improvement of Living and Working Conditions.

Caritas (2001) *Immrgrazione Dossier Statistico 2001*, Rome: Caritas.

Caritas di Roma (2002) *Remittances and Immigrants: Global Context and the Italian Case*, Rome: Caritas.

Castells, M. (1996) *The Rise of the Network Society* (vol. 1), Oxford: Blackwell.

Cox, R.. (2000) 'Exploring the growth of paid domestic labour. A case study of London', *Geography*, 85(3): 241–51.

Crawley, H. (2001) *Refugees and Gender. Law and Process*, Bristol: Jordans.

Daly, M. and Lewis, J. (2000) 'The concept of social care and the analysis of contemporary welfare states', *British Journal of Sociology*, 51(2): 281–98.

Dayan-Herzbrun, S. (2000) 'The issue of the Islamic headscarf', in J. Freedman and C. Tarr (eds) *Women, Immigration and Identities in France*, Oxford: Berghan.

De Hart, B. (1999) '"It just went according to the rules with us". Binational families, marriage, migration and shifting identities', paper presented at the Conference on Migrant Families and Human Capital Formation in Europe, Leiden, 19–21 November.

Dietz, G. and El-Sohoumi, N. (2002) 'Door to door with our Muslim sisters: inter-cultural and inter-religious conflicts in Granada, Spain', *Studi Emigrazione*, XXXIX: 77–105.

Dobson, J., et al. (2001) 'International migration and the United Kingdom. Recent patterns and trends', *RDS Occasional Paper 75*, London: Home Office.

Dumper, H. (2002) *Missed Opportunities: A Skills Audit of Refugee Women in London from the Teaching, Nursing and Medical Professions*, London: Refugee Women's Association.

European Commission (2003) *Immigration, Integration and Employment*, Brussels: Employment and Social Affairs.

Ehrenreich, B. and. Hochschild, A. (eds) (2003) *Global Woman. Nannies, Maids and Sex Workers in the New Economy*, New York: Metropolitan Books.

Esping-Anderson, G. (1990) *Three Worlds of Welfare Capitalism*, Cambridge: Polity Press.

European Industrial Relations Observatory (2003) *Migration and Industrial Relations*, available at: http://www.eiro.eurofound.eu.int/2003/03/study/tn0303105s.html [accessed 30 March 2004].

Fasano, L. and Zucchini F. (2002) *Local Implementation of the Consolidated Law on Immigration. The Seventh Italian Report in Migration 2001*, Milan: Fondazione ISMU.

Federal Institute for Vocational Training (2000) *New Employment Opportunities for Female Migrants*, Bonn: Federal Institute for Vocational Training.

Freedman, J. (2004) 'Secularism as a barrier to integration? The French dilemma', *International Migration*, 43(3): 5–27.

Friese, M. (1995) 'East European women as domestics in Western Europe – new social inequality and division of labour among women', *Journal of Area Studies*, 6: 194–202.

Hauge Byberg, I. (2002) *Immigrant Women in Norway. A Summary of Findings on Demography, Education, Labour and Income*, Norway: Statistics Norway.

Hess, S. and Puckhaber, A. (2004) '"Big sisters" are better domestic servants?!' comments on the booming au pair business', *Feminist Review*, 77: 65–78.

Hill Maher, K. (2004) 'Globalized social reproduction: women migrants and the citizenship gap', in A. Brysk and G. Shafir (eds) *People Out of Place. Globalization, Human Rights, and the Citizenship Gap*, New York and London: Taylor and Francis.

Hochschild, A. (2000) 'Global care chains and emotional surplus value', in W. Hutton and A. Giddens (eds) *On the Edge. Living with Global Capitalism*, London: Jonathan Cape.

Home Office (2002) *Secure Borders, Safe Haven: Diversity and Integration in a Modern Britain*, London: HMSO.

Hukum, P. and Le Saoult, D. (2002) 'Les femmes migrantes et la création des activités' *Migrations Etudes*, 104 (January).

Kingma, M. (2001) 'Nursing migration: global treasure hunt or disaster-in-the making?' *Nursing Inquiry*, 8(4): 205–12.

Kofman, E. (2002) 'Contemporary European migrations, civic stratification and citizenship', *Political Geography*, 21(8): 1035–54.

Kofman, E. (2003) 'Women migrants and refugees in the European Union', paper presented at EU/OECD Conference, Economic Effects and Social Aspects of Migration, Brussels, 22–23 January. Available at: www.oecd.org/documents [accessed 30 March 2004].

Kofman, E. (2004a) 'Family-related migration: a critical review of European studies', *Journal of Ethnic and Migration Studies*, 30(2): 243–62.

Kofman, E. (2004b) 'Gendered global migrations: diversity and stratification', *International Feminist Journal of Politics*, 6(4): 642–64.

Kofman, E., Lloyd, C. and Sales, R. (2002) 'Civic stratification, exclusion and migratory trajectories in three European states', *ESRC Project One Europe or Several?* Programme Report L21325201.

Kofman, E., Phizacklea, A., Raghuram, P. and Sales, R. (2000) *Gender and International Migration in Europe*, London: Routledge.

Kofman, E., Raghuram, P. and Merefield, M. (2005) 'Gendered migrations: Towards gender-sensitive policies in the UK', *Asylum and Migration Working Paper 6*. Available at http://www.ipprorg.uk/ecomm/migration wp6gender.pdf [Accessed 10 January 2006].

Lazaridis, G. (2001) 'Trafficking and prostitution: the growing exploitation of migrant women in Greece', *European Journal of Women's Studies*, 8(1): 67–102.

Menz, G. (2002) 'Patterns in EU labour immigration policy: national initiatives and European responses', *Journal of Ethnic and Migration Studies*, 28 (4): 723–42.

Morokvasic, M. (1991) 'Roads to independence. Self-employed immigrants and minority women in five European states', *International Migration*, 29: 407–20.

Morokvasic, M. (1996) 'Entre l'est et l'ouest, des migrations pendulaires', in M. Morokvasic and R. Hedwig (eds) *Migrants. Nouvelles mobilités en Europe*, Paris : L'Harmattan.

Morokvasic, M. (2003) 'Transnational mobility and gender: a view from post-wall Europe', in M. Morokvasic-Müller, U. Erel and K. Shinozaki (eds) *Crossing Borders and Shifting Boundaries*. Vol. 1: *Gender on the Move*, Opladen: Leske and Budrich.

Morokvasic-Müller, M. (2002) 'Post-communist migrations in Europe and gender', *Journal of Gender Studies*, 5: 15–45.

Morris, L. (2000) *Managing Migration: Civic Stratification and Migrants' Rights*, London: Routlede.

Mozère, L. (2002) *Les domestiques philippines 'entrepreneurs d'elles-mêmes'. Le marché mondial de la domesticité. Formes contemporaines de l'économie informelle*, Metz: Laboratoire ERASE.

Network for European Women's Rights (2003) *Background Report on Women's Social Entitlements*, available at: www.newr.bham.ac.uk [accessed: 1 June 2005].

Nussbaum, M. (2002) 'Women's capabilities and social justice', in M. Molyneux and S. Razavi (eds) *Gender Justice, Development and Rights*, Milton Keynes: Open University Press.

Parrenas, R. (2001) *Servants of Globalization, Stanford University Press: Women, Migration and Domestic Work*, Stanford, CA: Stanford University Press.

Pratt, G. and Yeoh, B. (2003) 'Transnational (counter) topographies', *Gender, Place and Culture*, 10(2): 159–66.

Raghuram, P. and Kofman, E. (2002) 'State, labour markets and immigration: overseas doctors in the UK', in *Environment and Planning*, A(34): 2071–89.

Riano, Y. (2003) 'Migration of skilled Latin American women to Switzerland and their struggle for integration', in Y. Mutsui (ed.), *Latin American Emigration: Interregional Comparison among North America, Europe and Japan*, Osaka: National Museum of Ethnology.

Runnymede Trust (1997) *Islamophobia: A Challenge to Us All*, London: Runnymede Trust.

Sainsbury, D. (ed.) (1999) *Gender and Welfare State Regimes*, Oxford: Oxford University Press.

Sargeant, G., et al. (1999) *Turning Refugees into Employees. Research into the Barriers to Employment Perceived by Women Refugees in London*, London: Industrial Society.

Sassen, S. (2000) 'Women's burden: counter-geographies of globalization and the feminization of survival', *Journal of International Affairs*, 53(2): 503–24.

Simmons, T. (2004) 'Skills, sexual citizens and the UK's family reunion provision', *Feminist Review*, 77: 175–9.

SOPEMI (2004) *Annual Trends in International Migration 2003*, Paris: OECD.

Trydegard, G.B. (2003) 'Les réformes des services de soins suédois dans les années quatre-vingt-dix. Une première évaluation de leurs conséquences pour les personnes agées', *Revue Française des Affaires Sociales*, 57(4): 423–42.

Ungerson, C. and Yeandle, S. (2003) *Gender and Paid Care Work in Modern Welfare States: Issues of Work-Life Balance*, available at: http://www.leeds.ac.uk/esrcfutureofwork/downloads/events/symposium_2003/Ungerson&Yeandle.ppt [accessed 1 June 2005].

UNICEF/UNHCR, OSCE (2003) *Trafficking in Human Beings in South Eastern Europe*, Belgrade: ODIHR.

Weeks, J., Heaphy B. and Donovan, C. (2001) *Same Sex Intimacies. Families of Choice and Other Life Experiments*, London: Routledge.

Wetten, J., et al. (2001) 'Female asylum seekers in the Netherlands: an empirical study' *International Migration*, 39(3): 85–98.

Williams, A. and Balaz, V. (2004) 'From private to public sphere, the commodification of the au pair experience? Returned migrants from Slovakia to the UK', *Environment and Planning*, A(36): 1813–33.

Williams, F. (2003) 'Rethinking care in social policy', paper presented at The Annual Conference of the Finnish Social Policy Association, Joensuu, 24 October.

Yeates, N. (2004) 'A dialogue with "global chain" analysis: nurse migration in the Irish context', *Feminist Review*, 77: 79–95.

Zappi, S. (2003) *French Government Revives Assimilation Policy*. Available at: http://www.migrationinformation.org/Feature/display.cfm?ID = 165 [Accessed 10 January 2006].

Zontini, E. (2002) 'Towards a comparative study of female migrants in Southern Europe: Filipino and Moroccan women in Bologna and Barcelona', *Studi Emigrazione*, 145: 107–34.

8
Violence as Violation: Understanding Domestic Violence against Women as a Matter for Human Rights

Audrey Guichon and Rebecca Shah

Domestic violence and its causes are socially embedded. Because victims of domestic violence have particular needs for social protection that are often inadequately met by existing social policy, domestic violence is a topic of particular concern in the field of women's social entitlements and rights. Domestic violence is a contested concept. Many types of violence occur in the home, including spousal abuse, child abuse and elder abuse. This chapter focuses on domestic violence as violence perpetrated by men against their female partners. This is not to deny other forms of family violence or violence within same-sex relationships or to imply that women are never violent to male partners. Rather, it is to acknowledge the contemptible fact that one woman in three will be the victim of violence from a male intimate partner in her lifetime (Amnesty International, 2005). Violence against women is one of the most widespread violations of human rights worldwide. Domestic violence is one of the most silent and pernicious forms of violence against women. It can prevent victims from fully accessing many of their human rights including rights to liberty and security of person, health, freedom from torture and to life. Yet human rights law has struggled to accommodate the complexities of women's experiences of domestic violence. The objective of this chapter is to determine whether the issues raised by domestic violence can be answered by international human rights law. This chapter takes a multidisciplinary approach to domestic violence in Europe, drawing on sociological, psychological and legal perspectives to address these issues.

The first section contextualises the legal discussion of the second section by exploring the realities of domestic violence. Domestic violence often manifests itself as physical, sexual and emotional abuse perpetrated repeatedly against the victim over time. While the impact of domestic violence resonates throughout the family and society, this chapter is primarily concerned with the impact on the psycho-social well-being of victims as individual women. This part goes on to reveal and discuss the multifarious causes of domestic violence. Recent approaches to domestic violence emphasise the structural gender inequalities of society, economics, law and politics that facilitate and perpetuate violence against women. Attempts to explain or understand the causes of domestic violence are inevitably political; it is necessary to understand the pervasive nature of violence against women without condoning or excusing it.

The second section presents the international legal framework relevant to violence against women and, more specifically, domestic violence. By its very nature, domestic violence most often occurs behind closed doors within the private sphere of the home. This has precluded victims from accessing the protection offered by the principles and mechanisms of traditional international human rights law. This part illustrates how traditional human rights law has evolved to reflect women's needs and rights better and to offer more effective responses to domestic violence. The evolution is not yet complete. International human rights law still fails to account adequately for the causes of domestic violence and the complexity of women's experiences. Yet, human rights are universal and with appropriate will can be developed until they reflect universal needs, including those of women.

Domestic violence – nature, impact and causes

The nature of domestic violence against women

The patterns of domestic violence and the responses of victims and societies vary across Europe. Considerable differences between and within the countries of Europe exist, but across all boundaries of nation, ethnicity, class, culture and education the greatest risk factor for experiencing violence in the home is simply being female. Women of Europe are united in this vulnerability and all over Europe victims experience domestic violence in three main forms: physical, sexual and psychological or emotional abuse.

Common expressions of physical domestic violence include slapping, hitting, kicking, beating with an object or burning. Despite the stark clarity of these terms, distinguishing 'normal' physical behaviour from abusive behaviour in a relationship remains a constant debate (Gelles, 1997). This may be particularly true for the abused, who are reluctant to identify themselves as victims, or for perpetrators, who feel that hitting their partners may be acceptable: 'Oh yes, I slapped her, but that wasn't violence' (Dobash and Dobash, 1998: 168). Domestic violence is notoriously difficult to measure for these reasons and because most cases are never reported to the police. With this in mind, lifetime incidence of violence from an intimate partner is approximately 20 per cent in Switzerland (UNICEF, 2000), whereas in Turkey as many as 90 per cent of married women experience physical violence from their husbands (Benniger-Budel and O'Hanlon, 2004). At an extreme, physical violence results in murder, and research suggests that as many as 70 per cent of women murder victims are killed by intimate partners or ex-partners (Amnesty International, 2005).

The incidence of sexual violence is even more difficult to assess, not least because of beliefs, which may be reflected in national law, that sexual violence and rape cannot occur within what are otherwise consensual or married relationships. Cultural myths about the blurred boundaries between consensual and forced intercourse and the rights of men to sexual gratification in relationships make women vulnerable to sexual violence in relationships and contribute to extremely low reporting rates. Research suggests that forced or coerced sexual acts are often used by abusive partners as part of a process of humiliation and domination, and that women are seven times more likely to be raped by an intimate partner than a stranger (Lees, 1997).

Domestic violence is differentiated from other types of violence in several respects. The perpetrator and victim are very well known to each other, the abuse itself often includes combinations of different types of violence, and violent events are not isolated but recurring, often with escalating severity over time. Research with victims and perpetrators suggests that unlike many other types of violence, domestic violence is motivated by a desire to control the victim's behaviour (Felson and Messner, 2000). The state of terror induced by physical and/or sexual violence at the hands of an intimate partner, often accompanied by threats, is a form of psychological abuse. Controlling emotional violence also exists in most abusive relationships and often precedes physical violence (Hoyle and Saunders, 2000). This type of abuse may include criticising the victim, her friends and family, limiting the victim's contact with these support networks, mistrust in her contact with other men and threats to her pets or children. Psychological abuse is used to undermine the victim's self-esteem, make the victim feel responsible for the abuse and to isolate the victim from potential sources of social and economic support (Burman and Chantler, 2004).

The impact of domestic violence

The effects of domestic violence are multiple and radiate from those involved to their families and societies. Domestic violence inflicts physical injuries on the victim such as bruising, bleeding, loss of consciousness, broken bones, burns and miscarriages (Dobash and Dobash, 1998). The scale of the physical harm caused by domestic violence is evidenced by the fact that domestic violence and rape account for one in five disability adjusted life years[1] lost in women aged 15–44 (UNICEF, 2000). The particular nature of repeated and systematic abuse from an intimate partner means that physical injury may not be the most harmful aspect of domestic violence for victims. Although the law often responds to violence at the hands of a known aggressor as less serious than that from a stranger, the impact on psychological well-being is more profound. For example, victims of sexual assault from known aggressors experience higher levels of distress, experience the distress for longer and are more likely to blame themselves than those assaulted by a stranger (Kelly and Radford, 1998).

Attempts to understand the psychological effects of domestic violence have not always proved beneficial. Lenore Walker coined the term 'battered woman syndrome' (BWS) in the late 1970s to explain the particular psychological responses of women who had experienced recurring domestic violence (Walker, 1979). Walker portrayed domestic violence as a cycle of tension-building, physical violence and temporary cessation and contrition that induced feelings of low self-esteem, depression and a state of 'learned helplessness' in victims. Learned helplessness is a term derived from experimentation with animals and is used to describe the passive behaviour of domestic violence victims and explain why they do not leave violent partners. Learned helplessness theoretically develops from the victim's experience that her behaviour cannot alter the repeated and unpredictable violence she is subjected to. In time it becomes a generalised belief that the victim does not have the capacity to change what happens to her.

BWS was sympathetic to the distress of domestic violence victims and employed to defend women charged with killing their abusers. However, the construction of a victim who is helpless yet able to kill was easily manipulated and used against defendants. BWS was heavily criticised for pathologising victims and implying homogeneous patterns of violence and psychological response that failed to account for the diversity of women's experiences (Schuller et al., 2004). Moreover, the phenomenon of learned helplessness was criticised as conjecture that was unhelpful in creating an image of female victims of domestic violence as passive and weak rather than active and adaptive survivors.

The symptoms of BWS are now understood as part of post-traumatic stress disorder (PTSD). PTSD is a clinically recognised condition that may occur after witnessing or experiencing an event that involves actual or threatened death or serious injury. Symptoms include re-experiencing the trauma through intrusive thoughts, dreams and even hallucinations, coupled with the avoidance of situations that are similar to or evoke memories of the traumatic event, a numbed emotional response and a heightened state of physiological arousal (DSM-IV-TR, 2000). Studies of female victims of domestic violence have found the incidence of PTSD to be as high as 45–84 per cent (Sharhabani-Arzy et al., 2005).

It is now understood that there is a broad range of psychological responses to the trauma of domestic violence. For victims who do not experience PTSD, feelings of low self-esteem, depression, self-blame and guilt are not uncommon. Women may develop coping mechanisms that others perceive as maladaptive, such as behaviour to please and placate the offender as well as behaviour to numb the pain, such as alcohol or drug use. The incidence of suicide in women who experience domestic violence is twelve times higher than in women who do not (UNICEF, 2000). Victims may deny or minimise the extent of the violence in order to cope or to avoid the shame and stigma that is associated with being a victim of domestic violence (Gill, 2004). Many women engage in adaptive behaviours to cope, to solicit help and to achieve safety for themselves and their children, such as active negotiation and strategic resistance (Lewis et al., 2000).

BWS implies that women stay in abusive relationships because of the abnormal psychological state induced by domestic violence, but women's attempts to secure safety from violence are often hampered by a wide range of factors. The social and economic isolation associated with domestic violence can leave victims with few options. Although shelters for abused women exist to some extent in most European countries, there are often too few places and shelters may be a long distance from where the victim lives. Without access to other social support networks or financial resources for transport, food, shelter and child care, women may be unable to leave violent partners. Without economic independence women may also risk losing custody of their children to their abusers. Social entitlements and rights are therefore crucial resources for women who experience domestic violence. As noted above, domestic violence is often motivated by a desire to control the victim's behaviour. The victim leaving the abuser is the ultimate threat to his control and may elicit extreme reactions. It is not uncommon for abusive partners to threaten to harm or take custody of the victim's children if she tries to leave. Perpetrators are most likely to rape and murder the victim during or after the break-up of a relationship, and one third of all women who leave violent men suffer harassment and attacks after separation (Lees, 1997).

Domestic violence affects other members of the family, particularly children. Even if they are not victims of violence themselves, children will witness abuse or live in an environment permeated by fear, aggression and gender inequality. The impact on their immediate and long-term psycho-social well-being and the normalisation of harmful beliefs about gender roles and intimate violence is profound (Margolin and Gordis, 2000).

The costs of domestic violence spread far beyond the family. Despite the extreme underreporting of domestic violence, it accounted for 22 per cent of all violent incidents reported in the British crime survey in 2002 (Amnesty International, 2005). This gives an indication of the burden domestic violence places on public services, including the doctors, nurses and counsellors who treat victims, the police and the criminal justice system, safe shelters for abused women and their children, and social campaigns for education and prevention (UNICEF, 2000). Domestic violence is an impediment to social development and erodes social capital. Abused women may be physically restricted to the home or prevented from active participation in society through fear and coercion. For victims who do work, it can contribute to decreased productivity, lower earnings and job losses, which in turn has a negative macro-economic impact.

The causes of domestic violence

Until the late nineteenth century the right of a man to chastise his wife physically or to restrict her movements was legally sanctioned in the UK. It was in the same century that feminists began to campaign on domestic violence within marriage, which they attributed largely to male alcoholism (Abrar et al., 2000). The feminist movement of the 1970s provoked a groundswell of research and critique on domestic violence and proffered alternative causal explanations, but the early beliefs about domestic violence tend to endure in popular perception. Victims and perpetrators of domestic violence often attribute the abuse to immediately contextual factors. These include stressors, such as male alcohol use, male job insecurity, poverty and relationship factors, such

as the incendiary female behaviour of excessive nagging or the derelic-
tion of matrimonial duties. Evidence from post-Soviet countries indicates that increased competition for jobs, lowered standards of living and
increased alcoholism certainly have correlated with high levels of violence, including domestic violence (UNICEF, 2000). Dobash and Dobash
(1998) also indicate that violent events are often precipitated by arguments over the victim's competence at domestic work, the perpetrator's
jealousy and possessiveness of the victim or the fulfilment of the perpetrator's sexual desires. The abuse may therefore be seen as justified, a
necessary form of disciplining the errant female or even an expression
of love, as articulated by the Russian saying: 'a beating man is a loving
man' (Benniger-Budel and O'Hanlon, 2004).

Environmental stressors and relationship dynamics clearly play a role
in situations of domestic violence. While they must be acknowledged
as contributory or contingent factors, they are wholly inadequate on
their own to explain domestic violence as the widespread and pervasive
phenomenon that it is. An alternative explanatory approach has been
to naturalise domestic violence as an expression of man's inherent
aggression, woman's inherent passivity and the natural hierarchy of
human existence in which the male is superior to and dominant over
the female. To a certain extent such an evolutionary perspective hits
the mark: there is no denying that a gender-based hierarchy predomin-
ates not only across Europe, but much of the world. There is nothing
to suggest, however, that this hierarchy is in any way natural. The
UN Declaration on the Elimination of Violence Against Women (1993)
understands violence against women as a 'manifestation of historically unequal power relations between men and women, which have
led to domination over and discrimination against women by men'.
The dominant contemporary approach to domestic violence acknowledges the myriad social, cultural, economic, legal and political factors
that conspire to discriminate against women, perpetuate the gender
inequality that makes women vulnerable to violence and limit their
options in dealing with violence. Some examples of these factors are
explored below.

Social/cultural factors include the devaluing of women and female
characteristics or the valuing of these characteristics only in a rela-
tional manner. Both men and women are socialised into gender roles
which present feminine virtues of passivity and sacrifice and masculine
virtues of strength and agency (Gill, 2004). This results in the valuing of
women in so far as their caring roles as wives and mothers are valuable
to others and the valuing of men as dominant and aggressive. The

traditional focus on the family or private sphere as the extent of the female domain makes women more vulnerable to violence. The major religions of Europe regard marriage as a promise to God and divorce as undesirable. In some countries divorce is not a religiously or culturally acceptable option, even in the face of domestic violence (Nason-Clarke, 2004). Customary beliefs also regard the family as a private space that should remain beyond public reproach, within which the man as the head of the family should have decision-making control and a mono-poly on violence (Benninger-Budel and O'Hanlon, 2004). The extreme result is the construction of women and female sexuality as male prop-erty or an indicator of male or family honour. As such violence against women outside the family may be perceived as an offence only against male property and violence against women within the family as no offence at all. Although this may appear alien to the liberated lives of many European women, it was only in 1994 that UK law acknowledged that it was a crime for a man to rape his wife, and the Turkish penal code still considers sexual violence against women an offence against public decency and family order, not against an individual (Arat, 2003).

Economic factors include the fact that women have less access to educa-tion and training than men and therefore fewer opportunities to engage in the job market. Women generally hold lower paid jobs and are paid less than men for equivalent work. As a result, in EU countries women's salaries are on average 20 per cent lower than men's (ICFTU, 2000). Even in Estonia, where females outperform males in education, women still face discrimination entering the job market and their salaries are just 75 per cent that of men's (Benniger-Budel and O'Hanlon, 2004). Women have restricted inheritance and property rights, for example in Turkey despite legal equality between the sexes, 90 per cent of property is owned by men (ibid.). The gender roles noted above negatively impact on women's economic independence from men, as the majority of women's labour is unpaid. Domestic violence and lack of economic independence cyclically reinforce each other; violence and the fear of violence inhibit women from seeking economic opportunities, and the consequent lack of economic independence impedes women's ability to leave, especially when they have dependent children. Interestingly, the converse argu-ment has been used, i.e. that the increased economic independence of women precipitates domestic violence by marginalising men's position in society and challenging male dominance. It is interesting to note that regardless of the actual economic status of women or the arguments used to explain the economic causes of domestic violence, the results are equally detrimental for women.

Legal factors include the fact that domestic violence is not recognised as a distinct offence in many countries. While women may make recourse to the law, their treatment under general assault laws fails to recognise the realities of domestic violence, particularly the special relationship between victim and perpetrator. For example, domestic violence differs from other types of violence in that the victim and perpetrator usually live together and share economic resources. This means the risk of recidivism is much greater and financial penalties will harm the victim as much as the perpetrator. Women are discouraged from seeking legal redress by policing practices and legal systems that tend to be insensitive to the realities of women's experiences of domestic violence. At worst these systems criminalise the victim or punish her through further physical, sexual or psychological abuse (Benninger-Budel and O'Hanlon, 2004). At best most legal systems are immersed in a patriarchal tradition in which attempts at gender-neutrality are based on the use of males as the 'standard measure', which result in a gender bias. If charges are brought, sentencing and conviction rates for domestic violence are typically weaker than similar crimes committed by strangers.

Political factors include the limitations on women's ability to participate in political organisations and engage in formal politics. Women are under-represented in positions of political power, the media, law and medical services across Europe. Their poor representation in policy-making arenas may perpetuate the gender-neutral approaches of public services that fail to recognise women's experiences. Domestic violence and other forms of discrimination against women are often not considered political priorities and may be treated as inevitable aspects of human life.

These examples serve to illustrate the multiplicity of factors that contribute to structural gender inequality beyond the dynamics of individual relationships. In light of this perspective, domestic violence should not be considered natural, but rather a symptom of an unbalanced and unequal society. This approach is able to explain the pervasiveness of domestic violence and situate it within a discourse of power, indicating that real change in domestic violence cannot be achieved without structural changes to patriarchal society. However, this approach can be criticised to the extent that it fails to account for the perpetrator as an agent who can choose and control his behaviour. Sørensen (1998) warns of the dangers of interpreting domestic violence either as a symptom of individual characteristics or of society. The former can excuse the perpetrator's behaviour by reference to his childhood, socio-economic conditions and so forth, denying the relationships between gender, violence and power. The latter focuses attention on the abstract entity of society, minimising the roles of individual perpetrators and victims. This can be used to exempt perpetrators from responsibility for their actions, neglecting the fact that they are capable of independent thought or action. Such an approach is also unhelpful for individual victims whose individuality is reduced merely to being female and therefore violable (Hagemann-White, 1998).

This debate illustrates that the pursuit of any causal explanation for domestic violence is an inherently political process. Any attempt to rationalise the causes of domestic violence may be used to political ends to excuse, legitimate or blame. It is clear that patriarchal structures give rise to gender inequality and the vulnerability of women to male violence, but it is also clear that within these structures men choose to engage in violent acts against women. Approaches to dealing with domestic violence must be sensitive to the political nature of the task as well as the realities of victim and perpetrator experience. The next section explores the validity of international human rights law as an approach to the complexities of domestic violence discussed above.

Human rights and domestic violence

The public/private divide

The Universal Declaration of Human Rights (UDHR) was constructed in the wake of the Second World War, and reflected contemporary concerns about state intrusion into the private lives of citizens by articulating the rights of individuals that could be held against states. As part of the desire to limit state interference in the lives of citizens, human rights instruments acknowledge the family as the 'natural and fundamental group unit of society' (International Covenant on Civil and Political Rights, ICCPR, 1966, art. 23(1)) that should be accorded 'the widest possible protection and assistance' (International Covenant on Economic Social and Cultural Rights, 1966, art. 10(1)) from the state. The family is not only granted special entitlements to state assistance, but privacy *within* the family is protected *from* state interference: 'No one shall be subjected to arbitrary or unlawful interference with his privacy, family, home or correspondence' (ICCPR, 1966, art. 17(1)). This creates a special distinction between the public sphere, where the relationship between state and citizen is mediated by human rights responsibilities, and the private sphere of the family and home, which is protected from the eyes of the state. This annexing of the private sphere from the remit of human rights puts women at terrible risk (Sullivan, 1995).

The uncritical distinction between the private and public spheres in the human rights framework reflects the concerns of those who articulated human rights law. The UDHR was mostly created by men for men who perceived little threat to themselves or the values of society from any act or actor within the private sphere. This dichotomy finds its origin in classical western liberal thought which has qualified the 'public' as 'political' and the 'private' as 'cultural'. Human rights focus on the individual as citizen and public actor, which is an inherently gendered role. The result is that the standard measure of a 'human' in human rights is androcentric, and the rights that have been prioritised are rights that relate to men and male interests. The public/private dichotomy reflects deeply held cultural beliefs and values about the natural status of the family unit. The family is portrayed as a sanctuary of nurturing, safety and love that should be protected from the sullying effects of external political influences. The family is also an important vessel for the intergenerational transfer of cultural knowledge and traditions. This romanticised ideal fails to acknowledge the distinctly political and gendered power relations within society that bind women to the private sphere by valuing them mainly as mothers, wives, carers and cooks, and allowing them little opportunity for economic independence and political participation, while enabling men to exploit the public sphere (Peterson and Parisi, 1998). It also ignores the gendered power relations within the private sphere that make the family the most common arena for physical, sexual and emotional violence against women.

The naturalisation of the family and disregarding of the risks this creates for women is not merely an unconscious omission. The pursuit of women's interests and human rights for women is most often criticised on the grounds that it poses a threat to culture and family life (Freeman, 1995). This prioritises the welfare of the family unit over the safety and security of women as individuals. Many commentators claim that states can and will interfere in the private sphere on issues that are not as inherently gendered as domestic violence (e.g. Peterson and Parisi, 1998). The crux of the matter is that female oppression is viewed as somehow natural or inevitable and therefore acceptable. An example is the criticism levied at the removal of the marital rape exemption in British law that suggested the 'marital rape exemption was one of the *pillars holding up the family*' (Lees, 1997: 118). The implication is that protection of a woman's physical integrity is secondary to the value of a woman's body as a family asset. The failure to understand female oppression as political has enabled the neglect of women's interests in traditional human rights doctrines (Bunch, 1995). The state-citizen focus of human rights is poorly adapted to account for the fact that most violence against women occurs at the hands of private, rather than state, actors. The establishment of the family as the natural and moral unit of society has therefore enabled states and the international community to decline responsibility for domestic violence. The following sections will present what the international legal human rights framework has to offer in addressing domestic violence.

The doctrine of state responsibility

The challenges the public/private sphere divide creates for women have resulted in a number of legal hurdles that make the recognition of domestic violence as a human rights violation difficult. The traditional purpose of international human rights law is to regulate the relation and (absence of) actions between the state and individuals. This understanding of international human rights law sees it as protecting individuals from the potential misconduct of their states. In this sense, the subjects of international human rights law are states and not individuals (Charlesworth et al., 1991) and this branch of international law regulates violations committed by the state through its officials such as the police and prison officers (International Law Commission, 2001). Domestic violence is not perpetrated by states or their officials but by private individuals or so-called 'non-state actors'. For this reason, domestic violence was not initially perceived as a human rights violation.

Nevertheless, the exclusion of acts committed by private individuals from the human rights remit is prejudicial to women because most of the abuses suffered by women are committed in the private sphere by non-state actors. International debates on the doctrine of state responsibility led to a questioning of its restrictive nature (Chinkin, 1999: 390). The Velasquez Rodriguez case (Inter-Am.Ct.H.R, 29 July, para. 174) states that '[t]he State has a legal duty to take reasonable steps to prevent human rights violations and to use the means at its disposal to carry out a serious investigation of violations committed within its jurisdiction, to identify those responsible, to impose the appropriate punishment and to ensure the victim adequate compensation'. The Inter-American Court of Justice in this case broadened states' responsibility by saying that 'an illegal act which violates human rights and which is initially not directly imputable to the State (for example, because it is the act of a private person or because the person responsible has not been identified) can lead to international responsibility of the State, not because of the act itself but because of the lack of due diligence to prevent the violation or to respond to it as required by the Convention' (para. 172). The use of this doctrine of 'due diligence' paired with disagreement on the apparent clear-cut distinction between violations committed by state actors and non-state actors led to a significant evolution of the international jurisprudence and the broadening of state responsibility for human rights violations committed by non-state actors.[2]

Feminist critiques were central to the evolution of the doctrine of state responsibility, which enabled the recognition of domestic violence as a human rights violation. This is illustrated by the adoption of CEDAW General Recommendation 19 and of the Declaration on the Elimination of Violence Against Women, which are both discussed below.

The legal reasoning behind the recognition of domestic violence rests on the fact that in such cases, 'the state's failure to prosecute can be shown to be rooted in discrimination along prohibited lines', i.e. gender (Thomas and Beasley, 1993: 42). It is because domestic violence is almost systematically targeted at women that a state's failure to intervene can be characterised as a human rights violation.

Women's rights activists have campaigned earnestly for the inclusion of domestic violence as a human rights violation because they believed that such inclusion was not only natural but would also result in more positive advance in this domain. Indeed, as Thomas and Beasley explain:

> [t]he human rights approach employs a pre-existing international system to bring pressure to bear on governments that routinely fail to prosecute domestic violence equally with other similar crimes. This provides an opportunity for local institutions and activists to supplement their efforts with support from the international community. (Thomas and Beasley, 1993: 61)

From the perspective of human rights theory, 'this dynamic ultimately may help transform the international human rights system so that it honors the Universal Declaration of Human Rights and protects more than just the rights of man' (ibid.: 62).

The non-discrimination (equality) approach of CEDAW

The main international women's rights instrument is the Convention on the Elimination of all forms of Discrimination Against Women

(CEDAW). Adopted by the UN General Assembly in 1979, CEDAW makes no specific mention of a prohibition of domestic violence or of violence against women. Nevertheless, the prohibition of domestic violence can be deduced from CEDAW's anti-discrimination (equality) approach. Article 1 defines discrimination against women as:

> [A]ny distinction, exclusion or restriction made on the basis of sex which has the effect or purpose of impairing or nullifying the recognition, enjoyment or exercise by women, irrespective of their marital status, on a basis of equality of men and women, of human rights and fundamental freedoms in the political, economic, social, cultural, civil or any other field.

A prohibition of domestic violence does not result from a specific clause in CEDAW but from the fact that it violates many human rights, including the right to physical and mental health (art. 25 UDHR), the right to be free from torture or other cruel, inhuman or degrading treatment or punishment (art. 5 UDHR, art. 2 CAT) and even sometimes, the most crucial of human rights, the right to life (art. 3 UDHR).

CEDAW goes further than simply providing a prohibition of discrimination by encouraging states to undertake proactive measures aimed at putting an end to discriminatory practices by, *inter alia*, introducing relevant legislation and repealing 'all national penal provisions which constitute discrimination against women' (art. 2). The absence of laws criminalising assaults committed within the home can consequently be denounced as a human rights violation under the terms of CEDAW. This was reaffirmed in the General Assembly's Resolution on Further actions and initiatives to implement the Beijing Declaration and Platform for Action (2000, para. 69(d)).

The Committee responsible for monitoring the implementation of CEDAW reinforced its mechanisms with regard to violence against women when it adopted General Recommendation No. 19 at its 11th session in 1992. Paragraph 6 of General Recommendation No. 19 states:

> The definition of discrimination includes gender-based violence, that is, violence that is directed against a woman because she is a woman or that affects women disproportionately. It includes acts that inflict physical, mental or sexual harm or suffering, threats of such acts, coercion and other deprivations of liberty. Gender-based violence may breach specific provisions of the Convention, regardless of whether those provisions expressly mention violence.

The adoption of General Recommendation 19 marked the beginning of a concerted effort dedicated to putting an end to violence against women, including domestic violence.

The first worldwide conference on human rights was organised in Vienna in 1993. While several international women's rights conferences had already been organised in conjunction with the UN decade on women's rights (Mexico City, 1975, Copenhagen, 1980, Nairobi, 1985), the Vienna Conference failed to integrate a women's rights dimension. In the preparation for the conference, women's rights groups lobbied for the inclusion of two main demands: first, the mainstreaming of women's rights in the different items of the conference; and second, the recognition of violence against women as a human rights violation (Bunch, 1995: 172). These efforts were successful in several ways. First, special mention of violence against women was made in paragraph 38 of the landmark Vienna Declaration and Platform of Action (General Assembly, 1993) in the following words: 'In particular, the World Conference on Human Rights stresses the importance of working towards the elimination of violence against women in public and private life . . . '; which specifically recognised violence against women, including domestic violence, as a human rights violation. Second, the Vienna Declaration called for the adoption of a UN Declaration on the Elimination of Violence Against Women (para. 38) and third, approved a decision of the Commission to appoint a Special Rapporteur on the Elimination of Violence against Women (para. 40). These last two achievements are quite significant in the UN system and merit further exploration below.

The Declaration on the Elimination of Violence Against Women

On 20 December 1993, the UN General Assembly adopted the Declaration on the Elimination of Violence Against Women (DEVAW). DEVAW is the result of an expert group meeting, following which the Draft Declaration was endorsed, with revisions, by the Committee on the Status of Women. The Draft Declaration was presented by the Economic and Social Council to the General Assembly and adopted by the latter at its 48th session.

DEVAW defines violence against women in article 1 as:

> Any act of gender-based violence that results in, or is likely to result in, physical, sexual or psychological harm or suffering to women, including threats of such acts, coercion or arbitrary deprivation of liberty, whether occurring in public or in private life.

DEVAW recalls that violence against women encompasses 'physical, sexual and psychological violence occurring in the family, including battering, sexual abuse of female children in the household, dowry-related violence, marital rape, female genital mutilation and other traditional practices harmful to women, non-spousal violence and violence related to exploitation' (art. 2(a)). DEVAW makes a specific reference to domestic violence and encourages states to undertake research on its incidence, causes and consequences.

While the adoption of DEVAW was extremely welcome, it also has a number of drawbacks. The main weakness of DEVAW is linked to its legal status: DEVAW is a declaration and not a convention that, once ratified, creates binding obligations that states have to comply with. The absence of obligations for states is visible in the way the DEVAW is drafted. For example, article 4 – on the measures that states should undertake to put an end to violence against women – gives an extensive list of actions that states are *encouraged* to undertake but does not specify any precise *obligation*.

Generally, it is regrettable that DEVAW does not clearly state that violence against women is a human rights violation. More specifically, it is regrettable that DEVAW does not recognise the equal right of women 'as to marriage, during marriage and at its dissolution, which may be impaired or nullified by various forms of domestic violence' (Sullivan, 1994: 167). The initial suggestion of the Expert Group to include a right to compensation for victims was not taken up and this would have represented a commendable step forward in combating domestic violence (Charlesworth, 1994). Compensation for rights abuses is now well established in the UN system, especially for victims of torture, and is being codified in a draft Basic principles and guidelines document (Commission on Human Rights, 2000).

The Special Rapporteur on Violence Against Women, its Causes and Consequences

The Vienna Declaration welcomed the Commission's promise to appoint a Special Rapporteur on violence against women, in its effort to bring women's rights into mainstream human rights (Sullivan, 1994: 154). Women's NGOs in Vienna lobbied for the Special Rapporteur to be able to investigate not only violence against women but also its causes 'in light of the interrelationship between violence and women's subordinate status in public and private life' (Sullivan, 1994: 157). The appointment of a Special Rapporteur represents a highly symbolic step and powerful legal procedure.

Radhika Coomaraswamy was appointed on 4 March 1994 as the first Special Rapporteur on violence against women and after extension of the mandate in 2003, Yakın Ertürk was appointed as the second. The Special Rapporteur has powers to investigate national situations with regard to her thematic mandate and write subsequent reports. The Special Rapporteur identified three spheres in which violence against women occurs (Commission on Human Rights, 1994, para. 117–315): in the family (including domestic violence); in the community (including sexual assault; sexual harassment in the workplace and in educational institutions and trafficking for purposes of sexual exploitation); and violence perpetrated or condoned by the state (including custodial violence, sexual assault during armed conflict and violence against refugee women) (www.stopvaw.org). In her preliminary report, Special Rapporteur Coomaraswamy set the framework around domestic violence and stated: 'There are many types of domestic violence. . . . the most prevalent is the violence of the husband against the wife' (Commission on Human Rights, 1994, para. 118).

In 1999 the Special Rapporteur produced her second report on violence against women in the family (Commission on Human Rights, 1999), following the Commission's request to do so. The report is extremely relevant in that it recalls that domestic violence clearly is a form of violence against women prohibited by international norms. The report also makes it clear that domestic violence, while potentially problematic theoretically, is without any doubt a human rights violation. The Special Rapporteur refers to three legal doctrines available to qualify domestic violence as a human rights violation. These include the doctrine of state responsibility and the equality approach, as discussed above. She further suggests that 'domestic violence is a form of torture and should be dealt with accordingly' (ibid., para. 22).

Assessing states' respect of international standards applying to domestic violence can be more difficult than in other cases of women's rights violations because of the theory of due diligence. How can it be determined whether states have been exercising due diligence with regard to adopting and implementing domestic standards on domestic violence? The Special Rapporteur identified a series of eight indicators useful to this purpose. They are:

1. Has the state party ratified all the international human rights instruments including the Convention on the Elimination of All Forms of Discrimination against Women?
2. Is there a constitutional authority guaranteeing equality for women or the prohibition of violence against women?

3. Is there national legislation and/or administrative sanctions providing adequate redress for women victims of violence?
4. Are there executive policies or plans of action that attempt to deal with the question of violence against women?
5. Is the criminal justice system sensitive to the issues of violence against women? In this regard, what is police practice? How many cases are investigated by the police? How are victims dealt with by the police? How many cases are prosecuted? What types of judgement are given in such cases? Are the health professionals who assist the prosecution sensitive to issues of violence against women?
6. Do women who are victims of violence have support services such as shelters, legal and psychological counselling, specialized assistance and rehabilitation provided either by the government or by non-governmental organisations?
7. Have appropriate measures been taken in the field of education and the media to raise awareness of violence against women as a human rights violation and to modify practices that discriminate against women?
8. Are data and statistics being collected in a manner that ensures that the problem of violence against women is not invisible?

By relying on its very specific procedural powers, the Special Rapporteur's work has greatly contributed to broadening the UN and the international community's views on domestic violence.

Beijing Platform for Action

The last significant step undertaken to combat domestic violence was the insertion of an item on this issue in the Beijing Platform for Action which was adopted following the worldwide women's conference in Beijing in 1995. The Platform uses the three spheres of violence against women (in the family, community and by the state) identified by the Special Rapporteur in her 1994 report. Strategic Objective D1 requires states to 'refrain from engaging in violence against women and exercise due diligence to prevent, investigate and, in accordance with national legislation, punish acts of violence against women, whether those acts are perpetrated by the State or by private persons' and, in doing so, makes it clear that domestic violence is a form of violence against women that states are responsible for eliminating under international human rights law. The reference to the due diligence doctrine reminds states that their obligation to do so is enshrined in international human rights law.

Strategic Objective D2 specifically encourages research on the causes and consequences of domestic violence.

A review of progress made since Beijing took place in 2000 under the form of a General Assembly Special Session, commonly know as 'Beijing + 5', which adopted the Resolution on Further Actions and Initiatives to implement the Beijing Declaration and Platform for Action. While some progress was noted, the general agreement was that the objectives of the Platform for Action had not been met. More particularly, with reference to domestic violence, the General Assembly noted at paragraph 14:

> Inadequate data on violence further impedes informed policy-making and analysis. Sociocultural attitudes which are discriminatory and economic inequalities reinforce women's subordinate place in society. This makes women and girls vulnerable to many forms of violence, such as physical, sexual and psychological violence occurring in the family, including battering. . . . Domestic violence, including sexual violence in marriage, is still treated as a private matter in some countries. Insufficient awareness of the consequences of domestic violence, how to prevent it and the rights of victims still exists. Although improving, the legal and legislative measures, especially in the criminal justice area, to eliminate different forms of violence against women and children, including domestic violence and child pornography, are weak in many countries. Prevention strategies also remain fragmented and reactive and there is a lack of programmes on these issues.

Human rights instruments and procedures have evolved to respond better to the necessity of making domestic violence stop. Progress has been made, especially in providing a legal framework to address domestic violence. Nevertheless, domestic violence is still widespread, victims are isolated and perpetrators left free. In this context, the 2005 Beijing +10 meeting certainly represents another significant opportunity in assessing progress made and bring the agenda forward.

Conclusion

The human rights doctrine was built with equality as its cornerstone, and this required neutrality with regard to gender. Yet, human rights are centred on the individual as citizen and public actor. The very assumption of the individual rights-holder as gender-neutral denies the different experiences that men and women have as public and private actors and in their experience of rights violations. Women's experiences of human rights violations are often gendered. They may have their rights violated simply because they are female, as in the case of female infanticide, female genital mutilation, honour killings or domestic violence. If women experience human rights violations for other reasons, the violation is often perpetrated in gender-specific ways, such as through rape or sexual assault (Bunch, 1995). Civil and political rights are of equal importance to men and women, but the typical victim of their violation is portrayed as male because men are more prominent political actors. This overlooks the fact that women are more often denied civil and political rights because they lack access to the public sphere (Bunch and Frost, 2000).

It is fair to say that international human rights law was not originally designed to apply to cases of domestic violence. Legal doctrines have evolved together with the realisation that human rights may be a universal and impersonal set of rules but that they are not implemented in a social vacuum. In the context of patriarchal societies steeped in gender inequality when 'man' is used as the standard measure of 'human', gender-neutral human rights law may fail to account for the realities of women's experiences and therefore fail to serve women's interests (Kaufman and Lindquist, 1995). The enactment of *de jure* equality may render the practical application of rights unequal (Thomas and Beasley, 1993). As such traditionally conceived human rights may convey a disadvantage to women, rather than a means to justice. New instruments have been adopted to allow the international community, states and women to denounce the perpetration of domestic violence as a human rights violation. Nevertheless, the lack of political commitment with regard to domestic violence combined with traditional beliefs about gender roles mean that domestic laws on domestic violence are still the exception. There is a need for firm and unconditional commitment on the part of states to translate the prohibition of domestic violence and the necessity for victim support measures provided for at international level into concrete measures for victims. Progress on this front is forthcoming. For example, in March 2005 Bulgaria passed a dedicated law on domestic violence that is the first of its kind in the region (http://www.cwsp.bg/htmls/home.php).

Beside the need to ensure better national implementation of the international standards applying to domestic violence, the international human rights framework also could benefit from further evolution. The adoption of DEVAW, the appointment of a Special Rapporteur and the strengthening of CEDAW's protection through the adoption of

General Recommendation 19 are all steps in the right direction. Yet, international human rights law can go further in offering an adapted and fair response to the specificities of women's rights. Proposals have been made towards the recognition of domestic violence as a form of torture (Copelon, 1994; Vesa, 2004). It is thought that doing so will ensure better visibility as well as a higher degree of moral and practical condemnation of domestic violence. The four constitutive elements of torture, as defined by the United Nations Convention Against Torture, are: '(1) severe physical and/or mental pain and suffering; (2) intentionally inflicted; (3) for specific purposes; (4) with some form of official involvement, whether active or passive' (Copelon, 1992: 122). These are applicable to the specific case of domestic violence, in which different forms of violence are used systematically for the purposes of controlling the victim's behaviour. Acknowledging domestic violence as a form of torture would enable the understanding that domestic violence is a crime of no lesser gravity than any other form of violence inflicted by the state. An alternative proposal would be to grant asylum to victims of domestic violence. The difficulty in doing so rests on the parameters stipulated by the 1951 Convention Related to the Status of Refugees. It states that a refugee must experience 'well-founded fear' based on one of five criteria: 'race, religion, nationality, membership of a particular social group or political opinion' (art. 1). Nowhere does the Convention mention gender as a criterion for obtaining refugee status, which would be necessary for granting asylum to victims of domestic violence. Nevertheless, many scholars have argued that belonging to a 'particular social group' does encompass gender (Seith, 1997; Blanck, 2000; Gallagher, 2006) thereby applying the criteria in a manner that meets the specific needs of women.

To date women have been excluded from reaping the full benefits of human rights. The human rights agenda may be criticised as another component of the patriarchal system that makes women vulnerable to domestic violence. The human rights framework is not yet equipped to challenge the causes of rights violations. Without addressing the structural and historical gender inequalities that contribute to discrimination against women, human rights can only ever achieve formal equality. Even if it were possible to eliminate domestic violence by the use of human rights this would not be enough to establish substantive equality that would stop the subjugation of women (Mandhane, 2004). Human rights may reflect their origins and be enacted within unequal societies, but they are not static and they are not the property of any specific group in society (Bunch, 1995). Human rights are universal, and with appropriate will can be developed until they reflect universal needs, including those of women.

Notes

1. Disability Adjusted Life Years (DALY) are a measure of healthy years of life lost to premature death or disability.
2. See also, *X and Y* v. *The Netherlands* (ECHR, 1985) and *Airey* v. *Ireland* (ECHR, 1979).

References

Abrar, S., Lovenduski, J. and Margetts, H. (2000) 'Feminist ideas and domestic violence policy change', *Political Studies*, 48: 239–62.

Amnesty International Stop Violence Against Women website, Available at: http://www.amnesty.org.uk/svaw/ [accessed 8 March 2005].

Arat, Z. F. (2003) 'A struggle on two fronts', *Human Rights Dialogue, Violence Against Women Issue*, 2(10): 32.

Benniger-Budel, C. and O'Hanlon, L. (2004) *Violence Against Women: 10 Reports/Year 2003*, Geneva: World Organisation Against Torture (OMCT).

Blanck, A. (2000) 'Domestic violence as a basis for asylum status: a human rights based approach', *Women's Rights Law Reporter*, 22(1): 47–75.

Bunch, C. (1995) 'Transforming human rights from a feminist perspective', in J. Peters and A. Wolper (eds) *Women's Rights Human Rights: International Feminist Perspectives*, London: Routledge.

Bunch, C. and Frost, S. (2000) 'Women's human rights: an introduction', in *Routledge International Encyclopedia of Women*, New York: Routledge.

Burman, E. and Chantler, K. (2004) 'There's no place like home: emotional geographies of researching "race" and refuge provision in Britain', *Gender, Place and Culture*, 11(3): 375–97.

Center of Women's Studies and Policies, The Law on Protection against Domestic Violence is adopted!, Available at: http://www.cwsp.bg/htmls/home.php [accessed 21 March 2005].

Charlesworth, H., Chinkin, C. and Wright, S. (1991) 'Feminist approaches to international law', *The American Journal of International Law*, 85: 613–45.

Charlesworth, H. (1994) 'The Declaration on the Elimination of All Forms of Violence Against Women', *American Society of International Law Newsletter*, n.p.

Chinkin, C. (1999) 'A critique of the public/private dimension', *European Journal of International Law*, 10(2): 387–95.

Cook, R.J. (ed.) (1994) *Human Rights of Women – National and International Perspectives*, Philadelphia: University of Pennsylvania Press.

Copelon, R. (1994) 'Intimate terror: understanding domestic violence as torture', in R. J. Cook (ed.) *Human Rights of Women – National and International Perspectives*, Philadelphia: University of Pennsylvania Press, pp. 116–52.

DSM-IV-TR (Diagnostic and Statistical Manual of Mental Disorders, Fourth Edition, text revision) (2000) Washington, DC: American Psychiatric Association.

Dobash, R. E. and Dobash, R. P. (1998) 'Violent men and violent contexts', in R. E. Dobash. and R. P. Dobash (eds) *Rethinking Violence Against Women*, London: Sage Publications.

Felson, R. B. and Messner, S. F. (2000) 'The control motive in intimate partner violence', *Social Psychology Quarterly*, 63(1): 86–94.

Freeman, M. A. (1995) 'The human rights of women in the family: issues and recommendations for implementation of the Women's Convention', in J. Peters and A. Wolper (eds) *Women's Rights Human Rights: International Feminist Perspectives*, London: Routledge.

Gallagher, A. M. (2006) 'Triply exploited: female victims of trafficking networks strategies for pursuing protection and legal status in countries of destination', in C. van den Anker and J. Doomernik (eds) *Trafficking and Women's Rights*, Basingstoke: Palgrave Macmillan.

Gelles, R. J. (1997) *Intimate Violence in Families*, third edition, London: Sage Publications.

Gill, A. (2004) 'Voicing the silent fear: South Asian Women's experiences of domestic violence', *The Howard Journal*, 43(5): 465–83.

Hagemann-White, C. (1998) 'Violence without end? Some reflections on achievements, contradictions, and perspectives of the feminist movement in Germany', in R. C. A. Klein (ed.) *Multidisciplinary Perspectives on Domestic Violence*, London: Routledge.

Hoyle, C. and Saunders, A. (2000) 'Police responses to domestic violence: from victim choice to victim empowerment?' *British Journal of Criminology*, 40(1): 14–36.

ICFTU (International Confederation of Free Trade Unions) (2000) 'Internationally-Recognised Core Labour Standards in the 15 Member States of the European Union Report for the WTO General Council Review of the Trade Policies of the European Union, Geneva 12 and 14 July 2000', Available at: http://www.erylmcnallymep.org.uk/international_confederation_of_f.htm [accessed 16 March 2005].

Kaufman, N. H. and Lindquist, S. A. (1995) 'Critiquing gender-neutral treaty language: The Convention on the Elimination of All Forms of Discrimination Against Women', in J. Peters and A. Wolper (eds) *Women's Rights Human Rights: International Feminist Perspectives*, London: Routledge.

Kelly, L. and Radford, J. (1998) 'Sexual violence against women and girls: an approach to and international overview', in R. E. Dobash and R. P. Dobash (eds) *Rethinking Violence Against Women*, London: Sage Publications.

Lees, S. (1997) *Ruling Passions: Sexual Violence, Reputation and the Law*, Buckingham: Open University Press.

Lewis, R., Dobash, R. P., Dobash, R. E. and Cavanagh, K. (2000) 'Protection, prevention, rehabilitation or justice? Women's use of the law to challenge domestic violence', *International Review of Victimology*, 7(1–3): 170–205.

Mandhane, R. (2004) 'The use of human rights discourse to secure women's interests: critical analysis of the implications', *Michigan Journal of Gender and Law*, 10: 275–325.

Margolin, G. and Gordis, E. B. (2000) 'The Effects of Family and Community Violence on Children', *Annual Review of Psychology*, 51: 445–79.

Nason-Clarke, N. (2004) 'When terror strikes at home: the interface between religion and domestic violence', *Journal for the Scientific Study of Religion*, 43(3): 303–10.

Peterson, V. S. and Parisi, L. (1998) 'Are women human? It's not an academic question', in T. Evans (ed.) *Human Rights 50 Years on: A Reappraisal*, Manchester: Manchester University Press.

Seith, P. A. (1997) 'Escaping domestic violence: asylum as a means of protection for battered women', *Columbia Law Review*, 97(6): 1804–43.

Sharhabani-Arzy, R., Amir, M. and Swisa, A. (2005) 'Self-criticism, dependency and post-traumatic stress disorder among a female group of help seeking victims of domestic violence in Israel', *Personality and Individual Differences*, 38: 1231–40.

Schuller, R. A., Wells, E., Rzepa, S. and Klippenstine, M. A. (2004) 'Rethinking battered woman syndrome evidence: the impact of alternative forms of expert testimony on mock jurors' decisions', *Canadian Journal of Behavioural Science*, 127–36.

Sørensen, B. W. (1998) 'Explanations for wife beating in Greenland', in R. C. A. Klein (ed.) *Multidisciplinary Perspectives on Family Violence*, London: Routledge.

Sullivan, D. J. (1994) 'Current developments: women's human rights and the 1993 Vienna Conference on Human Rights', *American Journal of International Law*, 88: 152–67.

Sullivan, D. (1995) 'The public/private distinction in international human rights law', in J. Peters and A. Wolper (eds) *Women's Rights Human Rights: International Feminist Perspectives*, London: Routledge.

Thomas, D. Q. and Beasley, M. E. (1993) 'Domestic violence as a human rights issue', *Human Rights Quarterly*, 15: 36–62.

Umberson, D., Anderson, K., Glick, J. and Shapiro, A. (1998) 'Domestic violence, personal control and gender', *Journal of Marriage and the Family*, 60: 442–52.

UNICEF (2000) 'Domestic violence against women and girls', *Innocenti Digest*, 6.

Vesa, A. (2004) 'International and regional standards for protecting victims of domestic violence', *American University Journal of Gender, Social Policy & the Law*, 12: 309–60.

Walker, L. (1979) *The Battered Woman*, New York: Harper and Row.

Cases

Before the European Court of Human Rights
X and Y v. *The Netherlands*, 91 ECHR (Ser. A) (1985)
Airey v. *Ireland*, 32 ECHR (Ser. A) (1979)

Before the Inter-American Court on Human Rights
Velasquez Rodriguez Case, Judgment of 29 July 1988, Inter-Am.Ct.H.R. (Ser. C) No. 4 (1988)

UN documents

From the UN Commission on Human Rights
The right of everyone to the enjoyment of the highest attainable standard of physical and mental health, Report of the Special Rapporteur, Paul Hunt, E/CN.4/2004/49, 16 February 2004.

Commission on Human Rights resolution 2003/45, 23 April 2003, Elimination of violence against women.

Report of the Special Rapporteur on violence against women, its causes and consequences, Ms. Radhika Coomaraswamy, on trafficking in women, women's migration and violence against women, E/CN.4/2000/68, 29 February 2000.
Violence against women in the family, Report of the Special Rapporteur on violence against women, its causes and consequences, Ms. Radhika Coomaraswamy, E/CN.4/1999/68, 10 March 1999.
Preliminary report submitted by the Special Rapporteur on violence against women, its causes and consequences, Ms. Radhika Coomaraswamy, E/CN.4/1995/42, 22 November 1994.

From the UN General Assembly

Draft Articles on the Responsibility of States for Internationally Wrongful Acts, A/CN.4/L.602/Rev.1, 26 July 2001.
Further actions and initiatives to implement the Beijing Declaration and Platform for Action, A/RES/S-23/3, 16 November 2000.
Beijing Declaration and Platform for Action, Fourth World Conference on Women, A/CONF.177/20 (1995) and A/CONF.177/20/Add.1 (1995), 15 September 1995.
Vienna Declaration and Programme of Action, A/CONF.157/23, 12 July 1993.
Declaration on the Elimination of Violence against Women, A/RES/48/104, 20 December 1993.
CEDAW General Recommendation No. 19 on Violence against Women, A/47/38 (General Comments), 29 January 1992 (11th session, 1992).
International Law Commission, Report on the Work of the 53rd session, 23 April–1 June and 2 July–10 August 2001, A/56/10. Available at: http://www.un.org/law/ilc/reports/2001/2001report.htm [Accessed 9 December 2005].

9
Women's Social Rights and Entitlements in Latvia and Lithuania – Transformations and Challenges

Tana Lace, Irina Novikova and Giedre Purvaneckiene

This chapter addresses some issues in women's social rights and entitlements in Latvia and Lithuania in the transitional period from the socialist welfare system, the Soviet model, to the welfare state structured by the demands of the capitalist market economy. The argument of the chapter draws on the presentations and discussions of the participants from Latvia and Lithuania at the workshops of the Network for European Women's Rights project on women's social entitlements in Athens (Greece) and Riga (Latvia).

In the 1990s the post-Soviet societies of Latvia and Lithuania experienced a dramatic process in which specific welfare regimes were formed. This process has exposed – depending on various political, economic, social, ethnic and historical factors – various strategies from different types of ideal welfare regimes (either categorised by Esping-Andersen, or described in Korpi-Palme's typology of social insurance institutions). This has been a benchmark decade in the period when, as Katherine Verdery argues:

> we have been both creating and living through an epochal shift in the global economy. Among its elements is a change in the operation of capitalism, responding to a global recession evident as of the early 1970s. ... Sometimes called a change to 'flexible specialization', it has produced a massive shift in the tectonic plates of the world economy; one sign of that was the 1989 collapse of Communist Party rule in Eastern Europe, and soon thereafter in the Soviet Union. I have suggested elsewhere how I think that happened, underscoring processes internal to the Soviet system that connected it more fully with international capital flows and, as a result, altered both the form

of socialist political economies and their place in global capitalism. (Verdery 1996: 24)

This process in the countries of East-Central Europe, and specifically the Baltic states, has been the subject of studies and analytical work (e.g. Pascall and Manning, 2000). However, there is still a notable absence of studies focusing on modern genealogies and transformations of distinctive gender regimes and corresponding gender orders in each society of the post-Soviet Baltic littoral, in particular, in the political discontinuities of the centuries century.

Gender policy in the Soviet period was based on several premises. Equality between the sexes was declared and supported by unwritten quotas for women's political representation. All citizens – men and women – had a constitutional right to a job and an obligation to work. It was always asserted that there were no unemployed. An individual who did not work could be punished as a sponger but this provision was never applied to women with children.

Socialist provision of citizenship rights had been based on the total state control of citizenship since the state was the possessor of resources and power. Thus, women's disadvantages as political, economic, social, reproductive citizens turned to be problematically combined with this specific form of citizenship. (Novikova, 2002: 69)

On the other hand, responsibilities of childrearing were exclusively granted to a woman-mother. Patriarchal traditions persisted in the home, but were also affirmed in the Soviet state legislation in social and family policies. Women were entitled to 56 (in certain situations 70) days' paid leave at childbirth. Mothers were entitled to have paid maternity leave until their child was one year old. A working place was preserved for a mother on a parental leave and this counted as part of her contribution period for which a woman finally received a pension. Since 1982 (in Lithuania) parental leave has been extended until the child is 18 months old, and a maternal allowance of half the minimal salary has begun to be paid until a child is one year old (Stankuniene et al., 2001). Family and social policies were built on a general assumption that women can reconcile family and work obligations by using nurseries and state-funded kindergartens. Free of charge after-school activities were available for all children. Trade unions provided summer camps for members' children, and trade union membership embraced nearly all of the working population. All these measures assisted women to reconcile work and family obligations. However, until the last decade of Soviet rule, there was a lack of places in kindergartens, and thus single mothers and low-income families took priority.

The Soviet paternalist system regulated women's working and emotional lives but provided them with support for child care as well as other benefits. A husband was one more patriarch in a family, and his patriarchal order in the family was ensured by cultural and ethnic traditions and values. Protection of women and their social entitlements in motherhood also had a negative effect on their employment and career. The retirement age was different: 55 years for women and 60 for men. It was assumed that women were exhausted by their double burden of work and family, so they should have earlier retirement. Therefore women were less attractive employees: according to the Soviet laws their participation in the labour market was shorter, and they had to take breaks for maternal leave and child care. In addition, there was a common understanding shared by men and women that all burdens connected with the health and education of children lay on women's shoulders, therefore they were more likely than men to be on 'flexitime' due to family duties. On the one hand, this convergence of tradition and ideology created open discrimination in the labour market, on the other, it facilitated the continuation of patriarchal relations within families.

However, '[d]uring socialism, full-time (eight hours per day) employment and social benefits (health care, legal and social protection of motherhood, liberal legislation governing abortion and family planning, and a network of public kindergartens) were considered rights that, once achieved, could never have been lost' (Gaber 1997: 143).

During the Soviet period Latvia and Lithuania were the end-link of a number of industrial chains. The restoration of political independence triggered the deconstruction of both national economies having been a well-integrated segment of the socialist economic circuit. The following privatisation and marketisation processes significantly lowered living standards and created conditions for rapid social stratification in both societies. Huge financial resources were involved and reallocated in the privatisation/marketisation process, as well as concentrated in the hands of a few economic groups. In both countries the consequence was the capture of the state levers, whereby these economic groups were able to influence and direct the legislative process to their own benefit.

From the early 1990s, the relation between state and women has been reconstituted into the relation between a re-nationalising state, market and family. Many protection measures were shifted from the state level to the local levels of enterprises, and this meant a certain, previously unknown, dependency mechanism for a woman as a repro- ductive, economic, social and political agent. Property as a crucial factor in the socio-economic underpinnings of political citizenship also unveiled gendered politics towards women on the part of the nation- state. Starting conditions for property acquisition and upward social mobility were beneficial for male-oriented echelons of power structured in the vertical gender segregation of the Soviet political and ideological hierarchies and labour market.

Marketisation, activities of global actors, gender equality policies and gender mainstreaming have been taking place with a radically different mindset for women and men in terms of their social citizenship, rights and entitlements. Soviet social policies were based on the identity of a woman as a worker and mother, thus shaping her social identity through granting her welfare protection and security in the production- reproduction relationship. The radical economic change exposed all the disadvantages women experienced under the socialist model of citizenship and affected the erosion of established social levels, values and expectations. On the one hand, its collapse and restoration rein- troduced patriarchal gender ideologies/contracts. On the other hand, women were continually and progressively finding themselves discrim- inated against in the labour market. Thus, economic transformation and liberalisation have culminated in complex gendered impacts, a deteri- oration of economic and professional prospects, and an increase in women's vulnerability to trafficking for sex due to low pay, transna- tional migration to the labour markets of the West, and impoverish- ment. One should also not underestimate the role and effect of the activities of global political actors in shaping residualist and privatisa- tion directions (Deacon, 2005), and such policies as social dumping. The reduction in women's entitlements and the rescinding of protec- tionist laws for women in the workplace and at home have dramat- ically limited a number of key opportunities for women in formal or informal employment. Occupational segregation – both horizontal and vertical – and a growing wage differential have become distinctive features of gendering the national labour market in Latvia and Lithuania. Gender asymmetry is also combined with a high degree of job insecurity. Discriminatory practices have been affecting all age groups, particularly young women entering the labour market and women of pre-retirement age who are particularly vulnerable to recruitment into part-time jobs and to impoverishment. The labour markets in the post-Soviet Baltic economies have exposed a mutually friendly encounter of a neoliberal economic framework and neo-conservative gender ideology. They used

the 'friendly fire' situation for a restatement of women's disempower-
ment through the politics of exclusion in terms of age, ethnicity and
class (Molen and Novikova, 2005).

The post-Soviet economic transitions have demonstrated that the
familiar concepts of the liberal democratic state are

> neither neutral nor impartial in the way in which they operate.
> Instead, they work in favour of some interests and against others.
> One of the groups to suffer disproportionately is that of women and
> it is because of this that the use of mainstreaming can be justified in
> order to redress this balance. (Beveridge et al., 2000: 386)

The degree of women's political solidarity for advocating their shared
social issues in employment or in the family, in care or in personal life,
has been especially low in Latvia. It is explained, on the one hand, as one
of major gender inertias after the Soviet so-called 'women's citizenship'
as well as one of the major gender effects of the post-Soviet political
citizenship regime. The latter literally divided society into two 'ethno-
political' communities to capitalise on the politics of emotions and to
succeed in advancing the residual welfare model. Women's NGOs have
been marginal in their activities to the international and supranational
funding for gender equality, and they are not considered serious and
influential stakeholders in the political life of the country.

In Lithuania, advocacy for women's rights has had a slightly different
scenario. The women's movement started early in the 1990s, was more
strongly organised, was led by women academics and therefore had
more influence in the political arena compared to Latvia. While the
predominant Lutheranism in Latvia implied 'softer' attitudes towards
women and their roles in private and in public, the revival of the Cath-
olic Church resulted in aggressive patriarchal pressure on Lithuanian
women. Probably this was one of the reasons for the stronger resistance
and activism of women there. Lithuania was the first Baltic country
to start building national gender equality machinery and to adopt a
National Action Plan for the Advancement of Women. Lithuania was
also the first to reach comparatively high political representation of
women (18.1 per cent of women in Parliament in 1996), to adopt
the Law on Equal Opportunities (1998) and to establish the office of
Equal Opportunities Ombudsman (1999). None of these achievements is
sustainable: parliamentary representation of women has had its ups and
downs and every new government starts with cuts in gender equality
policy followed later by some extension.

Nevertheless, both countries have shared the 'divorce' between gender equality policy and family policy. Both, gender equality and family policies were strongly affected by conservative ideas 'to return women to their families', and liberal ideas that 'the market solves all problems'. Equal opportunity policies and family policy are perceived to be in conflict rather than complementing each other. Thus, gender equality policy, aimed at equal rights in the labour market, has not created conditions for the reconciliation of work and family obligations.

Fertility, age, (un)employment and wage gaps in the labour market

In both countries the population is in decline. Even in the 1960s Latvia and Lithuania were not high-fertility countries but in the last 15 years fertility rates have fallen considerably (Figure 9.1). In Latvia the number of newborn children per 1,000 residents was 13.1 in 1991, 8.7 in 1995 and 8.6 in 2002. On the other hand, the number of deaths per 1,000 residents fell from 15.7 in 1995 to 13.9 in 2002. In Lithuania the numbers of newborn children per 1,000 population were 15.1, in 1991, 11.4 in 1995 and 8.6 in 2002. The numbers of deaths per 1,000 population in Lithuania was 11.1 in 1991, 12.5 in 1995 and 11.8 in 2002 (Lithuanian Statistics, 2003a). Hence the population decrease remains stable in both countries.

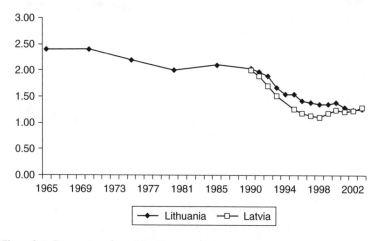

Figure 9.1: Dynamics of total fertility rate in Latvia and Lithuania
Sources: Department of Statistics, 1995, 1998; Lithuanian Department of Statistics, 1992, 1993, 1994; Statistics Lithuania 1999, 2001, 2002, 2003b, 2004a.

186   *Tana Lace, Irina Novikova and Giedre Purvaneckiene*

If the number of men exceeds the number of women in the age group under 32 years in Latvia, the number of women exceeds men of the respective age in the age group of 60 onwards by 1.9. In Lithuania, the same trend prevails: the number of men exceeds that of women in the under-thirties, whilst the number of women over 60 exceeds that of men by 1.76 times. Moreover, due to the earlier retirement of women, women comprised 68.8 per cent of the pension-aged population (Statistics Lithuania, 2004a). The mortality rates of women and men differ, too. If the crude mortality rate, i.e. the total annual number of deaths per 1,000 population, was 13.9 in Latvia, the respective numbers were 13.2 for females and 14.8 for males or 12 per cent higher for males. In Lithuania in 2003, the mortality rate was 10.4 for women and 13.5 for men per 1,000 of population (Statistics Lithuania, 2004a). At the same time life expectancy is growing in both countries (Figure 9.2), and is gender-specific. In 2003 the average life expectancy of residents born in Latvia was 71.4 years, within which the average for females was 76.9 years and 65.9 years for males. In Lithuania in 2003, average life expectancy at birth was 77.9 years for women and 66.5 for men (Statistics Lithuania, 2004a). That means that average life expectancy for women exceeds that of men by 11 years in Latvia and 11.4 years in Lithuania.

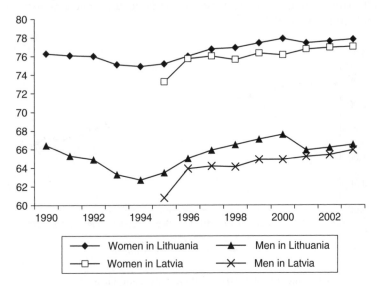

Figure 9.2: Average life expectancy at birth in Latvia and Lithuania
Source: Statistics Lithuania, 2004a.

There is an increasing need for new social and health services for the elderly and for increased funding for pensions – a challenge faced by women at work, in the family and in old age that none of the national governments has met in either country.

At present the economic situation of women is less advantageous than that of men in both countries. This is best demonstrated by the unequal situation in the job market which is characterised by vertical and horizontal gender segregation. Inequality can be observed when analysing the status of employment along with the resulting remuneration for work (the average female salary is 78.5 per cent in Latvia and 80.9 per cent in Lithuania of the male salary) (Statistics Lithuania, 2004a).

The example of wage differentials in Lithuania (Figure 9.3) illustrates vertical segregation in the labour market. Another factor cementing certain economic positions is the horizontal segregation of the labour market in the public sector or so-called 'female professions' (areas such education, culture, social and health care). They are lower paid than 'male professions' (manufacturing and construction). This is also related to the fact that women more frequently choose jobs in governmental and municipal institutions that are lower paid but have higher social guarantees.

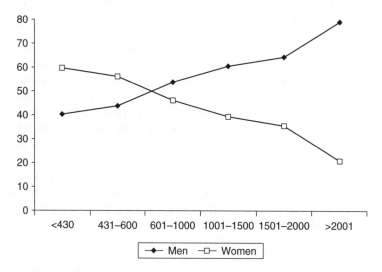

Figure 9.3: Distribution of female and male employees (%) by wages and salaries (in Litas) in Lithuania in 2003. Minimal wage – 430 Lt.
Source: Statistics Lithuania, 2004a.

The studies for the Baltic countries have shown that:

> The average wage for women in Latvia and Lithuania was around 80%
> of the average for men in 2000.... Between 1997 and 2000, women
> tended to reduce their relative disadvantage in Estonia and Lithuania,
> but only marginally so in Latvia. A closer scrutiny shows that the
> relative improvement experienced by women in that period mainly
> concerned white-collar jobs in Lithuania, but mainly blue-collar jobs
> in Estonia.... The gender-related pay gaps are particularly wide in
> sales and commerce jobs, while they are narrow for semiskilled
> manual workers (machine operators), for whom there is practically no
> gender difference at all in Latvia. Wide gaps are often found in occu-
> pations and sectors with high average wages (e.g. financial services,
> not shown in the table) and they mainly concern regions with many
> high-wage jobs. In Latvia in 1999, women earned on average at
> least as much as men in six of the poorest districts. Indeed, even
> controlling for all known factors other than the income level, the
> gender discrimination effect appears much stronger for medium and
> high-income groups than for low-income groups. (OECD, 2003: 5)

Some researchers confirm that they could find limited explanations for
the observed wage gaps (factors of education, economic sector and main
occupation groups).

> Baltic women are actually better educated than men on average, but
> they work more often in low-wage areas. Work experience is not
> important here because Baltic women have on average at least as long
> experience and tenure as men (albeit with fewer hours per week).
> Among the measurable characteristics, a principal factor operating
> to men's advantage is that wages are higher in some predominantly
> male activities (transport and communications, construction) than
> in some predominantly female activities (education, health care),
> and that public-sector employers, in particular, tend to give men
> the best-paid jobs. Remarkably, the wage premium for professional
> occupations in Estonia is substantially higher for women than for
> men (a difference of 19 percentage points, compared to 3 in Latvia
> and Lithuania). (OECD, 2003: 10)

In our opinion, vertical and horizontal segregation in the labour market,
shorter working hours for women (in particular, part-time work in
public or service jobs) alongside hidden discrimination of women due

to patriarchal attitudes can explain the pay gap. Nevertheless, the fact that the working-time gap is on average 1.5 to 2.5 hours shorter per week for women than men as full-time workers still leaves the entire gender pay gap in Lithuania, most of it in Estonia and about half in Latvia, unexplained. 'The wage gaps that remain after discounting the effects of controlled variables amount to around 10% in Latvia, 14 to 15% in Lithuania and 17 to 21% in Estonia in 2000' (OECD, 2003: 10). Although the authors of this study consider that there is a small wage gap between men and women, they do not consider the distribution of female and male jobs in the public and private sectors. The latter characterised by predominantly men's employment is also the sector in which part of an employee's salary is unregistered.

The unequal distribution of women and men between public and private sectors[1] puts the validity of official pay gaps in question. In the public sector earnings are relatively transparent, while in the private sector the 'shadow economy' and untaxed remuneration still exist, and is not reflected in statistics. The majority of actors in these shadow activities and sectors of economy are men. Therefore the income differences between men and women could be much higher (Purvaneckiene, 2004). The pay gap goes with unemployment risk.

In Latvia (Table 9.2), the analysis of the structure of the unemployed reveals that it has not changed much since the middle of the 1990s – the ratio of the long-term unemployed against the total number of unemployed persons remains very high, with considerable gender-based and age-marked differences. 59.6 per cent of all long-term unemployed were males but – as we argued above – an official status of 'unemployed' gives some opportunities, on the one hand, and this is also a way of finding a job in the 'shadow economy'.

The situation in Lithuania (Table 9.1) differs slightly. In the early 1990s, unemployment affected women much more than men due to the

Table 9.1: Unemployment rate in Lithuania for 2003

Age group	Women	Men
15–24	28.1	22.5
25–49	10.2	11.8
50–64	12.5	11.3
65+	8.9	2.7
Total	12.2	12.7

Source: Statistics Lithuania, 2004a.

Table 9.2: Unemployment rate in Latvia, 2002

	Women	Men
15–24	24.1	18.3
25–49	9.9	12.0
50–64	8.3	12.8
15–64	11.0	13.1

Source: Labour Force Survey data

shrinking state sector. Several years later, male unemployment exceeded that of women due to the collapse of big enterprises, as in Latvia. At present, male unemployment exceeds that of women only slightly. Concerning long-term unemployment, in Lithuania out of all unemployed women, 52 per cent are unemployed for more than one year. Out of all unemployed men, 49 per cent are unemployed for over one year. In 2002, there were 21.2 per cent unemployed young people aged 15–24 in the total number of unemployed persons; the unemployment rate among people of this age was 20.8 per cent. Youth unemployment also differs significantly by gender – 24.1 per cent of women (aged 15–24) were unemployed, which is 5.8 percentage points higher than the rate for men. The main reason for young people's – and young women's – unemployment is education that is not suited to and/or insufficient for the market's demands, as well as the fact that young men and women lack work experience and/or education, qualifying them for a job.

There is a high unemployment risk for women after maternal leave. This type of risk results from the necessity to improve their previous qualifications and skills as well as employer's stereotypes that women with children have lower labour productivity. Employers are not motivated to allow female employees to work part-time and to work at home (using information and communication technology, etc.). Another reason for the increased risk of unemployment for women after parental leave is insufficient public transport from and to the countryside. This hinders them from getting to the workplace and from using kindergartens.

There is also scientific evidence that opportunity to engage in part-time work has a positive effect on fertility (Coleman, 2004). Part-time work is quite often seen as a good option for a working woman with children. But it should be noted that part-time work hampers the professional career of a woman, lowers her income and consequently has negative effect on her pension. Therefore, after retirement women are effectively 'punished' for working part-time.

Balance between work and family life

Most women have to deal with a difficult balance between work and family life. Whether we like it or not, patriarchal attitudes in the Baltic countries place the majority of family responsibilities on women's shoulders. We can talk about equal opportunities and freedom of decision, but the reality is that if the state needs women in the labour market, it should ensure conditions for the reconciliation of work and family life. This is the task for family policy.

As mentioned above, the central issues in family policies in Latvia and Lithuania are those of the ageing populations and low fertility rates. Achieving the balance between work and family life should positively affect fertility rates, therefore, states need to take measures to enable a sustainable balance between work and family life. However, in Latvia and in Lithuania the main measures to support families have been directed towards increasing fertility rates, but their implementation has been affected by persistent patriarchal attitudes. For example, in both countries, typically, families are supported by several means: benefits, increasing the untaxed salary minimum with each child, maternity and parental leave, child care, etc. It should be noted that family policy in the last 15 years has been developed according to 'the best interest of child'. The common belief that a mother should stay at home with a child as long as possible still prevails among policy-makers. Therefore the policy-making emphasis was put on increasing and expanding various benefits as well as child care leave, but not on the development of a system of child care. Thus, a familial patriarchal attitude is sustained, and moreover, governments do not take responsibility for developing the social care system (the 'ghost' of the socialist social care system is thus buried under demonising rhetoric describing past times).

For Lithuania the dynamics of the numbers of day-care facilities are depicted in Figure 9.4, which shows that in the last years of the Soviet period the numbers of day-care facilities were increasing. In the 1990s, the numbers of day-care facilities dropped dramatically: in urban areas more than two times and in rural areas more than three times.

There were many reasons for this: fertility rates were decreasing, and enterprises and collective farms were closing day-care centres because of their own collapse. The conservative ideology calling women 'to return home' was channelled into mass media and elsewhere. The effectiveness of the pressure of public opinion can be illustrated by the dynamic of enrolment of children in day-care facilities in Lithuania (Figure 9.5). Due to ideological reasons the enrolment reached its low point in 1993, then

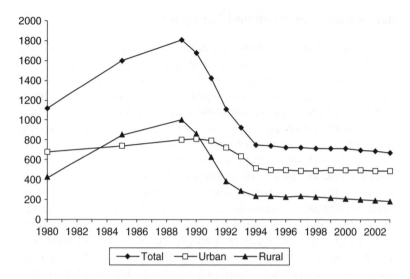

Figure 9.4: Numbers of child care facilities by year in Lithuania
Sources: Department of Statistics, 1995, 1998; Lithuanian Department of Statistics, 1992,
1993, 1994; Statistics Lithuania 1999, 2001, 2002, 2003b, 2004a.

started to increase and in 2003 had reached a higher level for children
over three years of age than in the Soviet period. For children under
three years of age, enrolment is still lower due to extension of child
care leave to three years in 1991. The comparison of trends in Lithuania
(Figures 9.4 and 9.5) is typical for the situation in Latvia. In both societies, the main obstacle to reconciling work and family life is a dramatic
lack of state-funded day-care facilities, the numbers of which are still
falling. In addition, there is a lack of day-care facilities for children under
three years and day care with long working hours. They cannot provide
care for children whose parents work in the service sector or who work
evening or night shifts. This is a serious problem for single-parent (in
the majority of cases single-mother) families, which comprise about one
fifth of all families with children.

In Latvia, the amount of maternity benefit is 100 per cent the average
insurance contributions wage. Paternity benefits are also granted: 80 per
cent of the average insurance contributions wage for the period of leave
(maximum ten days) related to the birth of child. In the first half of 2004
questions pertaining to the increase of childbirth and child care allowances enjoyed wide resonance among politicians and the general public
in Latvia. Along with the change of government and their unchanging
political stance, the document proposal has been returned for repeated

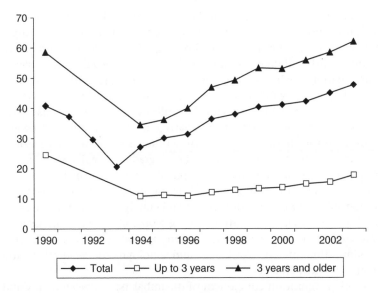

Figure 9.5: Enrolment in day-care facilities by year in Lithuania (in percentage)
Sources: Department of Statistics, 1995, 1998; Lithuanian Department of Statistics, 1992, 1993, 1994; Statistics Lithuania 1999, 2001, 2002, 2003b, 2004a.

examination, but no concrete decision has yet been made. A group of parents organised a petition and sent an appeal to the Prime Minister and to the parliamentary parties to support the increase of differentiated child care allowances. However, it should be noted that the opinion expressed in the mass media and by the public at large about the necessity of the allowance differentiation and the respective amount revealed stereotypes and social prejudices concerning the unification of low-income and socially disadvantaged families as well as mutually opposed opinions about the relationship between the amount of the allowance and social insurance payments made.

The amount of the allowance for employed parents taking care of a child up to the age of one year depends on the average taxed wage of one of the parents. Thus, as the amount of the allowance depends on the social insurance payments made by parents, it is assumed that the majority of citizens will eventually wish to legalise their actual earnings from which social insurance payments are made. Child care leave can be assigned to both parents and may actually promote the role of the father in the family. One of the reasons why women were assigned child care leave more often than men was that men have higher salaries. It is believed that the new rules will change that situation.

Another common problem for Latvia is that the low income level of the population and the comparatively high rental and utilities charges are the cause of the majority of housing-related economic problems. Families with children are among the least protected in this particular situation. Owing to lower income levels, families with children, in particular, single-mother families or all-women families, are at greater risk of incurring debts in paying for utilities, which are calculated on the basis of the total area of the apartment or the number of people residing in the apartment. At the same time, as in Lithuania, the social care and health system in Latvia is being gradually replaced by privatised services and, thus, the development of an informal household economy on the one hand, or recalling traditional patterns of women's responsibility for the care of children and elderly in their families. Both, marked with social polarisation among women, also raise the issue of gradually 'deskilling' consciousness among young women, their self-devalorisation in terms of career and employment perspectives and economic independence.

Another significant component of the imbalance between family and employment is the insufficient labour market flexibility in terms of part-time and temporary jobs. It has also been identified as a major culprit for limiting access to the labour market for the most vulnerable groups, namely older women and women with dependants. However, as wages are low, part-time jobs may be insufficient in most cases to lift people out of poverty, especially when no one else in the household has a full-time job.

The feminisation of poverty

The feminisation of poverty is a process that has to be seen in its various constituents. First, the Soviet model of provision of women's social rights in terms of their social entitlements was universal and secured from the state budget to provide an expected balance between a woman's work and her family life. Its model target was a nuclear, heterosexual two-breadwinner family, with a strong focus on legislation that protected the mother and occupational welfare. However, the Soviet labour market itself was gender-structured so that women were mostly concentrated in typically female industries. Their salaries, even with the formal legislations of 'sex equality', were lower than men's, and they never secured the principle of economic independence and security, either during working life or in the age of retirement. Impoverishment in single-mother families as in all-female households was

already a serious challenge in the 1980s, the time of economic stagna-
tion. The low fertility rates, increase in mortality and the negative net
migration from Latvia caused changes in the age structure of population.

Since 1991 the governments of Latvia have been implementing the
liberal model of economic development with a focus on the individual's
activity and responsibility. Economic development was not linked to
alleviation of poverty. The ruling parties and politicians were and partly
still are of the view that the market economy itself would eliminate
poverty and alleviate its negative consequences and that there was no
need to implement a socially oriented policy. The model of a residual
system of welfare (the liberal model) was introduced as a result of the
implementation of social policy reforms. The government declarations,
which set the main goals and objectives of the government, were characterised by an unwillingness to identify tackling poverty as a government
priority. The regularly changing governments hesitated to mention the
concept of poverty and tried to replace it with the concept of welfare.
The position of the government has been until recently that instead of
fighting the poverty they should increase the welfare of the people.

The Lithuanian social and family policy model was strongly influenced by liberal ideas, but they were not predominant (contrary to
economic policies where the market economy had the 'green light').
Due to the changes of governments, switching from the right to the left
with almost every elections social policy became eclectic. Today, poverty
reduction is set as one of the priorities of social policy in both countries.
The Poverty Reduction Strategy in Lithuania indicates the most vulnerable groups, namely, single parents, large families, the unemployed and
agricultural workers. The Programme of the Implementation of Poverty
Reduction for 2002–4 was approved by the government. Although it is
too early to draw conclusions about the achievement of the main target,
poverty did not decrease, and in 2003 it stood at 15.9 per cent (Statistics Lithuania, 2004b). This questions the effectiveness of social policy
as well making presumptions about insufficient attention to gender
differences in poverty level.

In this gender, demographic and economic context, we see the inter-
locking of at least three entitling positions for women:

1. 'Women as providers/carers' interlocked with – and affected by –
   'changes in social provision of health and education' (Pascall and
   Manning, 2000: 242) during economic transformations.
2. Women as a major part of the ageing population suffered detrimental
   cuts in their pensions.

3. Women as a substantial part of working force had to reclaim and adapt their skills in the labour market at the expense of their social and economic downward mobility.

At the same time, social security systems have had to be radically modified in both countries, again to the disadvantage of women as a sizeable old-age group. In the situations of declining and commodified health care systems, the family care exchange has already been reclaimed substantially, at the expense of women as traditional 'family carers'.

As we have shown, national family and social policies have been trying to change the situation, but have been failing to meet the demands of the gendered marketisation process. Poverty in Latvia and Lithuania is especially gender-related. In spite of the comparatively high level of female employment in Latvia and Lithuania, the trend of feminising poverty can be seen. For example, in Lithuania in 2003 19.1 per cent of households headed by women in comparison to 13.6 per cent of male-headed households lived below the poverty line (Statistics Lithuania, 2004a). Owing to women's low average remuneration, poverty tends to be sustained throughout their lifetime, as the amount of future material support or pension depends on their social contributions. However, the research data have revealed new groups which previously had not been analysed in the policy context. The highest risk groups in terms of poverty are families with children and single mothers. A significant poverty risk has also been identified for families with one or several unemployed members, especially long-term unemployed. A similarly high risk was identified for unemployed youth.

According to the Latvian Household Budget Report (HBR) data, the poverty risk index increases along with the number of children. For example, in 2002 the poverty risk index for a family with one child was 15 per cent, with two children it was 16 per cent, but with three or more children it was 26 per cent. The analysis of the households comprising a couple with children leads to the conclusion that such households are less vulnerable to poverty than single-parent households. Between 1997 and 2002 the poverty risk index for children from this type of household was 15–18 per cent, while for children from single-parent households it was 16–32 per cent. A worrying fact is that children under 14 are more at risk of poverty than in the above categories at 17–21 per cent. In 2002, 39 per cent of the total number of children lived in 20 per cent of the poorest Latvian households (Household Budget Survey, 2003). In comparison, in 1997, 40.3 per cent of the total number of children lived in 20 per cent of the poorest households.

The Lithuanian HBR data show similar trends (Statistics Lithuania, 2004b). The poverty level in single-headed household (the majority of which are women-headed) was 19.4 per cent in comparison with 13 per cent for two-parent households. The poverty level correlated to the number of children: for one-child families it was 12.6 per cent, two children 16.6 per cent, and for families with three or more children it was 30.6 per cent. The risk of poverty before social transfers, excluding pensions, decreased slightly in 2003 to 22.5 per cent (from 24.2 per cent in 2002). But the highest risk remains for single-parent families at 28.1 per cent and for families with three or more children at 26.5 per cent. Single persons over 65 years of age (the majority of whom are women) are also at high level of poverty risk at 23.8 per cent.

Sociological studies, as well as the HBR reports confirm that families with children, especially with three or more children, and single-parent families, in particular, are those most vulnerable to poverty and social exclusion. Single-parent families face the largest risk, as do those families with young children and where the mother is the breadwinner. As in the majority of cases the mother takes responsibility for bringing up her children after parents divorce, the feminisation of poverty emerges and children in these single-parent families are faced with an increased risk of poverty. It is important to note that for women, such poverty can last a lifetime. This is related to their mothers' low remuneration, which affects the level of insurance payments and thus results in women receiving lower pensions.

Poverty prevention in both countries is not linked to the main objectives of social policy. The main task set in the area of social assistance was assistance to those individuals who are facing insurmountable difficulties and cannot help themselves. Individual participation obligations are thus one of the preconditions for the receipt of social assistance. Within the framework of the social insurance reform was the American liberal model, and this process was heavily influenced by the World Bank experts. In all of this, governments have not acknowledged the feminisation of poverty, and this explains in part why governments have been choosing anti-women tasks and strategies in social policies.

As we have discussed, the economic downturn of the early 1990s and a growing ageing population meant that challenges were insurmountable, so Lithuania and Latvia raised the retirement age. Obviously, such a strategy for the provision of cheap and deskilled labour was made at the expense of women in the retirement ages of 60 for Lithuania and 62 for Latvia. These women's impoverishment does not stop as soon as they retire – they cannot enjoy the benefits of the pension reforms and, particularly, the advantages of private pension schemes.

Younger generations of women, due to the pressures of the European Union for gender equality legislation in Latvia and Lithuania during the enlargement process, can enjoy protection through anti-discrimination laws and equal opportunity policies. However, they confront the reality of persisting gender inequalities, a considerable and growing pay gap as well as vertical and horizontal segregation in both national labour markets. Young women mainly try to find full-time jobs and their working hours are among the longest of all OECD (Organisation for Economic Cooperation and Development) countries. All of this happens in societies with very low gender awareness, with a considerable polarisation of the society, deepening welfare gaps between urban and rural populations, social exclusion and poverty risk groups whose situation has not improved over recent years.

The case of Latvia, in which occupational welfare was reduced to a minimum and used for the residualist rhetoric of 'supporting the real losers', demonstrated strategies of what Jens Alber and Guy Standing conceptualise as social security dumping, and specifically, the example of androcentric social security dumping. 'Social security dumping refers to the extent to which transfers and services in social protection schemes are reduced or restructured by shifting the burden of financing. The main tendencies here are shifts from universalism and social insurance to selectivity and "social safety nets"' (Alber and Standing, 2000: 100). Secondly, national social policies in Latvia in the 1990s demonstrated a shift of a more general character – 'from universal to selective, means-tested social protection schemes and a trend towards 'residual' welfare states' (ibid., 101).

Alber and Standing consider that this process will finally be arrested as

policymakers in political democracies need to achieve a certain degree of legitimation. This implies that the social costs of the modernization process must be cushioned if governments want to stay in power and stabilize their regimes (for an early version of this argument, see Rimlinger, 1971). For the more extended welfare states, it has been shown that curtailing social standards is unpopular, because cut-backs are visible and concentrated on identifiable groups, whereas promised benefits from enhanced competitiveness and economic growth are diffuse and deferred to the future. (Pierson, 1996; ibid.: 102)

However, in societies with women as a very clearly identifiable group experiencing social costs, other levers of populist politics, supporting themselves through the gendered social and economic polarisation of the 1990s, are 'safeguarding' women as passive recipients of such politics.

Latvia in this sense is an explicit example of a society in which a meticulously constructed and supported regime of social divisions does all the work necessary to update the legitimisation of today's power-holders. Thus, all other 'reference models' are renegotiated in the light of 'historic specificity', and replayed into the national political representation in the European Parliament. It has been persistently done while women in the labour market have been used for recommodifying labour, cutting labour costs and ensuring international investments into the market with a cheaper labour force than, for example, Norway or Germany. In this post-socialist context of tremendous social losses, joining the European Union has exposed 'the relative indifference of the European Commission in the transition process which contracted out expertise and failed to push a European vision of social policy and a good society' (Alber and Staning, 2000: 110).

Challenges

The transformation of national welfare regimes and related gender orders, or their reformation in the former socialist countries of Europe, has impacted on women. European social policies follow market integration, and the market transformations due to the addition of ten economies are definitely resonant in the gender construction of the social policies in 'old' European economies and their respective social policy trends. The effects of this process are that it has never been researched in-depth and comparatively as a cross-cutting issue of gender concern in the EU enlargement. Very little comparative research has been made on the constraints 1) in mainstreaming gender by the EU in the enlargement process and by the ten states with regard to their policies and legislations; and 2) from the impact of the reforms, transnational labour migration and trafficking for particular groups of women, such as younger women, women over the age of 35, rural women and non-citizen women (with the status 'alien of Latvia'). Whether the gender equality policies and gender mainstreaming strategies in the enlargement group have been adequate in addressing these issues by discussing a 'paradox of gender mainstreaming', in which progress in legal-institutional terms is contrasted with the realities of women's diversity and limits of their participation in the national reformist agendas, must be seriously investigated.

In both countries it is important to strengthen the capacity of national machinery for the advancement of women and national human rights institutions to promote and protect women's rights through the development of institutional links and joint strategies as central policy coordinating units within government. However, a serious challenge is the national political setting in which legislative developments, and preparations of national action plans, strategies and policies for gender equality, are worked out. Another consideration is whether public discussion around gender equality issues is really accumulating critical mass to influence policy-making.

In terms of women's social rights, several aspects have not received sufficient attention in the mainstreaming process, such as women's citizenship, the social and political exclusion of women from the ethnic minority groups or the situation of older women. The lack of economic perspectives and the gradual elimination of women's social power from minority groups make these women increasingly vulnerable to trafficking for sexual purposes. This part of the 'reality' of European citizenship remains hidden behind official reports on gender mainstreaming. The question is whether mainstreaming agencies, national, regional and European, in the future will be able to show the complexity and diversity of women's constituencies in the enlarged European Union and the countries on its new borders.

For the new members of the EU, the process of adapting gender mainstreaming into governmental agencies is important. However, it is overlooked that gender equality and gender mainstreaming as operational categories in the EU historically have been affected by the activism of European women in politics, in academia, in grass-roots movements, in trade unions and in personal challenges to existing inequalities. It is not the EU that has brought gender equality to the countries of the Eastern enlargement group, but it is the experience of European women, with their achievements, losses and controversies. Thus, to be a success story, gender mainstreaming needs to incorporate the voices of women activists, experts and the socially excluded. This is also obvious in the absence of public policy analysis which directly links women's social rights to other objectives of national interest, such as security and economic development.

Note

1. In Lithuania in 2003 64.2 per cent of women worked in public sector and 43.7 per cent in private; 35.8 per cent of men were employed in public sector and 56.3 per cent in private (Statistics Lithuania, 2003).

References

Alber, J. and Standing, G. (2000) 'Social dumping, catch-up, or convergence? Europe in a comparative global context', *Journal of European Social Policy*, 10(2): 99–119.

Beveridge, F., Nott, S. and Stephen, K. (2000) 'Mainstreaming and the engendering of policy-making: a means to an end?' *Journal of European Public Policy* 7(3): 385–405.

Coleman, D. (2004) 'Facing the 21st century. New developments, continuing problems. Keynote address on population and development in Europe during the last decade: an academic overview', paper presented at the European Population Forum, Geneva, 12–14 January. Available at: http://www.unece.org/ead/pau/epf/present/ks1/coleman.pdf [accessed 30 May 2005].

Deacon, B. (2001) 'Prospect for equitable social provision in a globalising world', Available at: http://www.ceu.hu/cps/eve/globconf/papers/deacon2.rtf [accessed 30 May 2005].

Deacon, B. (1998) *Globalization and Social Policy*, available at: http://www.globalpolicy.org/socecon/un/unglobe2.htm [accessed 14 June 2005].

Gaber, M. A. (1997) 'Politics in transition', in J. W. Scott et al. (eds) *Transitions, Environments, Translations. Feminisms in International Politics*, New York and London: Routledge, pp. 143–52.

Hazans, M. et al. (2003) 'Determinants of earnings in Latvia, Lithuania and Estonia', in OECD, *Labour Market and Social Policies in the Baltic Countries*; short version available at: http://www.oecd.org/dataoecd/18/10/2493411.pdf#search='occupational%20segregation%20Latvia%20Lithuania [accessed 15 March 2005].

van der Molen, I. and Novikova, I. (2005) 'Mainstreaming gender in the EU-accession process: the case of the Baltic Republics', *Journal of European Social Policy*, 15: 139–56.

Novikova, I. (2002) 'Gendering post-socialist "reason": borders of nation, boundaries of identity politics and women in Latvia after 1991', in K. Komulainen (ed.) *Sukupuolitetut rajat. Gendered Borders and Boundaries*, Joensuu: Joensuun yliopisto, pp. 67–102.

Pascall, G. and Manning, N. (2000) 'Gender and social policy: comparing welfare states in Central and Eastern Europe and the former Soviet Union', *Journal of European Social Policy* 10(3): 240–66.

Purvaneckiene G. (2004) 'Gender dimension in the process of social change', in *Socialiniai mokslai*, 1: 11–19.

Stankuniene, V. et al. (2001) *Family Policy: Essence and Experience*, Vilnius: Institute of Philosophy and Sociology.

Stankūnienė, V. et al. (2001) *Paramos šeimai politika: samprata ir patyrimas*, Vilnius: Lietuvos filosofijos ir sociologijos institutas.

UNIFEM (2000) *Poverty Reduction Strategy Lithuania*, Vilnius: UNDP.
UNDP (2002) *Report of the Millennium Development Goals: a Baseline Study/ Common Country Assessment for Lithuania*, Vilnius: UNDP.
Verdery, K. (1996) *What Was Socialism and What Comes Next?* Princeton, NJ: Princeton University Press.

Reports and statistics

Statistics Lithuania (1999) *Women and Men in Lithuania 1998*, Vilnius: Statistics Lithuania.
Statistics Lithuania (2001) *Women and Men in Lithuania 2000*, Vilnius: Statistics Lithuania.
Statistics Lithuania (2002) *Women and Men in Lithuania 2001*, Vilnius: Statistics Lithuania.
Statistics Lithuania (2003) *DemographicYearbook 2002*, Vilnius: Statistics Lithuania.
Statistics Lithuania (2003) *Women and Men in Lithuania 2002*, Vilnius: Statistics Lithuania.
Statistics Lithuania (2004) *Women and Men in Lithuania 2003*, Vilnius: Statistics Lithuania.
Statistics Lithuania (2004) *Living Standard and Poverty*, Vilnius: Statistics Lithuania.
Central Bureau of Statistics (2003) *Report on Results of the Household Budget Surveys in 2002, 2003*, Riga: Central Bureau of Statistics.
Central Bureau of Statistics (2003) *Social Processes in Latvia*, Riga: Central Bureau of Statistics.
Central Bureau of Statistics (2003) *Labour Force Survey*, Riga: Central Bureau of Statistics.
Central Bureau of Statistics (2003) *Women and Men in Latvia*, Riga: Central Bureau of Statistics.
Central Bureau of Statistics (2004) *Women and Men in Latvia*, Riga: Central Bureau of Statistics.
Central Bureau of Statistics (2003) *Statistical Yearbook of Latvia*, Riga: Central Bureau of Statistics.
Central Bureau of Statistics (2004) *Statistical Yearbook of Latvia*, Riga: Central Bureau of Statistics.
Central Bureau of Statistics (2004) *Demography*, Riga: Central Bureau of Statistics.
Central Bureau of Statistics (2003) *Household Budget in 2002*, Riga: Central Bureau of Statistics.
Ministry of Welfare Republic of Latvia (2002) *Social Report 2001*, Riga: Ministry of Welfare Republic of Latvia.
Ministry of Welfare Republic of Latvia (2003) *Social Report for 2002–2003*, Riga: Ministry of Welfare Republic of Latvia.
Ministry of Social Welfare (2003) *Joint Inclusion Memorandum* Ministry of Social Welfare Latvia: Riga; available at: http://www.lm.gov.lv [accessed 30 May 2005].
UNDP (1999) *Human Development Report, 1998* UNDP: Latvia; available at: http://www.undp.riga.lv [accessed 30 May 2005].
UNDP (2000) *Human Development Report, 1999*, Latvia: UNDP.

10
The Impact of Globalisation on Women's Labour Market Situation in Eastern Europe

Osnat Lubrani and Elizabeth Villagómez

Central and Eastern Europe (CEE) and the former USSR (part of which is now known as the Commonwealth of Independent States, CIS) have undergone dramatic transformations since 1989. Political and economic processes of change have obviously been strongly influenced by the forces of globalisation. In general one can say that globalisation affects all spheres of social and economic life. It has brought new challenges to transition country governments in their task of mobilising and managing public finances. It has subjected economic and human development to greater uncertainties in the international environment and to the strong pressures of multilateral and financial institutions. It has also made the roles of transition country governments as actors in the provision of public goods and social services even more critical, but has weakened them considerably. These globalisation and regional transition processes have also influenced outcomes in terms of women's situation in society and the status of gender equality and women's human rights.

The United Nations Development Fund for Women (UNIFEM) has been working in the CEE and CIS since 1998 to respond to women's situation in the specific social and political context of the region. There remains a distinct lack of information and expertise on gender-sensitive economic issues, and across the region women are yet to be considered as key players in economic and policy-making arenas and are suffering as a result. Civil society in general and women's organisations in particular lack capacity for evidence-based advocacy, particularly on economic issues. UNIFEM has therefore focused its activities to advance women's economic security on supporting efforts to deepen analyses of women's economic situation and, concurrently, developing women's economic literacy so that they can become more effective and confident advocates for economic policies that are gender-sensitive. This chapter focuses on one initiative, which was specifically centred on the impact of globalisation on women in three countries in the CEE/CIS region – Bulgaria, Hungary and Kazakhstan. For the non-governmental organisations (NGOs) involved, engaging in research or advocacy on gender and labour market issues even at national or regional level was relatively new, let alone looking at these issues through the lens of globalisation. While further capacity-building is certainly needed to develop even deeper understanding of the impact of macroeconomic trends, trade agreements, etc. on women's lives on the ground, this project was important in increasing awareness of linkages and promoting debate on these issues.

The project concentrated on the development of national-level studies of women's participation in the labour market, and through advocacy and awareness-raising, hoped to influence policy in the three countries. Aside from the information obtained from the reports in these three countries, this chapter includes more recent information which is being analysed and prepared for a regional UNIFEM study titled 'The Story Behind the Numbers: Women and Employment in the CEE and CIS', which aims to probe more deeply into what the main labour market indicators mean, and where they seem to fall short in explaining the true situation of women – thereby hindering the specific policy reactions which are needed to address a number of problems.

The main trends in the situation of women in CEE

Evidence suggests that men have been better able to move into the fast-growing private sector in CEE and the CIS than women both because they have more time for training/re-skilling and because they are better able to work the longer hours required in the private sector firms, as more often than not men are not the primary care-givers within the family unit (UNICEF, 2001; Pierella, 2002; Pollert and Fodor, 2005). In addition, women have been much less able than men to establish small-scale enterprises of their own because of the lack of information on trends and markets and because of differential access to credit and other economic inputs, as well as their more limited mobility due to their traditional familial roles.

The work we review here focused mainly on the impact of globalisation on women's economic opportunities. It is important to keep in mind that the economic and social aspects focused on were mainly, but not exclusively, labour market issues. This is because other issues such as levels of education and availability of social services also play an important part in the labour market outcomes and because the interests of NGOs were also to have a more qualitative interpretation about women's situation in the labour market (and in the context of European Union (EU) accession in the cases of Bulgaria and Hungary). The NGOs that participated in the original project were coordinated by the Women's Alliance for Development (WAD) of Bulgaria. In Hungary the Social Innovation Foundation carried out the activities, and in Kazakhstan the Association of Businesswomen of Kazakhstan.

The main activities carried out were a scan of available relevant research, information and initiatives in the region and the creation of an International Advisory Group and corresponding list serve through which participants shared experiences and methodologies for conducting economic studies with a gender perspective. Based on this scan and the work of the advisory group, the three reports were completed focusing on: a) current skills profiles of unemployed and under-employed women in select sectors; and b) economic opportunities arising in each of the three selected countries (ABWK, 2003; Social Innovation Foundation, 2003; WAD, 2003). As for the methodology used, a single question-naire was agreed on the basis of which the in-depth interviews in the different countries were made. The structure of the reports, however, was very different, making it difficult for strict comparisons, and the results presented here draw on a subsequent analysis that was made in order to identify the common issues across the three reports.

The main idea around the assessments that the NGOs carried out was to concentrate on the way globalisation has affected economic oppor-tunities more specifically in an environment where governments work under these restraints and where foreign direct investment, on the one hand, and external competition on national capital on the other, create different demands on workers as well as opportunities: better for those who have adequate education and skills, and worse for those who do not have these.

The most important trends detected in the country reports were:

- General changes in the labour market (drops in activity and employ-ments rates coupled with increases in unemployment, as well as demands on age, skills and availability).
- Changes in education and training (educational choices, higher educational profiles and readiness for adapting to the demands of the knowledge economy and Information and Communication Technologies [ICT]).

- Changes in social security and social services (negative incentives for women through the benefit system, changes in the provision of social services and disadvantages in terms of pensions due to their worse position in the labour market throughout their working lives).
- Discrimination of various types (both age and sex, and the absence of specific laws or lack of mechanisms to enforce laws when they do exist).
- Changes in attitudes towards women's roles by society as a whole and by women themselves (such as drops in fertility rates and changes in the concepts of citizenship, which are also influencing the thinking about the type of work women can do).
- Increasing differences amongst women (public and private sector workers, rural and urban, young and old).

These issues are obviously connected to other social and economic changes that these countries have experienced, but here the focus was maintained on economic opportunities, mainly through the labour market, and how the changes experienced were being played out in the context of globalisation and increasing integration of geographical areas into trading blocs. This in itself posed a challenge to any gender mainstreaming strategy in policy, as decisions made under the pressure of these phenomena are many times outside the boundaries of nation states.

In what follows, each one of the trends enumerated above will be addressed in the light of the reports themselves and of literature and data that has been gathered to work on other UNIFEM projects currently under way or being planned.

General changes in the labour market

Although it is generally accepted that the decline in employment has disproportionately affected women during the first years of post-Soviet transition, gender differences on average remain smaller in transition countries than in many EU countries in the labour market. However, the reports have begun to unveil some of the hidden situations behind the numbers that have given rise to this difference in outcomes for men and women in the labour market. One example is the drop in activity rates that has taken place, which must be taken into account when interpreting differences in unemployment. The United Nations Economic Commission for Europe (UNECE) database[1] shows that women's activity rates (in the 15–64 age group) are roughly equivalent to or higher than the European Union average (60.1 per cent in 2002). In most countries there have been no significant changes recorded since 1995. However, there are some differences in the countries we analyse here, as those of Bulgarian and Hungarian women are significantly below 60 per cent (53 per cent and 57 per cent respectively in 2002).

Although all the reports made reference to the radical changes in the labour market that were prompted by the adjustments to the economies as a whole from centrally planned to market-oriented, what was missing to a greater or lesser degree was a more in-depth analysis of the aftermath in terms of the changes in the main labour market indicators, namely drops in activity and employment rates, and increasing unemployment (including long-term unemployment).[2] However, two main trends were found:

1. Drops in activity rates for both men and women which are having differentiated impacts on the two.
2. Changes in the sectoral composition of economic activity in the countries.

In general it is worth mentioning here that two questions which often get conflated should be kept in mind with respect to the results obtained from these studies: Has women's situation worsened since 1989? And, has women's situation worsened relative to that of men? The answer to the first question, as the following analysis shows, is yes, most definitely. As for the second question, the answer is 'not always' and that most standard indicators do not tell the whole story.

Although transition and globalisation can be seen as different processes that affect women's situation, they are really different sides of the same coin. While transition meant the dismantling of a system that in many ways encouraged women's economic activity but did not address underlying gender relations, globalisation has increased the pressure on economies to remain competitive either through lower salaries or high levels of innovation. Governments are increasingly pressured to maintain low levels of taxation and expenditure with the consequent loss of jobs and basic social protection and social services that affect women in very particular ways.

In the case of activity rates in the three countries, both older men and women (55 and over) have experienced very large drops in their likelihood of becoming employed again. The shutdown and restructuring of firms, the shedding of government jobs and the impossibility of looking for work in other regions means that a large proportion of older people leave the labour market for good. This has had different effects on men and women. Men in this age group have reportedly become sick (alcoholism or heart disease has affected many of these men) and higher than usual death rates have been reported (UNICEF, 1999).

Older women, on the other hand, have also struggled to live on benefits, in the cases where these exist, as they wait to reach pension age and, according to the opinions gathered in the report, demand that the government continue to look after them as they do not think that they are re-trainable for the new types of jobs that are being offered (this could, in principle, be described as the discouraged worker effect, but more in-depth analysis would have to be made).[3] Few of these older women, according to the information gathered in the reports, took on self-employment or were willing to re-train for new jobs. Again, the very large drops in activity rates of these age groups is testimony to this.[4] This is one of the differences among women that will be explained in more depth in the corresponding section below. Although the reports did not focus attention on this type of analysis, UNIFEM's present and future work in the region is being geared towards taking up this type of analysis and unveiling the facts behind the numbers in order to support advocates with strong evidence based advocacy.

As for younger generations, women face different pressures that explain their absence from the labour force. One of these relates to changes in attitudes towards the obligations of women in society (gender roles). Others have to do with younger women gaining higher educational levels which reduce their economic activity during their attendance at school (this has also happened in other similar EU countries) and the third and most worrisome from the point of view of gaining better future opportunities is their absence from the labour market during child-rearing (25–30) at the same time that child-bearing is being postponed and fewer children are being born.

Although this last phenomenon also has to do, in part, with changes in attitudes (to more conservative views about women's place in society), it is also linked to the drop or absence of child care facilities that could support women in going back to work after their maternity leave.[5] Other social services that look after dependent adults (the sick or elderly) also seem to be absent, but the ageing of society does not seem to be a significant issue according to the reports, although it is mentioned in some.

The financial difficulties that employers face in paying social security to cover maternity leave and higher absences from work of women who have small children is important in the context of changes in the labour market and the reduced role of the state. This will be discussed in the corresponding section below (social security) and is linked to the discrimination aspects that are discussed in the reports, which are discussed separately. In the context of EU accession and particularly in line with the European Employment Strategy, this issue is of particular importance.

Another important issue, which was not discussed in the development of the project, is the role of the informal market (except for a brief analysis in the case of the Kazakhstan report). This is important because it could have provided information on the way unemployment is accounted for (assuming that statistical office surveys are not designed to measure this) and on the strategies that women follow in order to survive and complement the family income in general, or their small wages, benefits or pensions.

With respect to the sectoral changes occurring from restructuring, privatisation and liberalisation processes, the restructuring of the industrial and agricultural sectors have been the most extensive; yet in most cases they still are a long way away from EU or OECD averages (in terms of gross domestic product share and employment), which are lower for agriculture and industry and higher for services. Although the reports give descriptive information on the sectoral distribution of women's employment, they do not make any detailed analysis of the changes that have occurred, although they do point to the growing numbers of women in the services sector.

Contrary to popular beliefs reproduced in some of the reports, women are concentrated in the higher and middle-level occupations (ranked by educational requirement), and not in lower occupations (European Commission, 2002). However, this does not mean that they are better paid or that within those higher categories they are not concentrated in the lower echelons. Some unskilled manual occupations in which men dominate the market may pay more due to labour market outcomes (demand and supply) or to specific government family and income policies (such as the 'male breadwinner model' which ensures that it is men who take home a high enough wage to support the family without the woman having to work or remaining a secondary or additional worker/income earner). In addition, although occupations are higher in terms of educational content, it may well also be that the conditions of work for those occupations are lower than those where men are concentrated (lack of unionisation, higher turnover, etc. may explain this). In this sense the possibility of 'social dumping' where women take up jobs with these worse conditions seems very likely as an explanation. In Bulgaria, for example, the report shows that jobs for women in new foreign-owned enterprises meant continuity in the labour market, but that the conditions were much worse than before and that women aged 40–45 had the greatest propensity to accept these lower quality jobs. In the case of Bulgaria lower wages, longer working hours and worse health and safety conditions at work seem to be the main aspects that reflect social dumping. In Hungary, as a result of the flexibilisation of the labour market, more women than men seem to take fixed-term contracts as well as a stronger occupational segregation into lower paid positions.

It is important to keep in mind that most of the employment gains in the last ten years for women in the EU has been in the service sector and it is expected that this will be repeated in EU accession countries. However, it is also a fact that some of these jobs are badly paid, do not require high levels of education and that employment conditions are worsening in terms of contract length, hours and benefits. The challenge is to capitalise women's higher levels of education so that unemployment, underemployment or inactivity do not hinder economic growth and that policies take into account women's and men's different roles which create inequalities but that can be changed in part by public policy.

Issues of education and training

Educational levels and choices were discussed in detail in the reports as this was also used as a characteristic to distinguish between different groups of women interviewed in the focus groups or to classify answers in the surveys that were undertaken. The three main trends that appeared were:

1. The educational choices made by young women might be putting them at a disadvantage compared to their male counterparts (e.g. humanities vs. engineering or business).
2. Higher average educational profiles of women are not reducing differences in pay or significantly improving labour market outcomes (this is not immediately translating into higher activity and employment on one hand and lower unemployment on the other).
3. Updating and introducing new skills as the new economy (knowledge and ICT) begins to introduce itself in all of the economic activities of the countries are only benefiting younger women (there seems to be no real strategy to apply active employment policies to older women).[6]

These findings, again, are not different from those that have been found in Western Europe and that have been at the centre of efforts by the European Employment Strategy. In addition to the formal side of higher education, there is a number of skills that were mentioned in all the reports which become much more important factors in obtaining and keeping a job, namely computer, communication and foreign language skills. Thus, equal access to obtaining these skills should be high on the advocacy agenda for all women, as currently only younger women seem to be benefiting from them (see below). While in the socialist era the CEE and CIS region was known for having less occupational segregation (more women working in 'masculine' jobs) there is evidence that occupation segregation is on the increase and the number of women in jobs which require a much more specialised knowledge (engineering, medical occupations, computer science, etc.) is declining. The problem arises when through self-selection or social pressures women choose studies that do not have a large demand.[7]

In spite of the higher average educational profiles of women, one observes that in these countries there are differences in pay and opportunities. This is something that is also happening in most of the EU and OECD countries (European Commission, 2001). Again, the gender roles with regard to the care of children and dependent adults as well as, in some cases, the lack of social services that support women in covering these needs do influence these outcomes, but gender pay gaps and occupational segregation, which is also behind this, are not discussed in detail in the reports.

Again, the reports did not offer a more detailed discussion of low paid occupations for women (what and where those are) and the role of the informal market. This is certainly more linked to the direct changes that globalisation is having in the region and the possible loss of human capital as women are more willing to take on lower paid jobs and lower educational level jobs (this underemployment also seems to be affecting men) which is only briefly mentioned in the reports.

Although it has already been pointed out that in the new economy skills are being highly valued, especially by transnational firms, in all the countries the qualitative evidence showed that it was younger women who were acquiring and benefiting from these skills as their expectation was to work for these foreign firms. A sense of economic security and the social and economic value of their work was detected in all countries for these younger women.

The wide differences in views and opportunities from older generations that this situation creates are discussed below. Furthermore, older women (and the not so old) who are facing difficulties in obtaining new training also face difficulties in accessing economic activity in general, and thus are put at a double disadvantage (triple, if you add their age). Firms can also be negatively affected by this situation, as the stream of younger people decreases as a result of migration or decreased fertility rates, or due to the fact young women with children who have the skills are not given the opportunity to return to work quickly through appropriate support services.

The complexity of preparing the workforce with the appropriate skills as part of education and labour market policy must be designed to reduce these inequalities, and raises once again the challenges of mainstreaming gender when two different ministries or departments are involved in the design and execution of policy.

Issues of social security and social services

In all the reports three issues with respect to social security or social services were observed:

1. High levels of contribution to social security or benefits by employers worsens the incentive to hire women if unaccompanied by other measures, such as extending paternity leave and making men more active in caring activities.
2. Changes in the provision of social services are influencing the economic activity of women.
3. Low wages mean low pensions (particularly for less educated and older women).

All the reports mention that tax benefit systems must be changed in order to reduce the negative attitude that employers have to employing women at different stages of their life-cycle. This is an important point that the studies have picked up and that is also linked to issues that are currently being explored under gender-sensitive budgeting such as the influence of taxation and of benefit systems on women's labour supply. A recent European Parliament study also points to the importance of changing these systems in order to increase women's participation and permanence in the labour market (Paoli and Parent-Thirion, 2004).

Policies that affect taxation and benefits that give incentives for the employment of women are being used in EU countries. In Spain, for example, where activity rates are still far below EU averages, studies have shown that women are encountering many more difficulties in finding and keeping jobs than men. Also, changes in the labour codes that allow men to respond to family needs and emergencies are being introduced in an effort to make the reconciliation of work and family life gender balanced.[8]

On the other hand, the fall in the provision of universal child care and care for dependent adults in these countries is also mentioned as one of the significant obstacles for women who wish to return to work after child-bearing and probably for those who have to look after dependent adults (again, this was not mentioned much in the reports but, given the demographic position of women, they may need to consider this. However, it might be true that it is not such a problem in these countries as it is in EU countries).

Three distinct reasons (interrelated to some degree) for the fall in child care services can be mentioned:

1. The drop in demand given the drop in activity rates of women (who now stay home to look after the children, independently of the reason).
2. The decline in the fertility rate.
3. The reduction in government budgets that has forced the shutdown of these services.

Given that these very different elements are at work, very precise studies need to be carried out that will inform government about the scope of the policies that need to be undertaken on all fronts. However, from the reports it is possible to say that there is enough evidence showing that a given proportion of women will return to work if given the appropriate support in training and in child care facilities.

Finally, the issue of pensions has been mentioned in all three reports as changes in all countries have affected the duration and level of pensions that are being received. In some cases the statutory pension age has been raised so that men and women have to wait longer to receive this income and in other cases the rules have changed so that the amounts received are far lower than the minimum living wage. This is a hotly debated issue from the point of view of gender equality and gender mainstreaming by women's NGOs in Bulgaria and Hungary. Where the pension age has been lowered, it is argued that changes have been introduced without acknowledging the advantages enjoyed by women under the previous pension regime. According to a recent ILO study:

the difficulties with this change will probably fall most heavily on those women who, closest to retirement, planned to retire under the old rules but find themselves nearing retirement under the new ones.... With the elimination of redistribution toward workers with low lifetime contributions, most women who exercise the option to retire early will receive substantially lower benefits than they would have before the reforms. (Fultz, Ruck and Steinhilber, 2003: 34)

This affects women in particular ways as women's life expectancy is longer and the prospects of living on these small pensions point to a high incidence of poverty (as has been shown in several studies in the region; UNICEF, 1999 and 2001; Pierella, 2002). In addition, the raising of the pension age puts pressure on both men and women to continue to be active in the labour force with great disadvantage to them. However, judging by the figures, there is a massive reduction of those over 55 in the labour force as they show low employment and activity rates and, in most cases, lower unemployment rates[9] than the rest of the population. So, the question must be, given their very small pensions or total lack of income, where and how are these people managing to survive? This is something that the reports leave unanswered to a large degree, although they do point out that this group is more likely to fall into poverty, as most of the institutional research has also shown (see Pierella, 2002; Pollert and Fodor, 2003).

One can think of informal markets as a refuge for women to carry out economic activities, but this is something that needs to be investigated further. In the case of rural women in Kazakhstan it seems that their work in family activities has been their retreat. Their work would have to be considered as unpaid, but it seems that they are in fact being counted in statistics as inactive. In any case Kazakhstan was the only country report where some of this analysis was made.

Discrimination

In the case of discrimination the main trend mentioned in the reports was age discrimination for both men and women, which is also accompanied by sex discrimination.

As was discussed above, young women have problems because employers view them as possible future mothers for whom they will have to pay certain social security contributions. In the case of both men and women lack of experience can also be given as an explanation for difficulties in entering the labour market for the first time. On the other hand, given the demand on newer skills, older men and women are being discriminated against perhaps more for their lack of skills than for their age *per se*.

Also, there seem to be large differences in the way discrimination is perceived depending on the sector of activity. There are no clear reasons why this is so, but it could be linked to the overall management and integration into a more competitive environment. It seems that larger transnational firms engage less in discriminatory behaviour and that it is more marked in smaller national firms (except perhaps the banking sector). However, the other side of the issue is that transnational firms are increasingly outsourcing to the case study countries as they can pay lower wages and maintain lower conditions than in their parent countries. This seems to be particularly true of textile-related activities, but also of other types of goods and services.

Although ethnicity is certainly one of the recognised additional causes of discrimination against women, the reports did not deal with this in depth. However, in the Bulgarian report we find the following excerpt from one of the in-depth interviews with a 55-year-old Labour office expert, in Sofia:

> The integration of Roma people is also part of the globalisation process. This is important for Bulgaria. However, a lot of attention has been paid to this issue: far too many programmes have been worked out, too much energy has been put forth. This could create an independent problem as the Roma people are artificially set apart from other ethnic groups. If half the people in one municipality are unemployed and money is allotted only for the Romany people, this inevitably causes and maintains tension. (WAD, 2003: 12)

Another important point that was mentioned with respect to discrimination in all reports was the lack of an explicit law covering this issue or, alternatively, that laws were in place but that proper mechanisms were not in order to make them effective. The case of a 35-year-old woman from Sofia illustrates this very well:

> It is a big problem for a woman when they ask her if she is married or if she has a child. Some years ago, I went to the store 'Detmag' and was interviewed by 'Byrzakov' (name of prospective employer) and he asked me about my experience. . . . Then he asked me if I'm married and if I have a child. It turned out that you should not

have a child if you want to work at that store. That is discrimination and this is at a store where goods for children are sold. (WAD, 2003: 3)

In the case of Bulgaria and Hungary, it can be expected that as they join the EU, the institutional side will be strengthened; however, there might be a need for greater public awareness of and debate on these issues, as it is clear from the analysis in these reports that discrimination links to many other issues that put women in a disadvantageous position with respect to men. But it is also clear that in some cases men and women are suffering from the same type of discrimination. Here the use of the Convention on the Elimination of all Forms of Discrimination Against Women (CEDAW) as an advocacy tool will be central both when submitting country reports and in terms of raising awareness of the population at large, given that that all three countries have signed the convention.

Changes in attitudes

Changes in attitudes about the role of women and changes in attitudes by women themselves is perhaps the most fascinating and interesting trend picked up in the reports on all three countries.[10] These changes are having a direct impact on labour market outcomes, and although much has been written about it, the wider economic implications would have to be further exposed by women's NGOs. Given the importance of gender mainstreaming as a tool to bring about increased equality, these attitudinal changes, which also affect political will in terms of the commitment to gender equality and the protection of women's rights, are of paramount importance.

These changes also explain some of the differences that have been observed between the situations of different groups of women. Here, the main trends that can be attributed these attitudinal changes are:

- Drops in fertility rates which will have serious effects on the future of the labour market accompanied by high expected or effective migration of the younger population.
- Transition from a static society to greater participation and higher awareness of rights and obligations of citizens and the state which have direct impact on claiming all kinds of rights, and in particular labour rights.

Before discussing fertility rates[11] as they affect future and present labour market outcomes, there is a special link to be made to the preceding sections. Changes in attitudes may well be affecting the drops in activity rates for the younger age groups of women as they 'freely' decide that their place is at home with small children or, as in the case of Kazakhstan women, decide that their place as housewives greatly increases the chances of family survival.

However, another attitudinal change is also at work among young women which activity rates lower as higher education is sought (20–24 years of age) and later raises it as the fact that having children for these women reduces the chances of career development and obtaining returns from education.

Therefore, lower fertility rates can be explained by the postponement of marriage in search of career opportunities, and capitalising on educational investments. However, lack of economic opportunities (higher instability in the labour market) and low incomes can also play against the fertility rate and women refusing to have children unless they are assured that the children can be properly looked after. This is what seems to have happened in Spain and other Mediterranean countries, for example (Adsera, 2002; Engelhardt and Prskawetz, 2002). From the reports it is obvious that these differences and the way they play out also arise from disparities in income and education and that location plays a strong role as well, with rural areas being more conservative than urban ones. To give one example, the WAD report points out that the analysis of the study survey and other surveys shows that while men have become more conservative than women (WAD, 2003: 5), in Bulgaria there is still wide acceptance of working women; in Kazakhstan, however, women themselves accept more traditional roles, especially those living in rural areas (ABWK: 2003: 16).

Although the reports mention that conservative governments and the new-found influence of various religious institutions are seeking to change attitudes towards the role of women, there are strong economic incentives at work to make young women disregard this. Education is a very strong tool to overcome this type of thinking and economic reasoning is an even stronger one. The evidence about the contribution of human capital and higher economic activity of the population to higher economic growth goes beyond feminist economics and makes good economic common sense. Making sure that all women and men can enter education on an equal footing is another issue that is equally important in obtaining better economic results.

On the one hand, the changes in political attitude that also affect labour market outcomes are reflected in the answers given in the surveys and in the focus groups. It is not surprising that, given the very bad situation in which older workers, both men and women, ended up during these transition years, they are being considered 'the old guard' who yearn for the return of communism; a different strategy of income support and continuation as productive workers would have most likely reshaped this attitude. On the other hand, educated younger men and women do not see a lot of problems in gaining access to the labour market and in having good prospects for the future. Political discourses that advocate protection of what they have achieved will surely attract them as voters.

In addition, the reports show that there is a general lack of knowledge about rights and this is where more work needs to be done in order to strengthen the positive changes that have come about with transition, including the ability of citizens to take their issues collectively to government. Labour market rights that are protected by recent changes in the law (or labour codes) and changes that still need to be made should be widely known and used by citizens (particularly those that protect equal opportunities and outlaw discrimination on the basis of age or sex).

Increasing differences amongst women

Although throughout the reports some differences among women have already been pointed out, they can be summarised in the following three trends:

1. A big difference in attitudes towards economic activity and economic independence between urban and rural women.
2. Different levels of economic security depending on the type of firm and sector that the women can find employment in.
3. Differences by age, especially in terms of the attitudes towards the labour market.

These differences are tied to a certain degree to the changes in attitudinal differences discussed above, but it is important to point out that the lack of economic opportunities will increase or decrease these differences. Also, these differences are influencing the labour market outcomes that have been discussed throughout this chapter.

In all the reports there was reference to different opinions about globalisation and even to EU entry depending on education, employment activity and income and also on the region of residence of the women.

Looking more closely at these differences one can see that there is a possibility of fracture among women as some retreat into more conservative attitudes given their poor chances of having economic independence and a career, and others choose to achieve higher educational levels, postpone child-bearing and marriage, and become 'winners' of globalisation. It is clear that a strategy to bring together common causes is central to obtaining better economic outcomes for all women.

EU accession expectations

In the case of Hungary and Bulgaria, expectations about entering the EU as full member states were also explored. Although Kazakhstan is excluded in principle from this process, one must keep in mind that it is an OECD country and that it has signed bilateral agreements with its neighbours on trade.[12]

The questions about joining the EU in the survey and the focus groups revealed a positive opinion. Having said that, in both the Hungarian and Bulgarian reports, 'globalisation' was not a term about which the population concurred when compared by age and educational level. Again, those that have the most to lose have the worst opinions about this process, while those who have not been affected or are likely to have gained seem to have a better opinion. Also, attitudes to migration and immigration reveal that younger people see EU accession as an opportunity to expand their job experiences, while most of the population do not welcome the idea of foreigners coming entering the country for work.

It is also important to underline that in the surveys the views of both men and women (but especially men) coincided in that women's rights in general would be better served by entry into the EU. The surveys did a good job in capturing some of the most relevant qualitative aspects in terms of expectations and opinions about how the most recent changes have altered the environment in which women now have to access employment (as employees or on their own).

Conclusions

The trends identified in this initiative have a direct link to the type of work that UNIFEM is carrying out in the region. From improving the knowledge about women's economic situation to advocating specific changes in polices, the reports seem to have achieved a great deal in addition to building up the knowledge of women's NGOs themselves. Also, use of the results as an advocacy tool by the NGOs and the contribution to advancing research of women's situations in the region cannot be ignored.

Recognising that the initiative was limited in the depth of scientific research and tools it applied, the importance for UNIFEM has been that it allowed gender equality advocates to work with experts and gradually gain confidence in delving into the complex financial economic issues and analysing their impact on the daily lives of women. The focus of attention has invariably drifted to the local, national and regional levels and focused less on the linkages with the global macroeconomic frameworks, trade agendas and financial architecture. Organisations such as Women in Development in Europe (WIDE), which have taken the lead in advocating women's rights in the context of globalisation, have recently strengthened their partnership with women's organisations in CEE and the CIS to work on gender and economic issues. Such partnerships should contribute to increased advocacy and action that ties the local to the global.

UNIFEM's work in other regions in bringing together women across social classes or generations can also be adapted and used here in order to articulate common causes, as differences among women seem to exist across all three countries and most likely the entire region.

Notes

1. http://www.unece.org/stats/gender/web/.
2. This is understood as being unemployed (available for work and actively seeking work) for one year or more.
3. The 'discouraged worker effect' is a well-established theory whereby looking for work has such a low expected payoff that the unemployed decide that spending time at home is more productive than spending time in job searches. This is also known as hidden unemployment. On the other hand, long spells of unemployment can cause demoralisation of the workers and stigmatisation from employers (they do not want to hire a person that has been unemployed a long time, interpreting this as a signal that they are 'bad' workers) (Ehrenberg and Smith, 1991; Layard, et al., 1991).
4. By 2000 the activity rate for women aged 55–64 in Hungary was 13.5 per cent and in Bulgaria almost 12 per cent; however, more recently the activity rate for this age group seems to be rising steadily but in both countries remains under 25 per cent in 2002.

5. Although in some of the reports the concluding demand is access to free child care, one must be careful to take into account the tight budgets that most governments now work under and focus advocacy on attaining free child care for those who cannot afford it and who need it the most. One can easily prove to governments that the investment in these facilities partly pay themselves as the employees of these services will also pay taxes and social security contributions. It is also possible to use economic growth and development arguments such as the fact that, according to academic studies 100 women in the labour force will create 15 jobs in the service sector (Esping-Andersen, 1999).

6. Active policies in employment are in counterbalance to passive policies which only include the handing out of benefits. Active policies include orientation services, training and follow-up that lead to increasing employability of those who have been unemployed for a long time and find more difficulties in keeping a job. It is important that these policies keep a gender focus and take into account time use of women who may not be able to attend training and other basic appointments if no alternative care services (for children and dependant adults) are offered.

7. These choices are also highly influenced by the expectations that young women have when making these choices. If the goal is to enter public sector employment because of the more flexible hours and benefits they might make educational choices that limit their opportunities later. Expectations of marriage and child-bearing and rearing are also important.

8. Entry into the EU has obliged these countries to introduce a number of directives, in our case those that deal with the reconciliation of work and family life are Council Directive 92/85/EEC and 96/34/EC. However, these laws remain to be fully developed and implemented in the new member states, there is currently very little documented case law around these transposed directives.

9. See first paragraph in General Changes in the Labour Market section above for activity rates. According to Eurostat figures for both countries, the employment and activity rate are practically the same in Hungary, which means that unemployment for this age group is very low. On the other hand, the differences in Bulgaria are larger, which means that unemployment will have a greater impact. Unfortunately, no information on unemployment rates by age is given.

10. Activities under the UNIFEM projects included a survey that illustrated a trend towards a more conservative view of women's role in society (women should be at home with children, should be married, etc). The survey undertaken by the UNIFEM partners was complemented, in the case of Bulgaria by the International Social Survey Programme surveys, which confirms these trends. See http://www.gesis.org/en/data_service/issp/data/2002_Family_III.htm.

11. According to Eurostat, for Hungary the fertility rate dropped from 1.78 to 1.30 between 1992 and 2003. In the case of Bulgaria, it dropped from 1.54 to 1.23 in the same period (Eurostat, 2004).

12. The Agreement On Free Trade between Government of the Kyrgyz Republic and the Government of the Republic of Kazakhstan going back to 1994 is just one example.

References

ABWK (2003) 'Women's economic opportunities and capacities in Kazakhstan', study report on UNIFEM Project No. RER/98/W02/B.

Adsera, A (2002) *Changing Fertility Rates in Developed Countries: The Impact of Labor Market Institutions*, available at: http://www.src.uchicago.edu/prc/pdfs/adsera02.pdf [accessed on 27 May 2005].

Almenara Estudios Económicos y Sociales, S. L. (2004) *Social Security Systems in the EU and Their Impact on Reconciliation of Work and Family Life*, European Parliament, Committee on Women's Rights and Gender Equality.

Ehrenberg, R. G. and Smith, R. S. (1991) *Modern Labour Economics, Theory and Public Policy*, London: HarperCollins.

Engelhardt, H. and Prskawetz, A. (2002) *On the Changing Correlations between Fertility and Female Employment over Space and Time*, available at: http://www.demogr.mpg.de/papers/working/wp-2002-052.pdf [accessed 27 May 2005].

European Commission (2002) *Employment in Europe*, Brussels: General Directorate for Employment and Social Affairs.

European Commission (2001) 'Equal pay', *Gender Equality Magazine*, Directorate General for Employment and Social Affairs, 11.

Paoli, P. and Parent-Thirion, A. (2003) *Working Conditions in the Acceding and Candidate Countries*, available at: http://www.eurofound.eu.int/publications/files/EF0306EN.pdf [accessed 27 May 2005].

Eurostat (2004) *Total Fertility Rate*, available at: http://epp.eurostat.cec.eu.int/portal/page?_pageid=1996,39140985&_dad=portal&_schema=PORTAL&screen=detailref&language=en&product=Yearlies_new_population&root=Yearlies_ new_population/C/C1/C12/cab12048 [accessed 20 May 2005].

Fultz, E., Ruck, M. and Steinhilber, S. (eds) (2003) *The Gender Dimensions of Social Security Reform in Central and Eastern Europe: Case Studies of the Czech Republic, Hungary and Poland*, Budapest: ILO.

Layard, R, Nickell, S. and Jackman, R. (1991) *Unemployment, Macroeconomic Performance and the Labour Market*, Oxford: Oxford University Press.

Open Society Institute (2002) *Bending the Bow: Targeting Women's Human Rights and Opportunities*, available at: http://www.soros.org/initiatives/women/articles_publications/publications/bendingbow_20020801/bending_the_bow.pdf [accessed 27 May 2005].

Paoli, P. and Parent-Thirion, A. (2003) *Working Conditions in the Acceding and Candidate Countries*, European Foundation for the Improvement of Living and Working Conditions. Available at: http://www.eurofound.eu.int/publications/EF0306.htm [Accessed 8 December 2006].

Pierella, P. (2002) *Gender in Transition*. Available at: http://europa.eu.int/comm/employment_social/employment_analysis/gender/gend_in_trans.pdf [Accessed 6 December 2005].

Pollert, A. and Fodor, E. (2005) *Working Conditions and Gender in an Enlarged Europe*, available at: http://www.eurofound.eu.int/publications/EF04138.htm [accessed 27 May 2005].

Social Innovation foundation (2003) 'Women's Economic Opportunities and Capacities in Hungary', Study Report on UNIFEM Project No.RER/98/W02/B.

UNICEF (1999) 'Women in Transition', *The MONEE Project: Regional Monitoring Report*, 6: 77–92.

UNICEF (2001) *A Decade of Transition*, available at: http://www.unicef-icdc.org/
cgi-bin/unicef/main.sql?menu=/publications/menu.html&testo=Lunga.sql?
ProductID=313 [accessed on 27 May 2005].

WAD (2003) 'Women's economic opportunities and capacities in Bulgaria',
Study Report on UNIFEM Project No.RER/98/W02/B.

Paci, P. (2002) *Gender in Transition*, available at: http://66.102.9.104/
search?q=cache:XBEuB6oZg0QJ:lnweb18.worldbank.org/ECA/eca.nsf/0/
F55E7337BA69423985256BFA0053F091%3FOpenDocument+Gender+in+
Transition+Pierella+Paci.&hl=en [accessed on 27 May 2005].

11
Current Approaches to Gender Equality in European Social Policies

Theodora Hiou Maniatopulou and Maria Katsiyianni Papakonstantinou

Introduction

This chapter is an attempt to illustrate the nature and implementation of European social policy in general, and its consequences on women and gender equality specifically. Since the early stages of the formation of the European Union (EU), it was very clear that social policy matters would remain within the specific remit of national states, while the EU would mainly focus on specific aspects of the field. As a result, the relation between gender equality, a principle increasingly protected by EU legislation, and matters of social security became of growing interest; it is the focus of this chapter.

The first section of this chapter explores the process of establishment of the principle of gender equality and equal treatment between men and women, especially since the EU enlargement of May 2004, which brought within the EU borders ten new member states. It presents and explains the various legal instruments in place today for the promotion and protection of gender equality and other women's rights in the EU.

The second section focuses on European social policy and more specifically on the rationale and conditions for a European system of social security, especially for women. It offers a thorough exposé of the various relevant legal documents and offers an analysis of the consequences of the present regime on the situation of women in the EU. It considers the balance between member states' competence and EU obligations with reference to the various elements of social security today.

The chapter concludes that the European system of social protection remains closely related to states' national legislation and we are witnesses of a strong *acquis national* in the field of social protection, in which the European Community's intervention is justified only to cover potential vacuums.

Strengthening gender equality in the enlarged EU

Facing the challenges of its fifth enlargement since its creation, the EU must implement equal opportunities legislation. Great expectations are attached to the enlargement policy and the consequences of the EU enlargement have been analysed from many points of view. While difficulties arose during the enlargement negotiations about the concept of gender equality, it was finally integrated into the corpus of the *aquis communautaire* (13th Chapter) at the end of the enlargement process.

Women's organisations across Eastern and Western Europe have expressed expectations and demands during the enlargement process from a women's rights perspective (Hantrais, 2000). Some of the most interesting proposals are described by Steinhilber (2002):

1. Fulfilling the commitment to gender mainstreaming.
2. Reassessing economic policy from a gender perspective.
3. Ensuring gender equality on the new labour markets in transition.
4. Promoting the implementation and enforcement of equal opportunity legislation in general.
5. Transforming the enlarged EU into a global actor for women's rights and gender equality.

In the enlarged EU, the gender equality principle has been strengthened by horizontal actions of gender mainstreaming, which inform the EU policies (Lisbon Strategy).

Gender equality and enlargement

EU institutions have repeatedly committed themselves to incorporating equal treatment of women and men in all EU policies and activities. The constitutions of the Central and Eastern Europe (CEE) candidate countries guarantee the equality of all citizens and the principle of non-discrimination. Likewise, EU members, as well as candidate countries, have subscribed to the core international agreements on women's rights and gender mainstreaming, such as the Convention on the Elimination of all Forms of Discrimination Against Women (CEDAW) and the Beijing Platform for Action and its follow-up documents. These national and international commitments form the broad legal framework for gender equality policies (European Commission, 2003).

The EU has formulated three basic criteria for EU enlargement (European Commission, 2003); these are political, economic and social. Progress towards fulfilment of these criteria is monitored by the European Commission, which publishes its assessments in annual Progress Reports. The first wave of enlargement negotiations, which formally opened in March 1998, looked into candidate countries' compliance with the *acquis communautaire*,[1] chapter by chapter, of which there are 31. Chapter 13 refers to 'Employment and Social Policy' and covers areas where there are substantial secondary sources of legal obligations at the EU level, such as health and safety issues, labour law, areas such as social dialogue, employment and social protection (convergent policies are being developed based on the Amsterdam Treaty) and equality of treatment between women and men. In these areas there are no specific legal obligations to implement precise policy measures but rather the political will of the member states to co-ordinate the respective policies in order to develop a homogeneous social framework in line with the principles and rules of the Amsterdam Treaty. The latest assessment of each candidate country's compliance with the *acquis communautaire* under this chapter heading can be found in the 2003 Regular Reports and in the Comprehensive Monitoring Reports (European Commission, 2003).

The present legal regime

Equality between women and men in the EU

European law has greatly contributed to promoting gender equality within member states, theoretically and in practice (Arribas and Carrasco, 2003). Starting with incorporating into the Treaty Establishing the European Community (EEC, 1957) the principle of equal pay for male and female workers for equal work, the European Community has, since 1975 and the EEC Treaty, concentrated its efforts mainly on ensuring gender equality in employment. The Maastricht Treaty also strengthened gender equality provisions. The Social Protocol attached to the Treaty of the European Community provides that the EU supports and complements national actions in the field of equal opportunities in the labour market. The Amsterdam Treaty constituted an important breakthrough in the concept of gender issues at Community level. So far gender equality has been limited to employment and consequently to a principle of social policy. Under the Amsterdam Treaty, gender equality is both a 'task' (Article 2 TEC) and an 'activity' (Article 3 TEC) of the EU. For the first time in the history of European treaties, article 3(2) introduced gender mainstreaming as an integral part of all policies, programmes, practices and decision–making, according to the Lisbon Strategy.

Another important contribution of the Amsterdam Treaty was a new article – article 13 TEC[2] – which established that the Council of Europe, acting unanimously and after consulting with the European Parliament, can adopt actions to combat all forms of discrimination based on sex, race or ethnic origin, religion or belief, disability, age or sexual orientation. This article is of crucial importance as it covers discrimination beyond the labour market. There have been two Directives based on article 13 so far: the Race Directive (Council Directive 2000/43/EC of 29 June 2000) and the Council Directive establishing a framework for equal treatment in employment and occupation (Council Directive 2000/78/EC of 27 November 2000). The legal content of these two Directives has greatly influenced the amendment to the existing Equal Treatment Directive. In fact, the New Equal Treatment Directive was amended in 2002 in order to respond to developments in the field of gender equality and to the case law of the European Court of Justice. The Directives that have been adopted under article 13 have contributed mainly to the definition of direct and indirect discrimination, which was not established before then. Another initiative of the two article 13 Directives is that it addresses the issues of moral and sexual harassment in the workplace, which constitutes discrimination on the grounds of sex.

Directive 2000/43/EC on the implementation of equal treatment between persons irrespective of racial or ethnic origin and imposing sanctions (by awarding compensations to the victims) complements the regime already established. Furthermore a six-year Community Action Programme (Council Decision 2000/750/EC, of 27 November 2000) on combating discrimination has been adopted by the Council for the period 2001–6. Overall, article 141(2) of the Amsterdam Treaty has entrusted the EU with a central role in combating discrimination, eliminating inequalities and establishing equality between women and men at work.

Gender mainstreaming in the EU

Under the Treaty of Amsterdam, gender mainstreaming became part of European law and, at the same time, binding on all its institutions (art. 3(2) TEC). The EU started adopting new strategies towards better implementation of equal treatment legislation in specific fields in close cooperation with member states. Gender mainstreaming is integrated in almost all EU policies, such as the European Employment Strategy, the Social Inclusion Process, Research Policy, Internal Market, Structural

Funds and Development Cooperation Policy, Energy, Environment and Sustainable Development Policy.

The European Parliament has also been very active in the promotion of gender equality in general and gender mainstreaming in particular. A Committee on Women's Rights and Equal Opportunities was established in 1984, and in February 2003 approved a Report on Gender Mainstreaming (European Commission, Decision 82/43 of 9 December 1981). This Report dealt with mainstreaming at the political and administrative level and made recommendations on concrete actions, e.g. the balanced participation of women in decision-making, working arrangements and reconciliation of family life.

The gender dimension of the EU is reinforced by the 'EU Community Framework Strategy on Gender Equality (2001–2005)' (European Commission, COM (2000)335 Final). The Framework Strategy considers gender as an integral part of economic, social and democratic development and specifies that gender must be mainstreamed across the Community's activities, within and outside the EU. The Framework Strategy involves policy analysis and planning, data collection broken down by sex, and training and awareness-raising of key actors. Finally, gender mainstreaming is incorporated in the European Constitution and thus was given crucial recognition in defining and implementing policies and activities, as outlined in Part III of the Constitution. Indeed, gender mainstreaming will be extended to cover the actions of Foreign and Security Policy, as well as Justice and Home Affairs.

The constitutional aspects of gender equality

While there have been intense debates on what the European Constitution has to offer women, one can say that it strengthens gender equality (European Women's Lobby, 2004). It retains all the existing provisions on equality between women and men, and provides the following:

- Equality as one of the Union's objectives (art. I-3).
- Gender mainstreaming clause (art. III-116).
- A legal basis for combating discrimination against gender, race or ethnic origin, religion or believes, disability, age or sexual orientation (art. III-118).
- The principle of equal pay for female and male workers (art. III-214).

The European Constitution also provides important improvements. In article I-2 equality between women and men is included in the core 'values' of the EU. The Charter of Fundamental Rights is incorporated in the Constitution and is legally binding at the European level. Further-more under article I-9, the EU shall accede to the European Convention for the Protection of Human Rights and Fundamental Freedoms. Article II-83 states that gender equality must be ensured in all areas, including occupation, employment and pay.

In Part III of the European Constitution, article III-116 provides for gender mainstreaming, which applies to all policies, as outlined in Part III. Article III-118 introduces a new provision of general application (with horizontal effects on all EU policies) to combat discrimination based on grounds other than nationality. Article III-124(2) establishes basic principles for incentive measures to support members' action in the field of non-discrimination. Article III-267(2-d) provides measures for combating trafficking in persons, in particular women and children. Article III-271(1) establishes a general legal framework, which determines minimum rules concerning the definition on criminal offences and sanctions in the field of trafficking in human beings and sexual exploitation of women and children (Declaration on Combating Domestic Violence, annexed to the Final Act of the International Governmental Conference, 2004).

The incorporation of all these new provisions is very important for upgrading the role of gender equality measures in the constitutional legal order of the EU, which is also accompanied by a strong legal status under article III-124. Finally Declaration 13, annexed to the Final Act of the Inter-Governmental Conference (IGC) which is related to the mainstreaming clause of article III-116, establishes the protection against gender discrimination, especially concerning domestic violence. The European Constitution, in conclusion, represents an opportunity for a new, strengthened system of promotion and protection of human rights at the European level. Accordingly, the European Constitution should be viewed as a positive step in the process of achieving full equality between women and men in European society.

Despite the gender pay gap that has prevailed in recent years and limited employment growth, the European Council (2004) estimated that positive trends towards closing gender gaps remain in some areas, such as education and employment in the EU 25. Thus, the Council, in considering 'that gender equality policies are instruments of social cohesion, as well as economic growth' (European Council, 2004: para. 29), decided to reinforce gender equality by adopting the following specific actions:

- Strengthening the position of women in the labour market.
- Increasing care facilities for children and other dependants.

- Addressing men in achieving gender equality.
- Integrating the gender perspective into immigration and integration policies.
- Monitoring developments towards gender equality (Beijing + 10).

Latest developments

The most important recent development has been the extension of the *acquis communautaire* on gender equality – which covers all rights and obligations deriving from the EU treaties and laws, soft law instruments, as well as the case law of the ECJ – beyond the field of employment. Directive 2004/113/EC, on the principle of equal treatment between women and men in access to and the supply of goods and services, also covers the principle of sex discrimination. The European Commission has also adopted 'a proposal of Directive on the clarification of the principle of equal treatment between men and women in matters of employment and occupation' by combining five existing Directives in a single text. Additionally, the Directive on the residency permit, which refers to Third Country nationals was adopted in April 2004.

A more recent development is the proposal by the European Commission to create the European Institute for Gender Equality, which represents an important step towards gender equality. The Institutes tasks will be:

- To develop further gender statistics and indicators in policy fields where such data are lacking.
- To pay specific attention to improving the provision of data on immigration and integration broken down by sex.
- To ensure the integration of a gender perspective in policy analyses inter alias by using data broken down by sex.

Finally, the European Council decided to invite member states to make efforts to integrate gender dimension into all policies (COM (2005) 44 Final). Specifically:

- To strengthen national machineries for gender equality.
- To ensure rapid implementation of the Directive on the principle of equal treatment for men and women in employment, vocational training and promotion, and working conditions.
- To continue co-operation with social partners.
- To increase women's labour market participation.
- To promote employment for immigrant women.

- To guarantee and respect the fundamental rights of immigrant women and to strengthening efforts to prevent and combat the specific violence to which women are victims.
- To examine pension systems carefully.
- To increase the care facilities for children and other dependants and reinforce strategies for reconciling work and home life.
- To use the full extent of resources available through the Structural Funds for the promotion of equality between women and men.
- To develop further the set of core indicators for monitoring progress towards equality between women and men, including the implementation of the Beijing Platform for Action.

After describing the development of existing gender strategies in the enlarged European Union, let us now look at the possibilities of a European system of social security. We will analyse the specific advantages and disadvantages for women in Europe of such a system.

Towards a common European system of social security?

The 50-year history of the European Community/Union in the field of social policy has been one of obstacles and difficulties. While one cannot talk of a coherent European social policy yet, some efforts have been made in this direction. European social policy is still fragmented and consists of the following:

- Equal opportunity and equal treatment between men and women in employment (article 141 of the consolidated version of the Treaty of European Community, TEC).
- Council Directive of 25 June 1991 measures to encourage improvements in the health of workers in fixed-term employment (Council Directives 91/383/ of the European Economic Community, EEC).
- The progressive implementation of the principle of equal treatment for men and women in matters of social security (Council Directive 79/7/EEC of 19 December 1978).
- The application of social security schemes to employed persons and their families moving within the Community (Regulations 1408/71/EEC of the Council of 14 June 1971 and 574/72).
- Framework Agreement on part-time work concluded by UNICE, CEEP and the ETUC (Council Directive 97/81/EC of 15 December 1997).

232 Theodora Hiou Maniatopulou and Maria Katsiyianni Papakonstantinou

The field of European social policy can be divided into two main categories: first, policies dealing with the enforcement and the development of social rights and employment, which constitute the *social acquis communautaire*; and second, policies relevant to unemployment in relation to physical or mental disability. The latter are implemented mainly through the granting of pensions and benefits, and are better known as the field of social security. The next section presents the nature and meaning of the European social policy with a gender approach deriving from equal treatment policies.

European social (security) policy before Maastricht

Social policies at the European level are based on article 136 of the consolidated version of the Treaty of European Community (TEC), (former article 117(1)), which states that the Community's competence is defined by article 136, para. 2 and limits the margin of action of the community by specifying that 'development will ensue not only from the functioning of the common market . . . but also from the procedures provided for in this Treaty and from the approximation of provisions laid down by law, regulation or administrative action'. This article shows that the Community's competence on social policy is concurrent under the principle of subsidiarity, which means that member states can object to the Community's initiatives when exercising these competences. This is true for the whole of the social policy agenda, and consequently, for social security matters too.

In fact, national laws and competences have prevailed in the field of social security until now. A key question for the development of European social policy is whether we should wait for enforcement mechanisms of the Common Market rules so that we can succeed in the convergence of the policy towards community-wide social security, or rather hope that the social-political circumstances will lead to the acceleration of Common Market procedures.

Reading articles 95, 96 and 136 TEC together makes the intervention of the Community in member states on social (security) matters possible in certain circumstances, but by no means obligatory. The provisions of these articles are to be examined in light of article 94 TEC, which gives power to the Council, after a proposal from the Commission, to issue unanimously 'directives for the approximation of such laws, regulations or administrative provisions of the member states as directly affect the establishment or functioning of the common market'. In this sense, the Community has been addressing labour law issues, but until now, has not done so for social security issues.

The adoption of the Single European Act in 1986 did not impact on the legal restrictions of articles 95, 96, 136 TEC. On the basis of adopting resolutions unanimously, article 94 TEC continues to regulate the legislative process in matters of concern for workers. Nevertheless the qualified majority of article 251 TEC can be used to harmonise national legislations on social security whenever there is a distortion of 'the conditions of competition in the common market' (articles 96 and 97 TEC).

The Community Charter of Fundamental Social Rights of Workers in 1989 brought new challenges for the social security system. The two main challenges were related to the provision of a minimum guaranteed income and the situation of migrants workers (Regulation 1251/70 and Directive 13/7/1980). The EC responded to these challenges by adopting a Draft Recommendation on the common criteria for social security; the criteria consisted of the existence of adequate resources for benefits and the convergence of the objectives of a social protection policy (Draft Recommendation 92/442). The Council subsequently adopted Council Recommendations 92/441 on common criteria concerning sufficient resources and social assistance in the social protection systems and 92/442 the convergence of social protection objectives and policies.

European social (security) policy after Maastricht

Following the adoption of the European Union Convention in Maastricht on 1 January 1993 and based on Common Market rules, the issue of harmonisation of social security measures became more urgent, especially in relation to the accession of ten new member states on 1 May 2004. Notwithstanding these difficulties, one can argue that a European model of social security has been developing, mainly through the adoption of two instruments:

- The Community Charter of Fundamental Social Rights of Workers, adopted in 1989; even though it is not legally binding, the text of this Charter contains provisions on social security issues at articles 10, 21, 25.
- The Charter for Fundamental Rights, adopted on 7 and 9 December 2000, in Nice, which contains several social rights provisions. Based on this Charter, Directive 91/383 on health and safety in the working environment was adopted and later completed by Directive 98/391.

The Treaty of Amsterdam came into force on 1 May 1999 and established the competence of the Community for the whole content of the social policy agenda. Under article 136(1), the Community and the 15 member states are subjected to the provisions of the European Social Charter, adopted by the member states of the Council of Europe on 18 October 1961 in Turin as well as to the Community Charter of Fundamental Social Rights for Workers mentioned above. Based on these provisions a *social acquis communautaire* came into being.

The combined reading of paragraphs 1 and 3 of article 136 TEC leads us to conclude that progress in social matters at the European level will result not only from the rules of the Common Market that will facilitate the harmonisation of social systems (as developed above), but also from the procedure that the Community has adopted, towards the convergence of legislative, normative and administrative provisions. Moreover, according to article 137 TEC, the Council can undertake unanimous decisions in the fields of social security and social protection of workers. Despite the establishment of the rules of competition in the Treaty of Amsterdam (articles 2, 3(g), 4, 81(1) TEC), this provision calls for a high level of social protection. In the Nice Treaty of 2000, the European Council emphasised the concept of 'equality' as a decisive element of 'competition'. Explicitly, it means that the notion and the content of the 'competition' of an economic model is not based only on the quantity of goods and services produced but also on their quality.

According to articles 143–145 TEC, the European Commission is entitled to submit an annual report to the Council accounting for the progress in the implementation of the objectives contained in the articles 136 TEC. This report should contain a special part on the present state of social security policy in the Community. The Commission submitted the Social Policy Agenda, later approved by the European Council in Nice, on 28 June 2000. The Social Policy Agenda is crucial because it deals with the updating of the European Social Model. The Social Policy Agenda provides for eleven activities to be undertaken by the European Institutions before 2005. We will focus, in this section, on the submission of proposals for the improvement of the social protection, which includes an emphasis on the pension status, central to systems of social security.

The European Parliament, in its process of approving the Commission's proposals for the Social Policy Agenda, recommended, among others, the inclusion of enforcement of action against social exclusion securing a decent standard of living by providing access to income, pension or to the lowest level of salary; and the improvement of social protection for posted workers.[3]

Other relevant European legal provisions

Several Council Directives are central to the field of European social security. They include:

- Council Directive 79/7 of 19 December 1978 on the progressive implementation of the principle of equal treatment between men and women in matters of social security.
- Council Directive 86/613 of 11 December 1986 on the application of the principle of equal treatment between men and women engaged in an activity, including agriculture, self-employment and in the protection of self-employed women during pregnancy and motherhood. This Directive also provides women who are not directly insured, when and wherever 'a contributory social security system for self-employed workers exists, in a Member State' (art. 6), to submit to a voluntary insurance system for them.
- Council Directive 92/85 of 19 October 1992 concerning the implementation of measures dedicated at improving the safety and health of pregnant workers, women workers who have recently given birth and women who are breastfeeding.
- Council Directive 94/33 of 22 June 1994 on the protection of young people at work.
- Council Directive 93/104 of 23 November 1993 concerning certain aspects of the organisation of working time.
- Council Directive 86/378, of 24 July 1986 on the implementation of the principle of equal treatment of men and women in occupational social security schemes.

The European Court of Justice's jurisprudence

The jurisprudence of the European Court of Justice (ECJ) has opened the door to adopting measures prohibiting the discrimination between men and women with regard to salary issues. According to the jurisprudence, benefits derived from the social security provisions are not always connected with the context of the working income.

1. In *Defrenne* v. *Sabena* (80/70), the ECJ stated that the granting of security benefits through pension schemes could not be considered as a salary from the employer as it is derived from national law. As a consequence, it is not subjected to the terms of article 141 TEC on equal treatment between sexes.

2. Other relevant decisions include the ECJ case *C. Razouk and
A. Begdoun* v. *European Communities* (ECJ, 75/82, 1984) together with
judgment ECJ 117/820 of 20 March 1984, in which under the principle of equality between male and female, the surviving member of
a couple is entitled to claim the pension of the deceased person. Likewise, parents or children are entitled to the pension of their deceased
child/parent irrespective of their gender.
3. The ECJ decision *Barber* v. *Guardian Royal Exchange Assurance Groups*
(IRLR 240 ECJ, 1009) is relevant to the issue of pension age in relation
with the principle of equal treatment.[4]

Main problems facing the European social security model today

The Social Policy Agenda reaffirms under Title IV (modernisation of
social protection), that 'the system of social protection stays in each
member state's competence'. The part on 'convergence of systems of
social protection' also emphasises the interdependence of the need to
increase the welfare state's commitments with the need to secure and
increase the competitiveness of enterprises, which opens the way to
new dilemmas. The first relates to the possibility of reducing employers'
social security contributions, which would result in a big increase to the
workers' financial burden. Moreover, such a reduction would have to be
compensated by an increase of the social security contribution from the
state. In the second case, economic compatibility would probably reduce
the development of social rights. At the national level, the economic
development of an individual also defines his/her ability to enjoy social
protection and rights (Tsatsos, 1988, p. 194). This is true at European
level as well.

The last phase of Economic and Monetary Union (EMU) has imposed
the obligation of reducing the deficit resulting from social policies.
At member states level, this theoretically means reducing social expenses,
which, pushed to the extremes, can be detrimental to the welfare state,
as protected by the EU. Indeed, there is a high level of interdependence between the level of national social protection and the economic
development of a given country, after taking into consideration the
high level of salaries. This is also shown by the fact that both lead
to greater social coherence and facilitate social changes. The Commission stresses, in two White Papers – 'On growth, competitiveness and
employment: the challenges and ways forward into the 21st century'
(White Paper COM(93) 700 final) and the 'European Social Policy –
a way towards the Union' (White Paper COM(94) 333 final) – the

importance of the financial burden linked to taxes and social security on the labour market. The only exception is the reduction of social expenses dedicated to encourage the employment of new persons. The European Council, which met in Lisbon on 23 and 24 March 2000 adopted measures in paragraph 31(b) aimed at maintaining the pension models (Presidency Conclusions, para. 31(b)) and at establishing a High Level Working Party on Social Protection, a body consisting of independent experts, responsible for examining national policy on social protection and for submitting annual reports. The European Council also asked this body to study the future of social protection policy and security systems in the European Union (Nikolakopoulou-Stephanou Iro, 2001). Its first report was published on 21 March 2000 and looked at the population size, economic and social changes that affect the national systems of social policy, the social expenditure of member states and the changes that took place during the 1990s. More precisely, the report emphasised changes in the social policy in order to:

- Encourage employment.
- Minimise the number of people that depend on the social benefits.
- Increase the number of the self-employed persons.

It also offered a comparative analysis of unemployment benefits and work income. These initiatives, combined with the adoption of a common European migration policy, mark the beginning of a social security review in member states. The link between social security systems and employment is obvious; it is estimated that social security systems could be secured until 2025 if employment rates increase by 1.26 per cent a year until 2020. In October 2000, the High Level Working Party on Social Protection (HLWPSP) introduced its study on the continuation and the perspectives of the social security systems of member states (HLWPSP, 2000).[5] It states that the social protection systems – the main component of the European Social Model – fall under each member state's competence and are confronted by modern challenges. It also says that these challenges will be overcome through modernisation, states' collaboration and assistance. The HLWPSP also suggested scheduling the following:

- The co-ordination of public dialogue on the sustainability of health-care systems, taking into consideration the ageing of the population.
- The scrutiny of trans-boundary access to quality products in hospital hygiene.[6]

Based on the Council Decision 2004/689/EC of October 2004, a Social Protection Committee (SPC) was established, repealing Decision 2000/436/EC (Official Journal, L.314 of 13 October 2004). The aim of this decision was to promote cooperation in social protection policies between member states and the European Commission. Among its main objectives, the SPC, a body with advisory status, has endorsed the following objectives:

• Making work pay and providing secure income.
• Guaranteeing pensions and making pension systems sustainable.

Through these various initiatives, we are witnessing the establishment of an institutionalised procedure to examine the national policies of social protection and security dedicated to reflecting the importance of the convergence of social protection objectives and policies, and to reaffirming the place of social protection among the common values of the European Union (EU).

A particular case: the status of migrant workers and the European social security system

The regime applying to migrant workers has become a crucial area of European social policy and indicates the point of convergence of social security systems in the EU. It is also closely related to the implementation of the principle of freedom of movement of workers within the EU territory and the abolition of obstacles deriving from national legislations. Therefore, the EU task of undertaking the initiatives required to implement the principles has translated into the adoption of a series of Regulations since 1971.

EC Regulations 1408/71 and 574/72

EC Council Regulation 1408/71, adopted on 14 June 1971 and Council Regulation 574/72 on the procedure for implementing Regulation 1408/71, adopted on 21 March 1972, relate to the application of social security schemes to migrant workers and their families within the EU territory. These Regulations are intended to coordinate the national social security system and to lay down the rules and principles which must be respected by all national institutions. Moreover, they aimed mainly at correcting those aspects of national legislation and administrative practice having discriminatory effects on European migrant workers and members of their family. The ultimate objective of these

Regulations was to remove the obstacles to the free movement of workers due to social benefits and family policy.

This legislation is based on article 51 of the Convention of the Economic European Community (EEC) and article 42 of the consolidated version of the Treaty of the European Community (TEC), and has been combined with Council Regulation 307/1999, adopted on 8 February 1999 to cover students. This regulation applies to:

- Member states' citizens working in another EU country.
- Refugees or persons without citizenship who stay and live in the territory of a member state and are submitted to the legal order of one or more member states.
- Members of the above persons' families.
- Public servants and other workers of similar professional status; these persons benefit from the same social security regime as the citizens of the member states.

In a report to the European Observatory of Social Security for Migrant Workers, the objectives of these community provisions have been codified as follows:

- To ensure equal treatment for the migrant worker in comparison with nationals of the Member State in which he is insured.
- To avoid the loss of entitlements gained as a result of qualified periods previously spent under the social security legislation of a Member State, by moving to work in another Member State.
- To ensure that the migrant worker and his family receive the most important benefits to which they are entitled, in whatever Member State they live. (Kremalis, 2003: 4)

Under this legislation, workers are protected by the principle of equal treatment. They also benefit from the export of benefits and aggregation of insurance periods. This regulation also deals with social security provisions, to include benefits for periods of sickness and maternity, invalidity, old age and death, accidents at work and occupational diseases, unemployment, family benefits and facilities, and benefits for dependent children and persons, as well as for orphans. The regulation applies to the general regime, as well as to special systems of social security; it sets obligations for employers. The exceptions to this regime relate to war victims' pensions and public servants' special security systems.

Recent developments at the European level

On 29 June 1998, Council Directive 98/49 was adopted to safeguard 'the supplementary pension rights of employed and self-employed persons moving within the Community' (1998: 46). The Directive's objective is to address the obstacles faced by workers posted to another member state, arising from the supplementary security systems. These provisions are applied individually to supplementary insurance and to persons entitled to it in one or more member states. These provisions deal with:

- The maintenance of the rights of the worker's country of origin legislation.
- The possibility of trans-boundary payments of benefits.
- The right to be insured in the social security system of the state from which a worker is coming for a short period of time.
- The creation of security funds dedicated to addressing the differences in social or supplementary security systems among European states.

The need for change

The need to revise the legislation on the coordination of the security systems for migrant workers was examined at the Edinburgh Council in 1992, which recommended its simplification. The Commission stressed in its 1997 Action Plan the need for the freedom of movement of workers and subsequently submitted its proposals for amending Regulation 1408/71 in December 1998. It provides for:

- The extension of the social protection to all citizens of a member state (e.g. students).
- The addition of more fields under the social security system.
- The amendment or revision of unemployment legislation.
- The application of the TESS information programme (Telematics for Social Security), which accelerates and simplifies the administrative procedure and the coordination of systems.

Pursuant to this proposal, the European health insurance card was adopted in order to replace forms E111 and E111B provided under the Regulations for Migrant Workers (Administrative Commission on Social Security for Migrant Workers, Decision 2003/753/EC, 18 June 2003).

Conclusion

We saw in the first section that the enlarged European Union, or Europe-25, has lofty aspirations on gender equality in the areas of work, care and equal pay. Moreover, gender equality has been the subject of recent initiatives to add momentum to the gender main-streaming agenda and the deepening of social research data on gender inequality in general and the status of migrant women in particular. However, the European system of social protection remains closely related to states' national legislation and we are witnesses of a strong *acquis national* in the field of social protection, in which the European Community's intervention is justified only to cover possible vacuums. Drawbacks can be noted throughout Europe in terms of the social protection accorded to part-time work, for example. Unions are lobbying for the inclusion in national legislations of high levels of social protection, or minimum standards of social protection, none of which seems possible under present circumstances. This means that the lobby for gender equality in the development of European-wide social policy remains an urgent item on the agenda of national and European-level organisations.

Nevertheless, the European Council that met in Lisbon on 23 and 24 March 2000 agreed that the target for this decade should be the combination of the highest level of competition and strength in the European Union's economy through knowledge and sustainable development with more and better status for employment and with more social cohesion (Lisbon European Council, 2000). The nature of these objectives gives an indication of the position of the EU in relation to this matter and highlights the need to face social cohesion gaps while working towards a strong European economy at the same time. From a gender perspective this gives some hope that similar progress may be made in building the European case for gender equality within and beyond social policy.

Notes

1. The *acquis communautaire* refers to the rights and obligations deriving from EU treaties, laws and regulations (Dinan, 1998: 2).
2. Consolidated version of article 6A, amended by article 2(2) of the Nice Treaty.
3. Under article 3(e) of Directive 98/49, '"posted worker" means a person who is posted to work in another Member State and who under the terms of Title II of Regulation (EEC) No 1408/71 continues to be subject to the legislation of the Member State of origin, and "posting" shall be construed accordingly'.

4. For other relevant cases, see the ECJ decision, of 13 May 1986, in the case Bilka/Weber and The ECJ decision in the case Kowalske/Freie and Haus-estadt/Hamburg on 27 June 1990
5. The Future Evolution of Social Protection from a Long-Term Point of View: Safe and Sustainable Pensions-.Communication from the Commission to the Council, to the European Parliament and to the Economic and Social Committee, Comm COM(2000)0622, 11 October 2000.
6. This refers to individuals' access to health services in a country other than the one they are residents in.

References

Arribas, G. V. and Carrasco, L. (2003) 'Gender equality and the EU – an assessment of the current issues', *EIPASCOPE*, 1: 1–9.
Dimitracopoulos, G. and Kremlis, G. (eds) (2004) *A New Constitutional Settlement for the European People*, Athens and Brussels: Sakkoulas-Bruylant.
Ehrhard, M. (1992) *Politiques et pratiques sociales en Europe: Valeurs et modèles institutionnels*, Nancy: Presses Universitaires de Nancy.
European Commission (1993) *White Paper on Growth, Competitiveness, and Employment: The Challenges and Ways Forward into the 21st Century*, COM(93) 700 final. Available at: http://europa.eu.int/en/record/white/c93700/contents.html [accessed 15 September 2005].
European Commission (1994) *European Social Policy A Way Forward for the Union A White Paper*, COM(94) 333 final, Available at: http://europa.eu.int/scadplus/leg/en/cha/c10112.htm [accessed 15 September 2005].
European Commission (2003) *Social Protection in the 13 Candidate Countries, a Comparative Analysis*. Available at: http://europa.eu.int/comm/employment_social/publications/2004/ke5103649_fr.html [accessed 15 September 2005].
European Commission and European Council (2003) *Adequate and Sustainable Pensions*. Available at: http://europa.eu.int/comm/employment_social/publications/2004/ke5303483_en.pdf [accessed 15 September 2005].
Hafner-Burton, E. and Pollack, M. A. (2000) 'Mainstreaming gender in European Union policymaking', in *Journal of European Public Policy*, Special issue on Women, Power and Public Policy, 7(1): 432–56.
Hantrais, L. (2000) *Social Policy in the European Union*, Basingstoke: Palgrave Macmillan.
Koukoulis-Spiliotopoulos, S. (2002) 'Towards a European Constitution: Does the Charter of Fundamental Rights "maintain in full" the *aquis communautaire?*' *ERPL/REDP*, 14(1): 57–104.
León, L. et al. (2003) *(En)gendering the Convention: Women and the Future of the European Union*, San Domenico di Fiesole: European University Institute.
Nikolakopoulou-Stephanou, I. (1992) *Convergence of Social Security Systems in Western Europe*, Athens: I. Sideris ed.
Nikolakopoulou-Stephanou, I. (2001) 'Development and employment', in G. Dimopoulos et al. (eds) *Introduction to European Studies Economic Integration and Policies*, Athens: n.p., pp. 567–695.
Pellny, M. and Horstmann, S. (2003), 'Outlook: enlargement and social protection', in *European Commission, Social Protection in the 13 Candidate Countries, a Comparative Analysis*.

Shaw, J. (2002) 'The European Union and gender mainstreaming: constitutionally embedded or comprehensively marginalised?' *Feminist Legal Studies*, 10(3): 213–26.
Steinhilber, S. (2002) *Women's Rights and Gender Equality in the EU Enlargement. An Opportunity for Progress*. Available at: http://www.igtn.org/pdfs/110_WIDEEUenlarge.pdf [accessed 2 September 2005].
Tsatsos, T. D. (1992) 'Constitutional Law (Vol. III)', in N. Sakkoula (ed.) *Fundamental Rights*, Athens: Komotini, pp. 194–216.
Tsatsos, T. D. (1998) *Constitutional Law – Fundamental Rights* (Vol. 3), Athens-Komitini: Ant. N. Sakkoula (in Greek).

EU legislation, directives and recommendations

Administrative Commission on Social Security for Migrant Workers, Decision No. 191 concerning the replacement of forms E111 and E111 B by the European health insurance card (2003/753/EC), 18 June 2003.
Council Decision 2004/689/EC establishing a Social Protection Committee and repealing Decision 2000/436/EC, 4 October 2004.
Council Directive 2000/43/EC implementing the principle of equal treatment between persons irrespective of racial or ethnic origin, 29 June 2000.
Council Directive 2000/78/EC establishing a framework for equal treatment in employment and occupation, 27 November 2000.
Council Decision 2000/750/EC, Community Action Programme on combating discrimination, 27 November 2000.
Council Directive 79/7/EEC on the progressive implementation of the principle of equal treatment for men and women in matters of social security, 19 December 1978.
Council Directive 86/613/EEC on the application of the principle of equal treatment between men and women engaged in an activity, including agriculture, in a self-employed capacity and in the protection of self-employed women during pregnancy and motherhood, 11 December 1986.
Council Directive 86/613/EEC on the application of the principle of equal treatment between men and women engaged in an activity, including agriculture, in a self-employed capacity and in the protection of self-employed women during pregnancy and motherhood, 11 December 1986.
Council Directive 86/378/EEC on the implementation of the principle of equal treatment for men and women in occupational social security schemes, 24 July 1986, amended by Council Directive 96/97/EC of 20 December 1996.
Council Directive 91/383/EEC supplementing the measures to encourage improvements in the safety and health at work of workers with a fixed-duration employment relationship or a temporary employment relationship, 25 June 1991.
Council Directive 92/85/EEC concerning the implementation of measures to encourage improvements in the safety and health of pregnant workers, women workers who have recently given birth and women who are breastfeeding, 19 October 1992.
Council Directive 93/104/EC concerning certain aspects of the organisation of working time, 23 November 1993.

Council Directive 97/81/EC concerning the Framework Agreement on part-time work concluded by UNICE, CEEP and the ETUC, 15 December 1997.

Council Directive 98/49/EC on safeguarding the supplementary pension rights of employed and self-employed persons moving within the Community, 29 June 1998.

Council Recommendation 92/441/EEC on common criteria concerning sufficient resources and social assistance in the social protection systems, 24 June 1992.

Council Regulation 574/72/ECC laying down the procedure for implementing Regulation 1408/71/ECC on the application of social security schemes to employed persons, to self employed persons, to self-employed persons and to their families moving within the Community, 21 March 1972.

Council Regulation 307/1999/EC amending Regulation 1408/71/EEC on the application of social security schemes to employed persons, to self-employed persons and to members of their families moving within the Community, 8 February 1999.

Council Regulation 1408/71/EC on the application of social security schemes to employed persons, to self-employed persons and to members of their families moving within the Community, 14 June 1971.

European Commission, Proposal for a Council Decision setting up a Social Protection Committee (2000/C 274 E/02), 15 March 2000.

European Commission, EU Community Framework Strategy on Gender Equality (2001–2005), COM (2000)335 Final.

European Commission, Report from the Commission to the Council, the European Parliament, the European Economic and Social Committee and the Committee of the Regions on equality between women and men, COM (2005) 44 Final.

Index